Praise for Richard G

"Everyone should read *The Greedsters* due to the wide popular interest in this topic. It is one that is genuinely important to us all. From students of economics to investors, business executives and heads of households--all will profit from it. This book is a primer for understanding the troubling developments that have occurred in banking and investing and their destructive consequences. I would hope this book will inspire our most promising students to realize more worthy ambitions than heading to Wall Street to make deals." *Dr. Alfred E. Kahn,* Professor Emeritus of Economics, Cornell University; Dean of Cornell University College of Arts and Science; chair of the Civil Aeronautics Board and chair of the Council on Wage and Price Stability under President Carter; and former Chief of New York State's Public Service Commission.

"This sweeping indictment of greed from past to present is important and timely. The knowledge gained from this book allows the reader to be a more informed and active citizen watchdog of corporate America." *J. Dayton Voorhees, MD,* Family Practice Physician; Medical Director, Amigos de las Américas.

"Every now and then a financial book comes along that says exactly what the business world and its boardrooms need to hear. Dick Gray has succeeded in peeling back the ugly truth about lax corporate governance in America's boardrooms. Gray confronts head-on the long-standing practice of company CEO's serving also as the board chair in Chapter 9, 'The Lax Standards of Boards of Directors.' Without a doubt, this book belongs in the hands of every CEO, board member, investor and student of business administration." *Blyth Berg Brookman* of Excelsior, Minnesota, currently serves as a board member and board chair of three non-profit organizations. She has been a financial advisor with a major brokerage firm for thirty-six years. She has seen first hand some of the dangerous practices that Gray addresses in *The Greedsters*.

"Reading this book made me feel outrage. I will no longer be a pawn to banks and corporations that feel they know more about finance than a woman who struggles to balance her family budget." *Sara Voorhees,* Board member, Broadcast Film Critics Association; Broadcast film critic and author of *Lumiére Affair.*

Copyright 2010 by Richard G. Gray Sr.

All rights reserved
Printed in the United States of America
First Edition

For information about permission to reproduce selections from this book,
Email: Greedsters@gmail.com
or visit the website: www.thegreedsters.com
The Cherry Creek Co., LLC
130 Holly Lane, Plymouth, MN 55447

ISBN-13: 978-1456576868
ISBN-10: 1456576860
Library of Congress Control Number: 2011901456
CreateSpace, North Charleston, SC

This book may not be reproduced, transmitted, or stored in whole or in part by any means, including graphic, electronic, or mechanical without the express written consent of the publisher except in the case of brief quotations embodied in critical articles and reviews.

THE GREEDSTERS

THE GREEDSTERS

WHEN ENOUGH IS NEVER ENOUGH

RICHARD G. GRAY SR., DSc, HON.

THE CHERRY CREEK CO., LLC
PLYMOUTH, MINNESOTA

Take Care and Invest Wisely!
Regards,
Dick Gray

Also by Richard G. Gray Sr.

Books

Passwords for All Seasons

Open Season

Pamphlet

The Making of a Present

TABLE OF CONTENTS

PREFACE 11
NOTICE OF BLOGSITE FOR "THE GREEDSTERS SEQUELS" . 17
CHAPTER 1: HISTORY OF GREED AND GREEDSTERS 21
CHAPTER 2: GREEDSTERS AND FRAUD TODAY 47
CHAPTER 3: GREEDSTERS PONZI SCHEMES 81
CHAPTER 4: GREEDSTER BERNARD L. MADOFF 127
CHAPTER 5: GREEDSTER STANFORD'S PONZI 183
CHAPTER 6: GREEDSTER BANKS 205
CHAPTER 7: GREEDSTERS ON WALL STREET 253
CHAPTER 8: GREEDSTERS ON MAIN STREET 285
CHAPTER 9: THE LAX STANDARDS OF BOARDS
          OF DIRECTORS 325
CHAPTER 10: THE FEDERAL RESERVE SYSTEM 357
CHAPTER 11: FINAL THOUGHTS 365
SELECTED GLOSSARY 373
SELECTED BIBLIOGRAPHY 381
INDEX 385
ACKNOWLEDGEMENTS 397

PREFACE

I take issue with anyone who proclaims, "Greed is good." Greed is inherent in all of us, but for most there is restraint from our baser impulses. From the earliest narratives of mankind to the enduring literature of the world, Man has been taught to guard against its temptations. Arguably, Eve's bite of the apple is no more than a cautionary tale of the consequences of greed.

For the purposes of this book, greed is defined as "when enough is never enough." Integrity and common sense should signal to any balanced person when they have acquired enough wealth to reach financial security or satiation. Those who keep on taking or even increase their appetite to the point of excess are classed in this volume as "Greedsters." Unfortunately, our world is full of them. The damage done by greedster ethics infects our culture and our national financial system. As individuals it invades our psyches and our financial security.

Dozens of greedsters are dissected in this book. Not all greedsters are guilty of fraud, but all fraud is perpetrated by greedsters. Today, we find greed unfettered and even sanctioned in the twenty-first century. My hope is that this book will instill in readers a healthy skepticism about investments with unrealistic returns and an awareness that successful investment requires a great deal of diligence on the part of the investor. After all, it is their investment of their hard-earned savings.

As you will learn from these pages, greedy individuals and the entities they represent walk among us in every sector of society. No profession is immune to the greed factor—even our moral and religious leaders are susceptible to it.

I was fortunate in my career. I was able to have four entirely different career paths that gave me insights into many facets of the business world during the twentieth century. I began as a young geologist exploring the geologic formations of Montana, Wyoming and Colorado for oil deposits and working in an oil refinery. After my military service, I started a manufacturing and sales company as an entrepreneur; that small business grew into an international company, which I sold in 1981. My lifelong interest in water, energy and nature led me to found a not-for-profit organization, The Freshwater Society, and to build and fund a major freshwater research facility later donated to the University of Minnesota's College of Biological Sciences. About the time I planned to retire, I was recruited to serve on several boards of directors of thirty-five mutual funds managed by Investors Group in Minneapolis. That commitment led to some years as CEO of Investors Group, one of the largest mutual fund complexes in the world at that time.

World War II prepared me for my business philosophy. As a U.S. Naval officer, I was stationed on an amphibious attack ship, the APA 234, and traveled 68,000 nautical miles in less than two years in the greater South Pacific. My service taught me the strength of teamwork, responsible leadership and loyalty. Those principles that preserve life in battle are similar to the ones that insure business survival. On February 20, 1945, during the second morning of the mayhem of the Iwo Jima invasion, I pledged to myself that if I survived that brutal landing, for the rest of my life I would devote as much time and effort as I could to causes that would improve American society.

There is nothing that can teach the basics of business like experience as an entrepreneur. I took an idea for a new type of mechanical variable speed control and patented it. We built a prototype and developed a manufacturing process in Minnesota. The company, Zero-Max, Incorporated, became an international manufacturing and sales distributor. The device in different sizes was used in applications as diverse as weaving devices and artificial lung and heart machines. The business grew steadily. After some sixty-three years there are many varied applications for the device today, and worldwide sales are still strong.

The principles that guided the conduct of this business were those I had defined as a World War II veteran: the business was run to produce an excellent product that supported a labor force with sustainable employment and benefits and investors with healthy returns on their investments. Zero-Max A.G. was formed to establish a European distribution point at the free port of Basel, Switzerland. The company's success has provided economic security for my own family and our employees. Eventually I sold the company to a firm that continues the manufacture and international distribution of Zero-Max and many related products.

For thirty-five years I was honored to serve on many financial boards of directors with outstanding individuals of impeccable integrity such as former President Gerald Ford; former Secretary of Defense Melvin Laird; The Honorable Hamer Budge (former federal judge and Idaho congressman); former Secretary of Defense Robert Froelke; Senator Muriel Humphrey (wife of Vice-President Hubert Humphrey appointed to finish her husband's Senate term following his death); three former SEC commissioners; and CEOs of companies such as 3M, General Mills and Pepsico. I made many friends including George Putnam of the Putnam funds, John Bogle of the Vanguard funds and T. Rowe Price of the T. Rowe Price funds.

As part of my corporate governance experiences, I served on all the board committees at one time or another, eventually becoming CEO of all thirty-five funds of the Investors Group. At that time it was one of the largest complexes of mutual funds in the world. My tenure as CEO gave me an insight into the "back office" of Wall Street and Main Street and provided me with first-hand exposure to the way inventive minds can create financial structures—and provide manipulative loopholes—that regulators have not anticipated.

My experiences as CEO of Investors Group and continuing interest in the world of finance motivated me to remain informed about the rapid changes occurring in that industry. Clipping newspaper columns of interest for years allowed me to observe how the conduct of business changed remarkably after my retirement. I began to note the obscenities of greed in corporate culture: excessive compensation for special employees even in years when a company delivered enormous losses; deceptive schemes designed by clever men and women to exploit investors; unscrupulous manipulation of value through mergers and acquisitions; unregulated creation of high-yield investment instruments with low quality and undisclosed risks.

Many Wall Street and Main Street boards of directors grew lax and lost their independence as it became common for the CEO to serve also as chairman of the company's board. Board members increasingly had "cozy" ties to management through multiple associations. Board service became so lucrative that professional directors served on multiple boards with frequent conflicts of interest. Boards and executive management failed to consider the interests of shareholders in their desire to increase share values and earn high ratings from analysts. This lack of board oversight and assessment of risks created record business failures and government bailouts of our financial system and automotive industry.

Finally multi-billion dollar frauds were revealed such as the Ponzi schemes of Bernard Madoff, R. Allen Stanford and many others as they unraveled in the Great Recession of 2007-2009 and the slow and painful recovery that has continued through 2012.

As an essayist my lifelong passion for preserving the environment and protecting our freshwater resources had led me to write a weekly column "Pass Words" for twenty-five years, along with dozens of articles and essays that have culminated in 1,300 pieces of writing collected in two books titled *Pass Words For All Seasons* and *Open Seasons*. I began to think of writing essays that documented the unwelcome changes I was seeing in the business world. I saw that nuggets of stories lay hidden everywhere waiting to be excavated and exposed to the light of day—in a way similar to my experience as a young geologist.

Fast forward to *The Greedsters*. A small dinner party with Denver friends in April 2008 featured a lively conversation that triggered discussion of our country's emerging financial crisis. Someone suggested that I write a book about the current business landscape of schemes, scandals, outlandish compensations and poor risk analyses of Wall Street and Main Street from the viewpoint of my own experience in running for-profit and not-for-profit enterprises since 1948.

I accepted the challenge, and *The Greedsters* is the result.

RICHARD G. GRAY, SR.
March 13, 2012

NOTICE

To enable all readers of "The Greedsters" to continue to follow the developments of the stories in this book, please see our blog called "The Greedsters Sequels." The blog is now available at http://the-greedsterssequels.blogspot.com. Because legal outcomes of the events described here can take years to adjudicate, appeals and final judgments for the many greedsters profiled in this book will be posted and updated as long as these developments remain topical.

HISTORY OF GREED AND GREEDSTERS

Chapter 1 – Synopsis

"Always Greed"

As early as the age of greedster King Midas of Macedonia (775 B.C.), mythology has identified greed as an affliction of humanity.

Greed is a complex human impulse, but it is most often expressed in the hoarding of precious metals, rare commodities, or in modern times, money. Power and domination are driven by greed. Emperors, generals, dictators and pirates have all suffered the disease of greed. But ordinary mortals are equally susceptible to it. The character trait of integrity, innate to us all at birth, provides immunity to greed. A sense of decency and awareness of having enough restrains us from taking more than we need. But when people become infected by greed, there is no satiation: the appetite for excess conquers integrity and all moral scruples.

Over the ages greedy people have been driven to take for themselves the wealth and resources that should benefit all mankind. In their ambition for power and wealth, they succumbed to a loss of integrity. History reveals numerous accounts of greedsters and their exploits and empires—from Alexander the Great to Julius Caesar to Genghis Kahn—and many more great and small despots throughout the ages.

The robber barons of the nineteenth century were greedsters—in spite of their great accomplishments and generous contributions to society. Prominent names like the Rockefeller, Carnegie and Duke families have left a legacy of philanthropy, but they attained their wealth through illegal manipulations and corruption. Greatness can be achieved without surrendering to greed, fraud and criminal behavior.

Despite your good works, if you are greedy so you shall be remembered.

Chapter 1

HISTORY OF GREED AND GREEDSTERS

GREED ENDURES

The concept of "greedsters" is as old as human history. Wherever there were valuable resources, be it gold or spices or tea, there have always been opportunists willing to commit crimes to acquire them.

The tapestry of history displays many examples of greedsters: explorers who destroyed entire civilizations in pursuit of power and fortune; monarchs and noblemen of medieval Europe who lied and cheated to enrich their families; pirates on the high seas who pillaged ships and murdered their crews to capture valuable cargo.

It is difficult to define the concept of greed. The Italian word for it *ingordigia* literally translated means "engorged"; the Greeks called it *pleonexia*, the insatiable desire to have what rightly belongs to others.

But the appetite for excess never changes whether in ancient or modern times. Our definition for greed is "when enough is never enough."

It's also very difficult to trace the history of greed way back in time. Some of its fundamental elements were totally different historically; some cultures survived only due to the protection of wealthy and powerful potentates.

Greed in the South American, African, Asian and Pacific Rim cultures is not being ignored but rather is undocumented in these pages as the elements of greed in our western culture afford a better opportunity to understand the nature of greed and greedsters in the modern United States of America.

History serves to identify four main areas where men and women have achieved power through greed:

Politics • Conquest • Religion • Commerce

All who climb the ladder of success to the top of their profession in order to live a life of privilege, wealth and power must guard against it.

There is a basic human condition that all of us have, to a lesser or greater extent, that differentiates us from one another. It is called integrity. Visualize each person having a ceiling or limit on this quality. Everyone has a different degree of integrity due to personality and environment.

Some break through this ceiling easily because their ceiling is low and their sense of right or wrong, good or bad, just or unjust, is warped. For these, greed is similar to a disease—the person becomes infected by power, consumed by money, twisted in his or her judgments and motivated by dreams of glory, fame and fortune.

But there are others who possess a high level or ceiling of integrity. We are all tempted by greed, but most of us do understand right from wrong, just from unjust, good from bad. Fame, fortune and power do not turn our heads; desire for fairness and justice rules our judgments. Concern for the welfare of others is never lost.

The disease of greed is often cured by failure and human loss or by the painful lesson that fame and fortune can be empty achievements. Greed has been with Man throughout the ages, is with us now, and will always be waiting in the wings to infect those with that lower ceiling of integrity.

ANCIENT GREED AND GREEDSTERS

Greed in western civilization is first documented late in the eighth century B.C. Therefore, for the purposes of this chapter we have defined "ancient greed" as occurring from about 800 B.C. to 1929 A.D. "Modern" greed in succeeding chapters is set from 1929 to the present.

That time frame should give us a fair reading of how old-time greed developed into the "western" greed of modern times.

A perfect example of ancient greed is the Greek myth of King Midas, who was born in about 775 B.C. Herodotus records that Midas was adopted as a child by King Pessinus of Macedonia and was pronounced King of Macedonia upon his father's death. King Midas became a fair ruler and an excellent gardener with a world-famous rose garden, each bush bearing sixty perfect blossoms.

In Greek mythology, King Midas received a "golden touch" from the god Dionysus, who granted Midas the gift that all he touched would turn to gold. Midas was delighted with his newfound road to wealth and quickly had a fortune in gold, but when the bread he was eating and the wine he was drinking turned to gold, he became frightened of his gift. He held his daughter to him and turned her to gold—as he did his rose garden upon touching the blossoms. Distraught, he died a broken man—deceived by the belief that having gold and wealth was the ultimate goal. He learned too late that greed was the death knell of a good and meaningful life.

Later, alchemists searched for a way to chemically create gold from base metals, calling the transmutation process *chrysopoeia*. For centuries, they spent lifetimes consumed by an obsession to mimic King Midas despite the object lesson of the myth. (The chrysalis or cocoon encasing a butterfly pupa is derived from the term chrysopoeia, and indeed, the Monarch butterfly has rich gold buttons surrounding the collar of its chrysalis.)

Another king of Macedonia, empire-builder Alexander the Great, was born into a royal family in 356 B.C. From his youth, he was a natural leader who could charm all those around him. At age thirteen, Alexander's tutor, the philosopher Aristotle, taught him medicine, religion, morals, philosophy, logic and art. At sixteen years he was made regent to rule Macedonia while his father, Phillip II, was off waging war against Persia. His father returned from the war only to be murdered soon thereafter. Alexander became King Alexander III at age twenty, the self-proclaimed "King of Kings," by ruthlessly murdering opponents to his accession (including his cousin). He is acknowledged to have been a tactical genius, and his battle strategies are still studied.

His insatiable greed for power and glory drove him to conquer more and more territory, and he became ruler of Syria, Egypt, Mesopotamia and Bactria. But Alexander the Great died on June 11, 323 B.C. at the age of thirty-three in Babylon (near modern day Baghdad). No one knows if his death was due to natural causes or assassination, but it is certain that he was entombed along with his ambition and greed. He left the throne of Macedonia bankrupt.

The Roman Empire can be traced back to 756 B.C. when King Romulus founded Rome as a monarchy. It lasted an incredible 2,209 years: from 756 B.C. to 509 B.C. as the Roman monarchy, from 509 B.C. to 27 B.C. as the Roman Republic, and as the Roman Empire under Emperor Julius Caesar and his successors until 476 A.D. From this date until 1453 A.D., the empire was split into the Western Roman Empire and Eastern Roman Empire.

Seven kings ruled the early monarchy over a 247-year period. Romulus created the Roman Senate, which in turn elected the king. These elected kings were alternately benign or ambitious but the seventh in the succession, Lucius Tarquinius, created such a scandal that the Senate established the Roman Republic with a chief executive called a "consul." From 509 B.C., the Roman Republic created a period of relative tranquility for its citizens that lasted about 400 years.

In 100 B.C. the ambitious Gaius Julius Caesar was born. In a series of foreign conquests, he expanded Rome's control from the Italian peninsula into what is now France and Spain, then across the English Channel into England. To the east his reach included Greece and Asia Minor. His campaign to include Egypt in the Roman Empire resulted in a liaison with its queen, Cleopatra, who bore him a son. Caesar, also a military genius, was eventually able to have himself declared "perpetual dictator" by the Roman Senate.

Julius Caesar hated the moneychangers of Rome and seized the power to coin money. He created a currency for the republic that usurped the control of the moneychangers—the bankers of their time. They retaliated by joining the conspiracy led by Caesar's friend Marcus Brutus and assassinated the dictator in 44 B.C. His death marks the end of the Roman Republic; his birth initiated a period of greed that lasted over 500 years.

Interestingly, Jesus Christ also hated the moneychangers for their rapacity and greed. The Bible tells us he drove them from the Temple in about 30 A.D., and they vowed to kill him. There is no direct evidence that the moneychangers were responsible for his crucifixion, but some historians have blamed them for effecting his execution.

A series of Roman emperors succeeded Julius Caesar. Many of their reigns were characterized by such greed, excess and debauchery that they eventually weakened the empire and made it vulnerable to barbarian invasion. The Roman civilization descended into chaos for almost a thousand years.

The Middle Ages had its greed-driven villains. This period began with the Dark Ages at about 500 A.D. and stretched until approximately 1000 A.D. when the Crusades and trade expeditions began. A feudalistic economy gave way to a period of conquests that began to reorganize cities and nation-states. In approximately 1500 A.D. the Western Roman Empire ended, and the rebirth of the intellectual, economic and artistic endeavors known as the Renaissance began. Throughout these times, political intrigue and greed set the moral compass of mankind low, and the appetite for power, glory and fortune high.

It is first documented in 1024 A.D. that the goldsmiths of England, realizing that all their precious metal assets were never called in at one time, began to lend money at the rate of ten times the actual gold they had on hand. They lent money to many who secured those loans with precious objects or property. If the debtor could not maintain regular payments, the lender seized the property or "collateral," originating the term "foreclosure." Sound familiar?

USURY AND GREEDSTERS

Lending money at interest brings us to the concept of usury and its role in the history of greed. Let us digress and trace usury prohibitions or "interest rate regulation" from ancient times to the present. It will be a recurring thread throughout the remainder of this narrative.

"Usury" is the name given to lending money and gouging the borrower by charging an illegal or exorbitantly high interest rate. In the Old Testament, Jews were forbidden from charging interest to one another. The prophets include usury as an "abominable" thing along with murder, robbery and worshipping false idols. Moneylenders have been regarded as predatory since the beginning of commerce—both ancient and modern—and usurious lending has been prohibited in many cultures.

Throughout history enlightened rulers have seen that usurious interest rates are destructive to the community as a whole. The Babylonian Code of Hammurabi, currently displayed in the Louvre in Paris, is one of the oldest records of codified law to survive in its original tablet form. The 282 laws of the code are carved into a stone tablet in the cuneiform script of Babylonia that dates from approximately 1750 B.C. One of the laws inscribed there regulates the maximum legal limit of interest as 20 percent on loans of silver and 33 percent on loans of grain. The word for "usury" in the Babylonian (or Akkadian) language means misery or hardship.

Aristotle taught that usury was immoral and unjust. The Romans set the highest legal interest rate to 8 1/3 percent, a law that lasted until 1543 A.D.

The Koran links the practice of usury to eternal condemnation.

By the time of Charlemagne, first emperor of the Holy Roman Empire, charging interest on loans was forbidden. In medieval times ex-communication was the penalty for realizing profits on lending.

King Henry I of England (son of William the Conqueror) solved the problem of chronic shortages of coinage in 1100 A.D. Bypassing the usurious moneychangers as lenders, he established a medium of exchange with "tally sticks" on which notches were cut to represent financial transactions. Tallies were an early verifiable form of bookkeeping and were honored in England until 1826—some 726 years.

St. Thomas Aquinas, a leading Catholic theologian (1225-1275 A.D.), campaigned against moneychangers charging interest on loans, claiming the practice was "double interest," charging both for the money and the use of the money.

During the reign of Henry VIII of England, the ban on usury was lifted while he battled the Roman Catholic Church. However, his daughter, Queen Mary, again restricted interest collection during her reign, and her half-sister, Elizabeth I, limited interest rates to 10 percent. This became the cap on interest in England until 1854.

William Shakespeare lived most of his life in sixteenth century England and died in 1616 at age fifty-two. Little is known of his personal life or experiences, but we do know he had serious periodic financial troubles. In his play *The Merchant of Venice,* the character Shylock is a usurious moneylender. Although Shylock is typically played sympathetically in modern versions of the play, there is no doubt that in Shakespeare's time he was viewed as a ruthless villain.

The new United States of America set an interest rate limit of 6 percent in 1776. By the 1900s banks were not making personal loans because they were unprofitable, so eleven states lifted the usury ban and several others raised the limit. After World War II all states had an interest rate cap, but the legal limit was different from state to state.

In 1978 the United States Supreme Court ruled that national banks could uniformly charge in their home state the highest interest rate allowed in any state where they did business. South Dakota promptly eliminated its interest rate cap and several banks with credit card divisions changed their corporate addresses to South Dakota so that they could increase interest charges on all their national accounts. This is how we reached 29.9 percent (and higher) maximum interest rates on our credit card accounts.

In 1980 control of interest rates by the states was taken over by Congress on all first lien mortgages. This allowed lenders to design "mortgage products" with the adjustable rates and interest-only introductory terms that have led to so many foreclosures. Since 1980 the Federal Government has fought the states and cities that attempted to adopt provisions to curb these predatory practices. Legislation proposed at the federal level has never made it to the floor of Congress for a vote.

Predatory lending gained speed in the recent sub-prime mortgage debacle, and the entire world economy has been rocked by the consequences. The notion of excessive interest rates creating financial "misery" and "hardship" (as first defined by the Babylonians) has become commonplace. The concept of limiting that excess has disappeared.

GREED AND GREEDSTERS IN THE MODERN ERA

As this history of greed reaches modern times, it is worthwhile to include a cautionary note left to us by none other than Karl Marx, who was born in 1818 in German Prussia and died in England at the age of sixty-four. His doctrines and beliefs have influenced thinking on a variety of philosophical, political and economic subjects. During his mature years he published *The Communist Manifesto,* and he discussed in it a theme that is relevant to this narrative:

The downfall of capitalism will ultimately be caused by greed.

This prediction causes shivers up and down your spine when you read, listen to or see today's financial events. Greed *is* gnawing away at the pillars of our capitalistic economic structure, no question about that.

Many would assert that greed, conquest and corruption were also the causes of the downfall of the communist economy of the Union of Soviet Socialist Republics. Remember Winston Churchill's famous remark: "Capitalism is the worst economic system—except for all the others."

The nineteenth century was also the dawn of new capitalistic economies. No longer was dominance maintained by assassinations of critics or opponents; no longer was it the norm to lie and cheat (at least openly) during Victorian times. In the Western world the industrial age introduced free enterprise. Manufacturing jobs led to prosperity for the working class. As the jobs necessitated training and education, an awareness of individual rights began to emerge. This more educated public demanded a voice. Legislation was enacted, enhanced and enforced so that no one would be above the law. Then came the dawn of a new breed of greed.

THE AGE OF THE ROBBER BARONS

The term may first have been used in medieval Germany to describe thieves who grew rich by imposing high tariffs on shipping up the Rhine River. E. L. Godkin described the ruthlessness of the magnates of the industrial revolution for an article in *The Nation* in

1867 and labeled them "robber barons." [http://riverdaughter.wordpress.com/2009/02/12/robber-barons/].

Matthew Josephson published an economic history about America's industrial age called *The Robber Barons* in 1934. [Matthew Josephson, *The Robber Barons: The Great American Capitalists, 1861-1901*, New York: Harcourt, Brace and Company, 1934.] He described the financiers and industrialists who had cleverly and deviously designed ways to exploit resources to their own profit. By 2008 the term "robber boomer barons" had entered the blogosphere and enlarged the historic notion of business tycoons exploiting the system at someone else's expense while taking exorbitant salaries and perquisites for themselves.

The use of the term in this book is to stigmatize those titans of American commerce in the nineteenth century who amassed their fortunes by the use of deceptive securities practices, insider information and political influence. The robber barons ruthlessly dominated the marketplace and quashed competition. Many individuals achieved wealth and success through legitimate endeavors in the financial and business worlds, but they were surpassed by the enormous power and wealth of the nineteenth century robber barons. The following is a list of that group:

OUR 23 ROBBER BARONS
(Our nation's first billionaires):

Astor, John Jacob – Furs
Carnegie, Andrew – Steel
Cooke, Jay – Finance
Crocker, Charles – Railroads
Doheny, Edward – Oil (Elk Hills)
Drew, Daniel – Finance
Duke, James Buchanan – Tobacco
Dwyer, Brian James – Coal

Fisk, James – Finance
Flagler, Henry Morrison – Railroads
Frick, Henry Clay – Steel
Gates, John Warne – Steel
Gould, Jay – Railroads
Harriman, Edward Henry – Railroads
Hershey, Milton S. – Chocolate
Hill, James J. – Railroads
Hopkins, Mark P. – Railroads
Morgan, J. P. – Banks
Rockefeller, John D. – Oil (Standard)
Sinclair, Harry F. – Oil (Tea Pot Dome)
Spreckels, John D. – Water (California)
Stanford, Leland – Railroads
Vanderbilt, Cornelius – Railroads

[Keys, C. M. (January 1906). "The Overlords of Railroad Traffic: The Seven Men Who Reign Supreme". *The World's Work: A History of Our Time* **XIII**: 8437–8445.]

The Worst: Jay Gould
The Richest: John D. Rockefeller
The Second Richest: Andrew Carnegie
The Best: Milton S. Hershey
The Nastiest: Harry T. Sinclair and Edward Doheny

In the next sections are profiles of some of the most well-known Robber Barons.

JOHN DAVISON ROCKEFELLER

John D. Rockefeller became the world's richest man—but he was not always the nicest. Born July 8, 1839, in Richford, New York (an apt town-name for things to come), he died in Ormond Beach, Florida, at age ninety-seven. He was an ardent Baptist who never used tobacco or alcohol.

His father, William A. Rockefeller, stated with apparent pride: "I cheat my boy every chance I get. I want to make him sharp." [Segall, Grant (2001). *John D. Rockefeller: Anointed With Oil*. Oxford University Press. pp. 14. ISBN 0-19-512147-3.] "Big Bill" was frequently gone from his family for extended periods and spent "considerable energy on tricks and schemes and avoided plain hard work." [Chernow, Ron (May 5, 1998). *Titan: The Life of John D. Rockefeller, Sr.*. Random House. p. 6. ISBN 978-0679438083.]

After graduating from Oswego Academy in New York, John D. was employed as an assistant bookkeeper for Hewitt and Tuttle, a small produce commission firm, where he learned to calculate with great accuracy the transportation costs of the inventory. He earned 50 cents a day and donated 6 percent to charity. Later in life, he always tithed 10 percent.

In 1863 at twenty-four he built a whale-oil refinery with a partner whom he bought out two years later. In 1866 he leveraged a majority interest in a petroleum refinery by borrowing heavily and reinvesting his profits. By 1868 Rockefeller, Andrews and Flagler owned the largest oil refinery in the world. The Civil War had ended and refined petroleum oil was destined to displace whale oil as an everyday product.

Mr. Rockefeller credited his success to his religious faith and stated publicly, "God gave me the money." He never apologized for the way he earned it.

In 1870 he formed Standard Oil of Ohio and became the largest *shipper* of oil and kerosene in the country. His dominating successes by age thirty-one made him a target of other copycat entrepreneurs, and he had to fight to hold his dominance. Fierce competition by new railroad lines led Rockefeller to form a secret cartel that forced lower rates and damaged his competition. It was later disclosed that Standard Oil of Ohio was a major player in the cartel.

In a period of four months in 1872, Standard Oil "absorbed" twenty-two of its twenty-six competitors. [Segall, (2001) p.44.] The period became known as the "Cleveland Massacre." By the end of the 1870s Standard Oil of Ohio had developed more than 300 products, from tar to Vaseline to chewing gum. Mr. Rockefeller was building pipeline transportation networks. He was now a millionaire.

His business practices were most controversial, but the company continued to undersell, price preferentially and employ secret transportation rebates. *The New York World* proclaimed in 1880 that Standard Oil was "the most cruel, impudent, pitiless and grasping monopoly that ever fastened upon a country."

In 1882 lawyers for Standard Oil created a new form of trust to avoid anti-monopoly regulations. Called the Standard Oil Trust, it was actually a corporation of corporations—forty-one companies in all.

The invention of the light bulb, which dimmed the use of kerosene for illumination, and the discovery of crude oil in other parts of the world again threatened Standard Oil. Mr. Rockefeller countered by buying up natural gas production and increasing promotion of the use of gasoline.

Mr. Rockefeller retired from business at age sixty-three, devoting his time and money to charitable causes. His enormous income grew, and his legendary philanthropy continued until the end of his life. In 1902, the year he retired, he earned $58 million in investment income. He died of arteriosclerosis two months shy of his ninety-eighth birthday.

ANDREW CARNEGIE

The most famous leader of industry in the late nineteenth and early twentieth centuries was Andrew Carnegie. Born in Dumferline, Scotland, on November 25, 1835, he died in Lenox, Massachusetts, at the age of eighty-three. His father was a weaver, and

Andrew's birthplace was a two-room cottage shared with another weaver's family. Fleeing hard times, his family immigrated to the United States in 1848 and settled in Allegheny, Pennsylvania.

Andrew was immediately employed at thirteen as a bobbin boy in a cotton mill, changing spools of thread twelve hours a day, six days a week, for 17 cents per hour. His father wove and peddled linens, and his mother was a binder of shoes.

In 1850 he became a telegraph messenger boy and doubled his hourly wage. His new job included free admission to a local theater, where he learned about Shakespeare. A quick and curious student, Carnegie pursued self-education throughout his life. He was attentive to the names of businessmen and the firms who sent messages. He learned Morse code by ear and could soon decipher messages without writing them down.

In 1853 Thomas Scott of the Pennsylvania Railroad Company gave Andrew a job as a secretary/telegraph operator at $4 a week (again more than doubling his previous wages), and he worked his way up to superintendant of the Pittsburgh Division of the Pennsylvania Railroad. Based on a piece of insider information, Mr. Scott induced Mr. Carnegie to invest in Adams Express, a rail and stagecoach freight shipper, and later in T. T. Woodruff's sleeping-car company. As the mentor to Mr. Carnegie's future successes and wealth, Mr. Scott continued to enable his protégé to invest profitably in iron, bridges, oil derricks and railroad rails. Mr. Carnegie gave Mr. Scott insider information on companies he learned about. They prospered together.

During the Civil War Mr. Scott became Assistant Secretary of War and was in charge of military transportation. Mr. Carnegie helped to restore the rail lines cut by rebels to Washington, D. C., and he rode the first train to bring Union troops to Washington. The war required munitions and supplies to be transported via railroads and extensive telegraph systems. It is presumed Mr. Carnegie, with his ability to "read" whole messages by decoding the sounds, had a leg up on some very special information.

In 1864 Mr. Carnegie invested $40,000 in the Story Farm on Oil Creek in Pennsylvania and reaped rich dividends in oil.

At the war's end Mr. Carnegie left the railroad business and concentrated on steel and iron. He started The Keystone Bridge Works and the Union Ironworks, companies that were heavily involved in supplying rails and bridges across the country. Mr. Scott stayed with Pennsylvania Railroad but was a stockholder in most of Mr. Carnegie's enterprises. Mr. Carnegie started Carnegie Steel Company in 1870 and twenty-one years later sold it to J. P. Morgan, who re-named it U.S. Steel. Mr. Carnegie also invested in rich iron ore properties in northern Minnesota.

He made a lot of money; he gave away a lot of money. Libraries, universities and schools of all sorts in the United States, England and Scotland were recipients. He retained his charm until his death in 1919, but forever will he be classed as a robber baron due to the immense size of his fortune and his abuse of insider information. He parlayed that advantage into enormous wealth. Today that kind of business behavior is unlawful.

JAY COOKE
Financier and Robber Baron

Jay Cooke, who was born on August 10, 1821, and died on February 8, 1905, is a lesser-known robber baron. Although history includes him with other robber barons, we do so because his name is on a state park in northern Minnesota, a park associated with one of the most famous kidnappings on record: that of Virginia Lewis Piper. On the afternoon of July 27, 1972, two masked men abducted Ginny Piper as she gardened at her Long Lake home west of Wayzata, Minnesota. Her housekeeper was taped to a chair with a ransom note nearby demanding $1 million for Ginny's safe release. Her husband, Harry C. "Bobby" Piper, paid it. Two days later Ginny was found alive, chained to a tree in the forest of Jay Cooke State Park, north of Duluth and about 200 miles from her home.

For five years no one was arrested. Then, a partial fingerprint, wisps of hair and the recovery of $4,000 of the ransom money provided the only evidence against two suspects, who were tried, sentenced and then released after a retrial in which an expert declared the fingerprint had been altered. The Jay Cooke State Park will never be just another park after this modern-day crime of greed.

Jay Cooke's early business experience was as a minor trader in a St. Louis office and in the booking office of a transportation company in Philadelphia. He switched to a private firm, E. W. Clark, when he was eighteen years old. Three years later he became a member of one of the largest private banks in the United States as well as a partner in two branches of E. W. Clark, in New York City and St. Louis.

On January 1, 1861, he formed his own company, J. Cooke and Company, and fortune again came his way—in part because of the Civil War. He had successfully floated a $3 million war loan for the State of Pennsylvania. In 1862 the Federal Secretary of the Treasury, Salmon Chase, was having trouble selling $500 million "five-twenty" bonds, bonds callable in five years and maturing in twenty years. Mr. Cooke was given the job of selling them, and he quickly topped the issue by $11 million.

By 1865 the Union needed more cash, and Mr. Cooke was commissioned to peddle three new "seven-thirty" bond issues. He raised a total of $830 million to pay Union soldiers and buy supplies for the rest of the war.

After the war he helped found the Northern Pacific Railroad and sought to develop Duluth, Minnesota, a place that he thought would become a new Chicago. To realize his dream he started to buy into railroads, using Duluth as a logical tie-in to Great Lakes freight moving by water and continuing the journey by rail. But he over-extended himself financially and went bankrupt in the Panic of 1873.

During the same time Mr. Cooke was tied to a financial scandal with the Canadian Government that resulted in Prime Minister John

Macdonald's defeat in the next election. The stock of the Northern Pacific Railroad was sold off for cents on the dollar.

By 1880 Mr. Cooke had paid off all his debts and invested in silver mines. Once again he became rich.

The residents of northeastern Minnesota loved Mr. Cooke, as he would bring scissors and small knives to the school children and lucrative business opportunities to the region. The Jay Cooke State Park has positive connotations to most people, although the name is in fact synonymous with greed, stock losses and other financial scandals.

JAMES JEROME HILL
The Empire Builder

Born in Rockwood, Ontario, on September 16, 1838, J. J. Hill led an average young life until his father died in 1852, ending the boy's formal education. In 1856 Mr. Hill left Canada for St. Paul, Minnesota, a mere frontier trading post at the time.

As a young boy he lost an eye in a bow-and-arrow accident, thus when in 1861 he tried to enlist in the Union Army, he was rejected. Instead he became an accountant for steamboat companies. Winter ice stalled the steamboats and forced him to deal in several small contracts, including one to supply firewood for Fort Snelling located at the juncture of the Minnesota and Mississippi Rivers.

In 1866 he started a freight forwarding business that supplied lumber for buildings in St. Paul. One story has it that he formed the Great Northern Railroad running due west along the north shore of Lake Minnetonka to tap into "The Big Woods" and its source of huge logs. He had the cargo of timber hauled east, back through Minneapolis, to encourage rival St. Paul to try to surpass Minneapolis as the "lead" city. St. Paul did become the state capital of Minnesota.

In 1866 Mr. Hill became a partner in the Red River Transportation Company, a company owning and operating a railroad carrying passengers and freight from St. Paul to Winnipeg, Canada. In 1887 Mr. Hill's partnership bought the St. Paul-Minneapolis & Manitoba Railroad and, in 1890, combined this railroad with the Great Northern Railway to become a major competitor to the Northern Pacific and Burlington rail lines.

Two innovations were used by Mr. Hill in his push west: he was one of the first to use long-lasting steel instead of iron in the railway track rails, and he used corporate stock instead of bonds to finance expansion. The purchase of the Burlington line in the 1890s caused the government to question such an acquisition as monopolistic and against the law. The case reached the United States Supreme Court, and it was ruled the acquisition was indeed anticompetitive.

Mr. Hill left the railroad company in 1904 after the court decision. He also left his original syndicate, which owned the Canadian Pacific Railway and the Great Northern Steamship Company. He died twelve years later. His only marriage was in 1867, and his ten children and their offspring have carried on the philanthropic use of his fortune.

JASON "JAY" GOULD
Worst of the Robber Barons

Born in Roxbury, New York, on May 27, 1836, Mr. Gould led a checkered and dynamic life. Many have called him the most skilled businessman they ever encountered. However, his unscrupulous use of insider information and stock manipulation (which was never condoned even though it was not illegal at that time) has earned him a reputation as a robber baron.

Even Gould himself stated at one point that he knew he was the most hated man in America, and he did not care.

His basic early business training did not prepare him particularly for the type of business he eventually entered, unless surveying and tanning of leather prepares one to be a wheeler-dealer in stocks and railroads.

He made his fortune by bettering Cornelius Vanderbilt for the purchase of the Erie Railroad. In 1867 Mr. Gould was brought aboard the board of directors of the Erie. Four railroads were in intense competition with each other for the freight and passenger traffic between New York City and Chicago. The Erie was a smaller railroad nipping at the heels of the New York Central Railroad owned by Cornelius Vanderbilt. Quietly, Mr. Vanderbilt was trying to buy up the stock of the Erie when its board caught wind of the action.

They quickly issued new Erie stock, whose volume effectively would drain cash from Vanderbilt and undercut his takeover bid. Mr. Vanderbilt was so furious at being uncovered that he had warrants issued for the arrests of the Erie's board members. The media at the time labeled the Erie as "the Scarlet Woman of Wall Street." The Erie board members and Mr. Gould beat it across the Hudson River and set up corporate headquarters in a hotel.

Mr. Gould then went to the state capitol in Albany and in a three-day period bribed enough legislators so that a law could be quickly passed to make the Erie stock sale legal. Vanderbilt was thwarted. The incident was called the "Great Erie War" by the media.

This issue represented but one of Mr. Gould's "Fancy Dan" financial and legal parlor tricks. Tuberculosis killed him on December 2, 1892, at fifty-six years old. Scratch another robber baron.

THE GILDED AGE ENDS

The "Age of the Robber Barons" is an uneven end to historical greed in the nineteenth century, but it was a tremendous growth period for America. What curtailed the domination of American business by the handful of powerful and enormously wealthy companies? Legislation had to be enacted to restrain anticompetitive business practices. Antitrust laws now restrict the efforts of individuals and corporations to monopolize resources, to reduce or suppress competition and to fix prices. Cartels or trusts that control production in order to artificially effect price discrimination are also prohibited.

There *were* positive effects from the robber baron era. Barons amassed enormous, efficient production facilities and reduced the chaos of many small operators. The huge companies they founded increased the amount of capital devoted to innovation and mass production of goods and services.

But major problems that threatened free enterprise came from greed: the robber barons wanted to control the means of production to obtain more substantial profits. They tried to wipe out competition and control markets. In addition, their exploitation of the labor force of the United States resulted in dangerous, cruel and inhumane working conditions. The labor union movement and national legislation eventually reformed these scandalous practices.

The robber barons as a group helped advance the industrial output of the United States, by rightful means or not, with major strides forward in banking, railroads, shipping, real estate, coal, timber, agriculture, oil, gas, iron, steel, mining, and tobacco. This was accomplished by combining political, religious, military and corporate entities. The resources of the nation were utilized for a boom in transport, communication, manufacturing and construction. The gross national product of the nation tripled from 1869 to 1910.

However the scars the "barons" left on the face of the United States are a sad testimonial to reckless greed. The consequences of their business conduct spanned the late nineteenth century and into the twentieth, triggering major tragedies followed by powerful legislative acts. Cruel events such as the Civil War; the Johnstown Flood of May 1889; the Homestead Strike of 1892; the Ludlow Massacre of April 20,1914 (in the Colorado coal-field war); World War I, ending in 1918; the Tea Pot Dome and Elk Hills Oil Field petroleum scandals of 1921; and even the stock market crash of 1929 can be blamed, at least in part, on the robber barons.

An event with lasting effects occurred in 1886 when the United States Supreme Court held that a public corporation had "personhood" in matters of law and taxes. By 1890 the first anti-monopoly legislation was enacted to insure fair trade practices and consumer protection: The Sherman Antitrust Act. It is still the primary law used by the Department of Justice to break up monopolies such as AT&T, Alcoa and Kodak. It was cited in suits against IBM in the 1970s and Microsoft in the 1990s.

Later legislation included the Clayton Antitrust Act, passed in 1914, which defined illegal activities outside the scope of the Sherman Act. It prevents price discrimination, exclusive dealing agreements, vertical integrations, anticompetitive tie-in agreements and anticompetitive mergers and acquisitions that substantially affect the free enterprise marketplace.

President Woodrow Wilson introduced legislation that created the Federal Trade Commission to protect consumers and regulate anticompetitive business activity.

Many legislative acts resulted from the Great Depression of the 1930s such as the Glass-Steagall Act of 1934, which forbade banks from being both commercial and investment banks (a law struck down in 1999 and arguably the cause of the 2007-2012 financial crisis in the United States and the world). Other legislation included the Securities Act of 1933; the Bank Holding Act of 1933; the Securities Exchange Act of 1934, and the Revenue Acts of 1934, 1935 (Wealth Tax Act) and 1936.

A more difficult consequence to assess is our national fascination for the lifestyles of the wealthy. One can make the conjecture that the cycles of excess that seem to be a pattern in American culture come from our national fantasy of achieving enormous personal wealth. As a nation we flock to the only "palaces" built by Americans: the lavish and grandiose residences of the robber barons. They have become our American nobility despite the fact that their fortunes were gained by greed, avarice and ruthlessness.

GREED IN THE INTERNET AGE

Now we pass from the era of the general history of greed into the modern era of the computer, the Internet and instant communications. This new era has not only changed our lives, but the advent of immediate information and instantaneous computer-programmed transactions has made it possible for greed to be easily perpetrated in the financial world and to harm the investing public with intricate schemes and fraud.

In all too many instances companies, commercial and investment banks, arbitrageurs and hedge fund managers have manipulated the assets and share values of businesses using complex and innovative financial strategies. The net result is the destruction of healthy companies and the conversion of assets into enormous wealth for executive management and their financial advisors. This is criminal fraud on a scale never before seen.

In the modern era, greed has been at the core of many of the bankruptcies and corporate scandals that continue to occur at an alarming rate. The following is an attempt to summarize the business cycle when manipulated by corporate greed:

- A successful business or corporation is created by highly disciplined execution of an innovative business plan
- A shrewd and aggressive CEO or president is hired
- The board of directors is expanded to include members with "cozy" ties to management
- A business plan is designed to produce rapid growth based upon fraudulent premises or accounting practices which must be shrouded in secrecy
- Other firms and corporations are acquired using highly leveraged assets and inflated stock values
- Executive compensation and stock values rise rapidly
- Global growth of the enterprises permits commerce without oversight or regulation

- Graft and corruption are committed and ultimately exposed by a whistleblower or by financial losses too large to conceal
- Stock value drops precipitously
- Contractual payout of excessive bonuses to executives continues
- Insolvency pushes the company into bankruptcy
- A federal investigation ensues
- Indictments are issued and the perpetrators are, sometimes, tried for their crimes

There are many paths to success. The above scheme is not one of these. The result is usually that the principal authors of the fraud serve brief sentences or no prison time, and new legislation is enacted to curb the fraudulent behavior. Sadly, the legislators and regulators are always a step behind the inventive minds of the greedy.

Why should anyone succumb to fraud when the actual production of goods and services can generate real income for labor and management and real returns for shareholders? Business success can be achieved honorably and be sustained indefinitely to the benefit of all. Does old-fashioned work ethic and integrity still exist in this age of greed?

GREEDSTERS AND FRAUD TODAY

Chapter 2 – Synopsis

"More than Ever"

Greed and fraud abound at all levels of society with various degrees of severity. Many examples of greed and fraud exist today, most of a minor variety, but they are very serious cumulatively because so many people have been hurt financially or stripped of their assets.

Greed is one of the historical Seven Deadly Sins, which date back to a fourth-century monk who defined them as the cardinal sins of the early Christian church. Three have been added by us to make a list of ten deadly sins for the modern era: Power misused, indifference to the needs of others and self-aggrandizement. Some thirty types of greed and fraud cited in this chapter made it clear the historical Seven Deadly Sins needed to be updated and expanded.

Examples of this are Elizabeth Monrad, CFO of General Re, who helped cook the books of infamous AIG; Dr. Scott Reuben, who falsified the results of important medical research; Kyle Foggo who, as former Director of CIA in Washington, D. C., steered contracts for bottled water for troops in Iraq and Afghanistan to friends; and Pat Forciea, who committed forgery to buy two semi-professional hockey teams.

Those committing smaller-scale greedy frauds are no less evil than those who practiced major versions of Ponzi schemes and other elaborate types of greed and fraud. Destroying the trust of your fellow man is the real crime.

Chapter 2

GREEDSTERS AND FRAUD TODAY

TODAY MORE THAN EVER

Whether in conversation with a friend, in a newspaper, magazine, or on television or the Internet, monetary values are typically denominated in millions, billions and, increasingly, trillions of dollars. Many commercial and investment banks, major corporations and even individuals like Warren Buffett, Bill Gates and the Mars family all measure their assets in billions.

It is breathtaking to think of the sums tossed around in Wall Street and elsewhere in the world. The budgets of nations have always been in huge numbers, but now it is the norm to read corporate financial statements whose figures are expressed in billions, not millions, of dollars. Our nation's budgets, surpluses and deficits are routinely in the trillions.

The total value of the so-called credit derivatives is estimated to be around $12 trillion, a sum larger than the entire economy of the United States. No longer is it valid to say, "As goes General Motors so goes the country;" it could be said more accurately, "As credit swaps and derivatives go, so goes our country."

A column in the *Denver Post* on January 21, 2009, by Al Lewis of Dow Jones aptly described many of our country's financial ills and the greedy few who prosper due to them. He wrote, "We are, after all, a Ponzi nation, relying on new investors to pay off the old, building up fortunes on paper, pretending the market only is up."[http://www.denverpost.com/ci_11505209]. Mr. Lewis further cites Mr. Bill Gross, Managing Director of PIMCO, the largest bond fund in the world, who has written:

> The U.S. and many of its G-7 counterparts over the past 25 years have become more and more dependent on asset appreciation...we became a nation that specialized in the making of paper instead of things.... We have met Mr. Ponzi and he is us — all of us.
> [Due credit goes to Walt Kelly's *Pogo*] (http://www.denverpost.com/business/ci_11505209#ixzz0fqMRPLuT)

Lewis went on, "The Ponzi word is used to describe Social Security, our bailout-happy government, our banking system and our financial markets."

It is assumed that "all of us" refers to the financial community and the wealthy one percent or less of the population (per the Occupy Wall Street movement) who make the headlines and fatten their net worth at the expense of the many. To the greedy, the majority of us ordinary people are "patsies" not "Ponzis."

Still our capitalist economy has done more to create wealth at every level of society than any other system has been able to do—it's worth repeating Winston Churchill's dictum, "Democracy is the worst form of government, except for all the others." Competition and the profit motive keep capitalistic economies innovative, efficient in their use of resources and responsive to markets.

So, when does the accumulation of money become greed? Chapter One of this book documents the fact that greed has been prevalent throughout prehistory and recorded history—and it is alive and well today. Sadly, it will always be a major part of the lives of the species *Homo sapiens*. This book documents the behavior of those humans and their companies that can be classed as greedy, and, in too many cases, the antics that turn to fraud or intentional deception to satiate the appetite for wealth.

THE ORIGINAL SEVEN DEADLY SINS

The Roman Catholic Church placed greed on this list of its Seven Deadly Sins (or Cardinal Sins) as the sin of excess. The list is given below with the opposing Seven Holy Virtues or Contraries:

SIN	VIRTUE
GREED (Latin: avaritia)	CHARITY
LUST (Latin: luxuria)	CHASTITY
GLUTTONY (Latin: gula)	TEMPERANCE
SLOTH (Latin: acedia)	DILIGENCE
WRATH (Latin: ira)	PATIENCE
ENVY (Latin: invidia)	KINDNESS
PRIDE (Latin: superbia)	HUMILITY

Thomas Aquinas included a sub-listing in his interpretation of the Seven Deadly Sins that incorporates the shadings of gluttony, for example:

> Eating too soon, eating too expensively, eating too much, eating too eagerly, eating too daintily, eating wildly...

In a certain sense, all the Seven Deadly Sins can have components of greed. Wrath can mean using anger to control or overpower others with greed as the purpose. Even the concept of sloth implies that others will be manipulated to provide the necessities of life to the slothful. In the narrowest sense, greed is an insatiable desire for money, but more broadly it is an appetite for any material thing or an emotional desire that leads to excess. All too often, greed is demonstrated in the willingness to compromise the well being of others, the creatures of this planet or the planet itself for the benefit of the greedy.

As an example, a person asked "Do you like pancakes?" would respond greedily, "Yeah, I'll say—I have a whole closet full of them." Greed is indulging desire to the point of meaninglessness; collecting things to the point of absurdity; hoarding beyond prudence or reasonable caution. Any action to corner supply, whether of prized paintings, first editions of a book, or commodities of any kind, smacks of greed.

The standard homily "less is more" is a laughable concept to the greedy, who always believe "more is more." It takes a huge sack of money to bid up the prices of treasures such as the items mentioned above in order to indulge one's vanity and sense of privilege. But even though it is possible, there is something amiss in using power and prestige to deprive the world of its historical artifacts or objects of beauty.

In the modern era, the Seven Deadly Sins probably should be expanded to *ten* to reflect our present culture. The expanded list would include three additions: power misused, indifference to the needs of others and self-aggrandizement as explained in the next sections.

POWER MISUSED

Enlargement of power includes the manipulation of business operations to operate above the constraints of prudent management, the striation of society into classes of privilege, the corruption of the sanctity of marriage, and abuse of other obligations of trust.

INDIFFERENCE TO THE NEEDS OF OTHERS

Greed breeds a distancing or separation between the members of humankind. The greedy ignore the plight of the less privileged in favor of pursuing their ambition for wealth. The few with almost unlimited resources often ignore the loss of basic human rights and security for the many. This disconnect causes ever-widening disparities in society as some prosper while others fall further and further behind in their ability to provide health care, education and the necessities of life for themselves and their families.

SELF-AGGRANDIZEMENT

Making oneself more powerful or wealthy by self-promotion, vanity or an egotistical desire for recognition is self-aggrandizing behavior. Gifts made from the desire to improve communities shouldn't require grand gestures such as naming buildings, roads, museums or kids' camps for the donor. Altruism is its own reward to the truly generous person.

The overuse of naming opportunities to link the mighty with their legacy to society or history goes back as early as the time of Alexander the Great. This practice persists into the modern era and it is a misuse of the spirit of philanthropy. In

Israel, for example, it is carried to extreme: Virtually every room, hallway, auditorium or stairwell in a hospital is named for a donor, and an advertisement is run in the donor's local newspaper proclaiming gratitude for the gift and the generosity of the donor to all in the community. This pandering to ego smacks of manipulating the need for self-aggrandizement instead of expressing gratitude.

Although deplorable, the desire for excess does not necessarily lead to criminal abuses. Greed can be categorized as these four types:

- Non-fraudulent greed—acts of excess that are insensitive or offensive to society-at-large
- Borderline greed—acts that border on criminal intent
- Fraudulent greed—illegal acts
- Obscene greed—abhorrent excess that is depraved or morally reprehensible

Greed is so pervasive that we recognize its effect throughout our personal and business lives. We know that greed can cause many psychological ills, such as neuroses, depression and suicide, and can lead to criminal acts like larceny, theft and premeditated murder. It perverts love and increases sexual misconduct. It even compromises religious leaders.

Each of the following segments of our society incorporate examples of one or more of the four types of greed: Sports, Health, Medicine, Politics, Education, Real Estate, Banking and Finance, Insurance, Stock Markets and Investment Management, Energy and Business. There is virtually no trust that will not be breached by the impulses of greed.

The next sections illustrate the variety of individuals seduced by one of the four types of greed.

GENERAL RE
Chief Financial Officer's Accounting Fraud

It's not every day a competent and successful businesswoman is charged, convicted and sentenced to eighteen months in federal prison. Ms. Elizabeth Monrad was Chief Financial Officer of General Re of Stamford, Connecticut, from June 2000 until July 2003. During that time, an apparent conspiracy occurred between AIG and General Re. AIG paid General Re to create a paper trail that appeared as if re-insurance policies had been bought in order to prop up the per-share price of AIG stock. Over a yearlong period, these actions served to increase AIG's stock price because the insurance policies sold and issued by AIG in large amounts were ostensibly protected by re-insurance. This caused an inflation of about $500 million in AIG's reserves.

Insurance companies purchase such reinsurance policies to insure, completely or in part, against the risk they have assumed for their customers. In this case, it was an accounting sham to assure a rise in AIG's stock price, a transaction devised by the parties to create an impression that the company had larger reserves for claims than it actually did.

Ms. Monrad, as the CFO, had to know about this arrangement. Judge Christopher Droney said she had plenty of opportunity to stop the deal and had to be involved from the beginning. "She was the financial expert for General Re in this case," he stated. "A message must be sent to the business and financial communities that this kind of conduct will not be tolerated."

Almost everyone involved was found guilty. General Re's Chief Executive has been sentenced to two years in prison and fined $200,000. AIG's Vice President Christian Milton earned himself four years in prison and a fine of $200,000. General Re's former Senior Vice-President Christopher Garand was sentenced to a year and a day in prison and fined $150,000.

Most would agree these fines and prison sentences are small compared to the cost to the American taxpayer of the AIG debacle.

HOCKEY TEAMS ICED BY FRAUD

Pat Forciea will walk out of federal prison in 2012 after serving eight years. Maybe he'll try to resume owning hockey teams with more success than in the past.

Mr. Forciea was a golden boy in Minnesota politics. He made his mark by playing a prominent role in the victory of underdog Paul Wellstone in the 1990 United States Senate election in Minnesota. Late in 1992, Mr. Forciea was helping the election campaign of Mr. Roger Moe in his attempt to become governor of Minnesota when he abruptly stepped off the Moe campaign trail.

He had other problems distracting him. Mr. Forciea was trying to buy the Rough Riders, the Cedar Rapids, Iowa, minor league hockey team. In order to do so, he received loans from three Minneapolis and St. Paul banks by committing acts of forgery. Shortly after the purchase, he sold 75 percent of the team to a Chicago venture capital firm for $2.1 million.

In the spring of 2004 he purchased another minor league hockey team, the River City Lancers of Omaha, Nebraska, by supplying fraudulent information to Marshall Bank of Minneapolis in order to borrow $2.56 million. He dug a deeper financial hole by embezzling $750,000 from SW Florida Restaurant Holdings as an officer in a Dairy Queen partnership. These funds were put to personal use. In the late 1990s he was investigated for stealing $10,000 from a University of Minnesota sports–promotion campaign. By 2004 the fraud and theft caught up with him and he was slammed into prison for an eight-year sentence.

Mr. Forciea's problems have been attributed to bipolar disorder, which causes drastic mood swings from elation to depression. He has sought treatment for this condition.

DOCTOR FAKES IMPORTANT MEDICAL RESEARCH

Members of the medical profession historically have taken the Hippocratic Oath (or modern versions revised to be more medically correct in our times) as part of their graduation ceremonies. The essence of the oath has been distilled to the phrase "First, Do No Harm." We expect our physicians to abide by the medical ethics of their profession.

Before marketing a medical product, any company in this field must perform exhaustive tests to prove the product is safe and will do what the label states it will do or not do. Patients rely on full disclosure from the medical profession. Medical fraud is chilling to the average person because of the implicit trust between patient and doctor. The next example illustrates how that trust was breached by greed.

Dr. Scott S. Reuben is an anesthesiologist who was chief of the acute pain service at the Baystate Medical Center in Springfield, Massachusetts. Jane Albert, the spokesperson for Baystate Medical, states that since 1996 he has been the respected author of results of at least twenty-one clinical trials. Much of the doctor's drug trial work has been done under grants from pharmaceutical giant Pfizer Inc. Specifically, Dr. Reuben was influential in proving that the multimodal analgesia drugs Celebrex and Lyrica (both marketed by Pfizer) were effective against post-operative pain and promoted faster recoveries.

Questions were raised concerning two of Dr. Reuben's recent trial study abstracts in *The New York Times* on March 11, 2009. Dr.

Reuben then admitted that much of his underlying work had been fabricated. Steven L. Shafer, MD, and editor-in-chief of *Anesthesia and Analgesia*, has said, "Dr. Reuben set back knowledge in the field tremendously."

It was reported in *Anesthesiology News* that in addition to falsifying data, Dr. Reuben appears to have forged another doctor's name as a co-author on two retracted papers.

One colleague, who spoke on the condition of anonymity, recalled that in Dr. Reuben's work over a fifteen-year period, he had never had a study with negative results.

As in many other cases of fraud of long duration, none of Dr. Reuben's peers critically questioned the perpetrator about the integrity of the work—even though there was reason to doubt such overwhelmingly positive data.

JAPANESE SONGWRITER FACES THE MUSIC

You wouldn't dream that a composer who has sold more than *170 million* recordings in Japan alone would commit fraud by selling copyrights to songs that he had already copyrighted—and sold. This is greed on steroids.

Tetsuya Komuro, also known as "TK", is a well-known Japanese keyboard artist. He owned the discotheque Velfarre in Roppongi, Japan, and is credited with introducing dance music to the average Japanese.

He was the most influential J-Pop figure of the 1990s. He had the top five songs on the Oricon record singles chart in April 1996. In that year he approached a private investor who agreed to pay him ¥1 billion, or $10 million, for copyrights to 806 songs. The investor advanced ¥500 million up front. Perhaps it would have been a good deal for all—except that TK couldn't deliver the copyrights; he had already sold them. He was sued for the advance but he had already used most of it for alimony.

According to Japanese law, he had to be arrested and charged with fraud. However, since he was a national figure and was able to restore the advance plus damages to the investor, he received a suspended three-year prison sentence.

SENIOR ACCOUNTANT PUSHED FRAUDULENT TAX SHELTERS

BDO Seidman, the United States member of BDO International, the largest global accounting and consulting network outside of the "Big Four" (Price Waterhouse Coopers, Deloitte Touche Tohmatsu, Ernst & Young and KPMG), is an old and esteemed accounting firm. It was big news when one of its senior partners pleaded guilty to charges of pushing a bogus tax shelter plan that made it possible for wealthy clients to evade more than $200 million in federal taxes.

Mr. Michael Kerekes (now an ex-partner of BDO Seidman) worked out of the Los Angeles office. On Friday, February 13, 2009, he pleaded guilty before Judge Harold Baer of Federal District Court in Manhattan. He will always remember how unlucky that day was for him.

One of the hot issues in corporate accounting today is offshore accounting and its special treatment of tax liabilities. Mr. Kerekes was found guilty of conspiracy and tax evasion. These offshore schemes have cost the Federal Government billions of dollars of lost revenue since the late 1990s. Because of this particular suit, the government will have new reasons to pursue tax-plan dodges of accounting firms—and of the big international banks as well.

The New York Times on June 9, 2009, reported that related charges were brought against two former employees of Deutsche Bank, two former lawyers and a former BDO Seidman partner. Both Deutsche Bank and BDO Seidman have declined to comment on the investigations into their involvement in the scheme.

CONGRESSMAN PRACTICED PERSONAL ENRICHMENT

A former Democratic Congressman with nine elected terms serving the constituents of the Second District of Louisiana, William (Bill) J. Jefferson of New Orleans, was sentenced on Friday, November 13, 2009, to thirteen years in federal prison for bribery, racketeering and money laundering. He received double bad luck—a thirteen-year sentence handed down on Friday the thirteenth.

Congressman Jefferson sought re-election to his Louisiana congressional seat in Washington, but lost it after being convicted in August 2009 for his crimes. His attorney, Robert P. Trout, says he'll appeal the conviction: "Mr. Jefferson ascended from humble beginnings to the nation's finest educational institution [Harvard Law School] and the highest corridors of power [U. S. House of Representatives]." The attorney didn't mention the jury verdict that declared him guilty of eleven of sixteen felony counts after a six-week trial.

After eight years in the Louisiana State Senate, according to *The New York Times*, Mr. Jefferson became "the first black person from Louisiana elected to Congress since Reconstruction." As a member of the Ways and Means Committee, he accepted bribes from companies to foster business in Africa and for personal enrichment.

In August 2005, federal agents raided his house and found $90,000 carefully wrapped in foil and stuffed into veggie-burger cartons in his freezer. The bribe was intended for the Vice President of Nigeria, who had suddenly left town without the money. A further raid on Mr. Jefferson's Congressional Office in May 2006 was declared unconstitutional as the Justice Department's first-ever intrusion on a Congressman's office.

PROFESSOR DUPES NASA
NASA Defrauded of Millions

Professor Samim Anghaie, a professor of radiological engineering, founded the University of Florida's "Innovative Nuclear Space Power and Propulsion Institute" in 1985. Agents of the Federal Bureau of Investigation raided the institute on February 25, 2009, and accused the professor of illegally applying for and receiving thirteen government contracts totaling $3.4 million.

Dr. Anghaie had formed a private company, New Era Technology (Netech), whose president was his wife, Sousan Anghaie. This company applied for several research grants from the National Aeronautics and Space Administration under the guise of the institute. Fraudulent invoices for hours worked by employees were also submitted on its behalf.

The professor and his wife diverted hundreds of thousands of dollars of illegally obtained monies from Netech to their personal accounts and to accounts of their two sons, Ali and Hamid Anghaie.

Dr. Anghaie, who was born in Iran, came to the University of Florida in 1980 and has served as a consultant to the American government in the areas of space propulsion, nuclear power and propulsion, advanced reactors, thermal hydraulics, computational fluid dynamics and heat transfer. He has published more than 500 papers and reports.

Despite using the millions for some research, the FBI claims that Dr. Anghaie bought six cars and six pieces of real estate in Fort Lauderdale, Gainesville and Tampa, Florida, as well as in Manchester, Connecticut.

On November 2, 2009, a Federal Grand Jury returned a seventy-one count indictment charging the Anghaies with conspiracy to commit wire fraud, fifty counts of wire fraud, conspiracy to commit money laundering, seventeen counts of money laundering and one count of making false statements to the government. They were arrested the same day.

GERMAN BILLIONAIRE
Commits Suicide After Losing Family Fortune

One of the richest men in Germany was a lawyer who practiced investing instead of law. Mr. Adolf Merckle of Blaubeuren committed suicide on January 5, 2009, by jumping in front of a train. He was seventy-four years old. He had bet that Volkswagen's stock would drop. A few days before his death, Porsche announced that they were buying 50 percent of Volkswagen and intended to increase their investment to 75 percent by year's end. Mr. Merckle lost hundreds of millions as the Volkswagen stock soared. The stock went from €120.85 per share to over €900 in less than two days.

Most of Mr. Merckle's money came from inheritance. His grandfather and father owned chemical and pharmaceutical wholesaler companies as well as generic drug, cement and vehicle manufacturing concerns. He took over the family companies in 1967 and had parlayed them into 120 companies with a work force of 100,000 and a net asset value of €30 billion. His own personal fortune was estimated to be €9.2 billion. He was ranked the ninety-fourth wealthiest individual in the world on the *Forbes* list of the world's 1,125 billionaires.

Mr. Merckle, normally known for his secretive and cautious business style, stunned Germany when it was revealed that he had taken huge risks in stock speculation and gone down in the financial turmoil of 2008-2009. He was negotiating to obtain major loans at reasonable interest rates from British and American banks to shore up his large debt loads. One of the conditions requested by the foreign banks was that he sell his majority interests in his main companies to secure the loans.

By January 2009 his financial situation must have grown so hopeless that he stepped in front of a train to end his life. A conservative businessman all his life, Adolf Merckle was thus destroyed by pride and greed.

75-YEAR-OLD NAILED
Another Mini-Madoff

Mr. Arthur Goeffrey Nadel at age seventy-five should have known better. He was indicted on April 28, 2009, and charged with fifteen counts of mail fraud and securities fraud. If convicted on all counts he would face 200 years in prison.

His alleged Ponzi schemes defrauded at least 371 clients who had invested a total of $397 million in Mr. Nadel's six hedge funds and two management companies. His business solicitation statements portrayed that his companies had generated more than $271 million in gains, whereas the U. S. Attorney's office of the Southern District of New York stated that the companies had an overall net loss.

When the Bernard Madoff Ponzi scheme hit the media with its immediate frenzy, two investors of Mr. Nadel's companies asked for an audit of the hedge funds. Mr. Nadel agreed to the audits—and then disappeared. A suicide note was found in his office-shredding machine after his fifth wife called authorities and reported him missing on January 14, 2009. Court documents show that the note read in part, "The avenues to money for you will likely be blocked soon. Sell the Subaru if you need money."

Federal agents were suspicious and tracked Mr. Nadel to Slidell, Louisiana, and arrested him in Tampa, Florida, on January 27, 2009, when he turned himself in. Mr. Nadel had transferred $1.25 million out of his hedge funds into his private account shortly before he went missing.

Michael D. Zucker, Mr. Nadel's accountant, admitted he was not licensed as a Certified Public Accountant. Gains on investments were purported to be as high as 21.6 percent in 2001. Donald Rowe of *Wall Street Digest* has stated Mr. Nadel's funds had "the best of track records." How would investors know that anything was amiss without proper audits by a licensed CPA?

SLAUGHTERHOUSE EMPLOYS UNDOCUMENTED ALIENS

On Armistice Day, November 11, 2009, Mr. Sholom Rubashkin, manager of Agriprocessors, Inc. in Postville, Iowa, was indicted by a jury in federal court on eighty-six of ninety-one financial fraud charges and soon will face a second trial on seventy-two immigration charges stemming from employing illegal aliens in the company's slaughterhouse.

This financial-fraud trial had been moved from Postville to Sioux Falls, South Dakota. Mr. Rubashkin could face a sentence of several hundred years in prison for the financial fraud, and if found guilty on any or all of the second trial charges, could face a combined prison sentence of over 2,000 years [Lynda Waddington, *The Iowa Independent*, February 24, 2009].

Employees of the slaughterhouse testified that Mr. Rubashkin directed them to create false invoices for loans to show St. Louis-based First Bank that the processing plant had more cash flow than it really had. They also said that a few days before the immigration raid by the Feds, Mr. Rubashkin scrambled to get new documents for at least 389 workers found to be illegal immigrants.

After the raid, the company filed for bankruptcy and has since been sold, according to an Associated Press article in *The New York Times*.

BALLOON CHASE BRINGS US ALL DOWN

On the afternoon of October 15, 2009, CNN started tracking a relatively large silver-saucer balloon as it careened its way northward along the eastern plains and Front Range of the Colorado Rockies. Details of its flight from location to location and why and how it had gotten loose, had cluttered the network most of the afternoon, reaching fever pitch when the mother of the family involved in the making and flying of the balloon stated that she thought her six-year-old son was aboard it.

No one watching the coverage could help having their heart in their throat as they saw the saucer dip and dive—never once turning over—as it flowed above the mile-high ground surface while reaching a peak altitude above ground of as much as 2,000 feet. It was dramatic and unbelievable that a young boy would be inside the "cabin" suspended below the balloon, tipping sideways, partially collapsing, wheeling and sailing on air currents until it lost enough buoyancy near the ground to have chasers grab the trailing tether lines that had somehow broken loose.

About the time the chase mob settled the saucer on the ground and raced to free the boy from the cabin, it was announced the boy had been found hiding in the garage attic. Nobody and nothing was in the cabin of the balloon, and that wasn't the only thing deflated. As watchers and followers expelled a collective sigh of relief and reality sunk in, it became obvious that all of us had been hoodwinked. The report of the boy in the balloon was a falsehood perpetrated on a gullible public to gain publicity for a possible reality television show. What about the hundreds of thousands of dollars of local and federal government funds used for the chase? We all paid dearly for that trial balloon.

Fortunately, the little boy did not know how to lie. When asked why he had hidden, he told the truth: "We did it for the show."

As a Christmas present from Larimer County, Colorado, District Court Judge Stephen Schapansk sentenced Richard and Mayumi Heene on December 23, 2009. Mr. Heene received ninety days in jail (with a daytime work release, spending nights in jail) and Mrs. Heene was slapped with twenty days in jail (with a modified family-care release, spending ten weekends in jail). They began serving sentences on January 11, 2010.

After being sentenced, Mr. Heene said, "I do want to reiterate that I'm very, very sorry. That's it." The pair could be fined the $50,000 in costs incurred during the chase.

The allure of fat fees for a dramatic television episode caused a family to mobilize an extremely costly rescue and to ask their six-year-old son to lie to authorities for a publicity stunt? Greed at work.

GREEDY JUDGE KICKED OUT FOR KICKBACKS

Senior Judge Arthur E. Grim said, "I've never heard of anything remotely approaching this." The issue was a sentence handed down by Judge Mark A. Ciavarella, Jr. to a seventeen-year-old student for writing a satirical spoof of her high school's Assistant Principal. The sentence? Ninety days in a juvenile detention center after being led from the courtroom in handcuffs. The incident occurred in Wilkes-Barre, Pennsylvania.

An investigation into a separate issue disclosed Judge Ciavarella and a sidekick judge took kickbacks of some $2.6 million over a seven-year period from operators of two privately-owned detention centers for juveniles called Pennsylvania Child Care and Western Pennsylvania Child Care. In December 2002 the two judges ruled for the shutdown of an existing public detention center because of its "poor condition."

Since 2003 Judge Ciavarella has sentenced 5,000 juveniles to the new private detention center. He was known as a tough judge. According to lawyer Marsha Levick, "there was a culture of intimidation surrounding this judge and no one was willing to speak up about the sentences he was handing down."

At the conclusion of the recent personal trial of Judge Ciavarella, a plea agreement was reached that inflicted a lesser penalty on the judge than he might have received in a jury trial. When the plea agreement was announced in court, someone amidst the eighty spectators in the courtroom yelled, "Bull!" Apparently, judges are judged differently than average citizens—especially if only a teenager has been harmed.

BEST BUY PURCHASING SCAM

Was $31 million in kickbacks worth being charged with five counts of mail fraud and money laundering carrying a possible sentence of twenty-five years of total jail time? You wouldn't think so.

Robert Paul Bossany, Vendor Relations Manager of Best Buy, Inc., admitted to investigators from the U. S. Postal Inspection Service, the Internal Revenue Service—Criminal Investigation Division and the Federal Bureau of Investigation that he did indeed defraud his employer, Best Buy, Inc. of Bloomington, Minnesota, of $31,000,000.

The scheme worked like this: Best Buy would solicit bids from computer parts companies. Company A (conspiring with Mr. Bossany) would bid low with no intention of supplying the parts at bid prices. At times they bid on parts that they didn't have in their possession. Their low bids were accepted and a purchase order sent. When filled, the order would be billed to Best Buy through Company B at a much higher price. Company A admitted they had billed through Company B, and Best Buy paid invoices for more than $60 million for the parts. Best Buy paid approximately $31 million in excess of the bid prices. Company A compensated Bossany with cash and other property hidden in gifts of magazines, CDs or DVDs. The checks and items were sent to Bossany's house.

Apparently, Company A was The Chip Factory and the fraud went unchecked from 2003 to 2007. Weekly packages were delivered to Bossany's house via Federal Express and UPS. Best Buy appropriately fired Mr. Bossany. The investigation begun by Best Buy ended in an official charge of fraud against Bossany and The Chip Factory.

IRAQ AND IRAN BOTTLED-WATER CONTRACTS FRAUD

Mr. Kyle D. Foggo should have been aware of the consequences of his actions since he is the former Executive Director of the Central Intelligence Agency. He steered lucrative bottled-water contracts to Brent R. Wilkes of San Diego, in return for which he received expensive vacations, meals at fancy restaurants and was even offered a job when he retired.

Under an agreement with federal prosecutors to plead guilty to a single count of wire fraud, he was eligible for a federal sentence of seventeen months—which he served.

Bottled water for our troops in hot countries like Iraq and Afghanistan is a necessity. One battalion alone consumes 6,000 bottles daily. The empty bottles can't be burned. Many caps are left on and the heated oxygen and expanded vestiges of water cause the bottles to explode from expansion, creating havoc amongst the troops, who think they're under attack. Millions of empty bottles must be buried daily.

Lawyers for Mr. Foggo maintained that in spite of his mistakes, he was a resourceful and loyal CIA officer who served his country well.

OIL AND GAS LEASES
Colorado Springs, Colorado

Mr. Donald H. Allen founded at least two companies: H & M Petroleum and American Energy Resources. These entities sell oil and gas leases to individual investors. Between March 2002 and December 2006, Mr. Allen and his companies raised at least $9.9 million from 350 investors who were promised return on their money ranging as high as 354 percent annually.

When accepting their money, Mr. Allen did not tell investors that neither he nor his companies had ever generated any profits for any investor from oil and gas leases, that securities were improperly sold in unregistered transactions and that Mr. Allen was acting as an unregistered broker.

What did he do with about $10 million of the investors' money? In addition to such costs as salaries, travel and operating costs, he was accused of spending nearly $3 million of investors' money on fancy speedboats, ski vacations, jewelry and the latest in fitness machines, according to SEC charges.

The SEC settled the case out of court without Mr. Allen admitting or denying any of the allegations. The case was settled for a fine of $510,000.

So, he took in $9,000,000 from investors, spent about $3,000,000 on personal goods and services and paid a fine of about $500,000. Where did the remaining $5,500,000 go in those four years of business? Certainly, the investors received not one dollar of it.

In four years he managed to bilk $5.5 million for himself. Nice and greedy.

RUSSIAN TYCOON JAILED FOR UP TO THIRTY YEARS

Mikhail Borisovich Khodorkovsky at age forty-five has a fraud and jail record almost longer than his full name. He was born in Moscow, made high grades in school, and while in college at Mendeleev Institute of Chemical Technology, became deputy head of Komsomol, the Communist Youth League.

He parlayed that position, with friends, into ownership of a private café, opened a "Center for Scientific and Technical Creativity," and through the Scientific Center developed a brisk trade in importing Swiss vodka (made in Poland) and French brandy (not made in France). Using cash from these operations, which included computer buys and sells, he founded the Bank Menatep in 1989.

With large deposits, the government awarded the bank the right to manage Chernobyl nuclear accident victims' funds, whose fees carried an exempt status, an extremely convenient vehicle for evasion of taxes and import duties. For more than ten years, Menatep and Mr. Khodorkovsky bought and maneuvered many companies, including a major interest in Yukos, the Russian oil company. The purchase of a major state-owned fertilizer company, Apatit, was his downfall.

A rosy future turned bleak when he was arrested in October 2003 and charged with fraud and tax evasion. His trial ended with conviction and up to thirty years in prison after judges (by Russian custom) read aloud all 662 pages of the indictment—which took from May 16 to May 31, 2005. In prison, Mr. Khodorkovsky has been denied early parole because he refused to take sewing lessons. Russian justice is uncompromising.

MORGAN STANLEY TAKES A FRAUD HIT BY AN EMPLOYEE

Just because Morgan Stanley is a major investment house on Wall Street doesn't exclude it from being subject to fraud by an employee.

Mr. Richard Garaventa, Jr. was entrusted with the authorization to approve corporate payments from the company's in-house accounts. He set up a company called the New York Transfer Company and had up to fifty checks ranging from $8,670 to $74,812 and totaling $2.5 million sent to it. According to Assistant District Attorney of New York, Jeremy Glickman, Mr. Garaventa "spent the money almost as fast as it came in."

With cash in the account of New York Transfer, in a period of time on and after September 5, 2001, he purchased Mercedes and Lexus cars and expensive jewelry, renovated his house, dined at fancy restaurants, and took luxury vacations in Florida, Aruba and other locations.

Morgan Stanley called Mr. Garaventa "a rogue employee" and stated that the actions spelled out in the indictment were "in direct violation of the firm's values and policies." He has been charged with forty-three counts of grand larceny, possession of stolen property and falsifying business records.

As a Morgan Stanley employee, his 2008 salary was $125,000 with a $50,000 bonus. Mr. Garaventa won't make that much from Morgan Stanley in 2009. He was fired on January 7 of that year.

HEDGE FUND HEAD HEDGED HIS DEATH

Samuel Israel III in effect died twice and yet still lives. First, he faked his death by abandoning his GMC Envoy on a bridge in 2008, with a note on the seat that read, "Suicide is painless." He reappeared four weeks later in an apparent change of heart.

The second "death" occurred when he entered federal prison for more than twenty years for his misdeeds. He will be at least seventy years old when released from prison, provided he survives the anxiety and danger of life in a secure federal penitentiary.

Mr. Israel is a scion of a wealthy and well-known family in New Orleans who made it big with a hedge fund until his Bayou Group collapsed. His faked death was an attempt to escape from furious investors who lost $450 million when defrauded by Mr. Israel after his elaborate promises of huge returns proved to be falsehoods.

Mr. Israel and girlfriend Debra Ryan planned his first death by leaving a getaway van in a rest area off I-684 early in the morning of his disappearance on June 10, 2008. He stashed his car on the Bear Mountain Bridge and wrote his message on the hood of the car. Picking up the van, they drove to the Prospect Mountain Campground RV Park in Granville, Massachusetts, where Mr. Israel holed up for nearly a month.

He finally gave himself up by riding his motor scooter to the police station in Southwick, Massachusetts, walking inside, and saying, "I'm a fugitive. I'm supposed to go to jail."

The police didn't argue. The girlfriend has been charged for her role in the disappearance. Mr. Israel's mother was influential in his decision to give himself up.

TEDDY BEAR COLLECTION WORTH $80,000

Mr. Paul Greenwood and his investment partner Stephen Walsh were wise guys when the market was surging and they attracted hundreds of millions of dollars from public and university pension funds. Sums invested with WG Trading included $339 million from the Iowa Public Employees Pension Fund, $65 million from the University of Pittsburgh, $49 million from Carnegie Mellon and $90 million from the Sacramento Employees' Retirement System. The Pennsylvania Employees System was getting ready to invest $1 billion in W G Trading when the roof fell in on the traders.

In the 1980s the investment pair devised a special computerized trading system called Shark, which enabled traders to spot trading opportunities in the stock, bonds and futures markets. In 1986, Wang Laboratories bought Shark from them and the twosome then bought a stake in the Islanders hockey team and formed two investment companies, WG Trading and Westridge Capital.

According to *The New York Times,* when the Madoff scandal hit the media some investors with Mr. Greenwood tried to redeem their investments. It was too late—the capital was gone. The SEC entered the picture. An audit found that the two partners had taken "loans" from their funds totaling $554 million and had invested $147 million in companies they controlled.

Their extravagant life style had included the purchase of a fifty-four acre horse farm from Paul Newman and Joanne Woodward, horses and an $80,000 collection of Steiff teddy bears that was later priced at $1.9 million for a Christie's liquidation auction.

Mr. Greenwood and Mr. Walsh were arrested on February 25, 2009. The total amount of the money missing was $667 million. Their trial is pending.

GREEDY FUNDS

The wide variety of greedy fraudulent schemes has resulted in many possible criminal acts. The United States Department of Justice has accumulated a list that pertains to the resolution of claims under the False Claims Act, but does not include claims of tax fraud, insurance fraud, inheritance fraud or estate fraud:

- Phantom billing—billing for work not performed
- Double billing
- Distribution of unapproved devices and drugs
- Forgery of physician's signature
- Falsifying prescription records
- Contract kickbacks
- "Upcoding"—stating more work done than was done
- Fraudulent cost reports
- Inadequate care (use of untrained personnel)
- "Unbundling"—charging each item when one charge suffices
- Performing inadequate or unnecessary work
- Charging for equipment never used or ordered
- Billing for brand-name drugs and using generic drugs instead
- "Defective testing"—test not completed but billed anyway
- Use of substandard equipment
- Reporting fraudulent research
- Making false statements on grant applications
- Improper use of federal grant money
- Illegal dumping of chemicals and other substances
- "Yield burning"—deflating yields by inflating costs
- Using phantom employees and charging for them
- Creation of phony insurance companies
- Using unauthorized foreign products

MINOR FRAUD AND GREED

It's a fine line between major and minor frauds and greed. Determining factors include the amount of money lost, the period of time the scam was in operation, the number of people involved on both sides of a scam, the notoriety of the perpetrator(s) and the overall severity of the crime.

For the purposes of this book, we have collected hundreds of minor cases involving thousands of people. To do justice to these many minor cases, we briefly present vignettes of twenty-three instances of minor frauds and the inherent greed in those acts:

New Jersey: A recent corruption sweep in New Jersey indicates how people from every walk of life may be involved in fraud and greed. A two-year corruption and international money-laundering investigation charged forty-four people, including three mayors, two state assemblymen, five rabbis and others. Their egregious actions involved the illegal sale of body parts, as well as passing of cash in diners, parking lots, boiler rooms and even in a box of Apple Jack cereal stuffed with $97,000. Their trials are pending.

Brooklyn, New York: In an unrelated case a Brooklyn man was accused of enticing people to give up a kidney for $10,000. Later, he sold the kidneys for $160,000 each.

Washington, D. C.: Michelle, a supervisor in the Department of Revenue, fell in love and stole money from the department by creating false businesses and tax returns. In all she stole $11,000,000 and gave most of it to her boyfriend, who bought expensive jewelry, land, cars and fancy trips. She was sentenced to twenty-four years in jail. The prosecutor stated, "She had a pretty smile, but threw all the money away for a prize who was not worth so much."

East Brunswick, New Jersey: Jerome O'Hara and George Perez were arrested for helping Bernard Madoff pull off his giant Ponzi scheme. They computerized an elaborate paper trail to conceal his frauds for years. They used a special computer labeled "House 17" on the seventeenth floor of the Lipstick Building in New York City—the off-limits offices of Mr. Madoff. These two gentlemen each face twenty-four years in prison.

Greeley, Colorado: Mr. Mark Strodtman was found guilty after a twelve-day trial for theft and forgery. He fled the country to avoid prosecution but was found and arrested in Mexico. He could face forty-eight years in prison. He solicited fraudulent mortgages for Spanish-speaking people and charged extravagant fees.

Denver, Colorado: Mr. Howard Kieffer was facing a thirty-five-year prison term and a fine of $1.25 million for impersonating a federal attorney in court. He was charged with wire fraud, making false statements and contempt of court. He advertised over the Internet as to his ability as an attorney. In May 2008 he took $70,000 to represent an Aspen, Colorado, woman who was charged with trying to have her son's father killed. She was convicted of the crime but is appealing the verdict.

Beijing, China: We call this a minor fraud even though it totaled $34 billion. During the first eleven months of 2009 sixty-seven senior officers and 164 others were turned over to judicial authorities for misappropriating funds. The official audit covered more than 20,000 government officials. Where the money went is still being examined. "Official corruption is one of the main causes of social unrest in China, and the country's leaders have publicly warned that it has become so widespread that it now threatens Communist Party Rule," according to *The Wall Street Journal*. This is a possible hole in the "great wall" of China's governing structure.

Helena, Montana: Four resorts have sued Credit Suisse Bank and real estate company Cushman and Wakefield under a class action of $24 billion. The eighty-four-page claim of artificially inflated real estate values has made it impossible to refinance mortgages in trouble. One such resort is the famed Yellowstone Club, whose members include Bill Gates and former Vice President Dan Quayle. The suit is being tried in Boise, Idaho.

Upper Red Lake, Canada: Four men from Wisconsin were in Canada fishing for walleyes, when a law officer stopped to see how they were doing. They had twelve walleyes in their two fish houses. "Nobody was sure how many fish they had," said the officer, so he checked their onshore cabin freezer. He found forty-four more fish—way over the legal limit of sixteen fish. They were fined $50 per extra fish plus $900 each for breaking the law.

Fishers, Indiana: Marcus Schrenker had problems—security violations and an unhappy wife. On January 9, 2009, he lost a $533,500 suit brought by a dissatisfied investor. His wife had divorced him eleven days before. On January 11 he took off in his Piper plane, set it on autopilot and jumped. The plane continued empty for 200 miles and crashed in Florida. Schrenker disappeared for two days and was arrested in Florida in his pup tent. He faces twenty-six years in prison, $500,000 in fines and millions of dollars in lawsuits.

Philadelphia, Pennsylvania: Do you have an empty house? Be careful; it may be sold without your knowledge. Fifteen criminals fraudulently sold eighty-two empty houses over a five-year period, mostly to immigrants and non-English-speaking buyers. The suspects were arrested and charged with theft, forgery, burglary, conspiracy and tampering with public records.

Telluride, Colorado: Shahin Kashanchi of Telluride helped his brother-in-law, Hassan Nemazee (also of Telluride), defraud three banks in excess of $290 million. In 2008, Nemazee was national finance chairman of Hillary Clinton's presidential campaign and later raised money for Barack Obama. One of Mr. Nemazee's fake documents was a statement for a non-existent account that held $623 million in U. S. Treasury securities. Mr. Kashanchi told authorities "a fifteen-year-old could figure out what we were doing." Charged with bank fraud, he could serve thirty years in prison.

Beverly Hills, California: Mr. John Goodin was a real estate promoter who hoped his fortunes would change after digging a deep hole of debt in his business. On June 10, 1992, he figured a way out of his troubles: In the afternoon, Mr. Goodin walked into his house, entered the bathroom, put the barrel of a twelve-gauge shotgun to his face—and pulled the trigger. He left behind three children. Subsequent research showed he had at least eight lawsuits filed against him in ten years, including slander and failing to pay construction expenses.

Indiana: Mr. Timothy S. "Bull" Durham lived a lavish lifestyle that included ownership of about 100 exotic and fancy cars (including a 2008 Bugatti Veyrona) and a 30,000-square-foot mansion. He was a large contributor to the Republican Party. He has been charged with running a Ponzi scheme and using investors' money in part to make $160 million in loans to his self-owned companies. When asked how he could justify lending money from one company to others of his companies, he said, "Because I knew them better."

Singapore: It's difficult enough to swindle a company or an individual, but it's really difficult to swindle a whole country. That's what Nigerian Paul Gabriel Amos tried to do. Living in Singapore, he and others created official-looking documents to extract large sums of money from Citibank remotely. Citibank held a major account for the National Bank of Ethiopia in New York. In October 2008 Mr. Amos sent twenty-four faxed messages to Citibank ordering transfers of a total of $27 million to accounts in Japan, South Korea, Australia, China, Cyprus and the United States. Signatures and other documents seemed to match their files, so Citibank honored the requests. The fraud was discovered after the fact, the perpetrators were caught and Citibank credited Ethiopia for any lost funds.

United Kingdom: Under the newly promulgated Freedom of Information Act, a Mrs. Brookes requested information regarding expenses of members of Britain's House of Commons. A direct result was the ouster of the Speaker of the House of Commons, the first such drastic action since 1695. Among expenses disclosed were $40,000 spent to renovate a member's house, monthly mortgage payments, the clearing of a country house moat, an electric massage chair and the installation of a Kit Kat bar—whatever that may be. It is clear that Ms. Brookes is a heroine of sorts to the British people.

Minneapolis, Minnesota: The Saint Elizabeth Seton Catholic School had Joyce A. Klevence as a favorite principal from 1995 to 2007—until it was discovered that she had stolen from church funds to the tune of $350,000. Hennepin County District Judge John Holahan said, "The theft was particularly egregious because its victims were countless school children." The parents of the school children learned a lesson, too!

Denver, Colorado: Mr. Michael Wise was chairman of the failed Denver-based Silverado Savings and Loan, which cost taxpayers more than $1 billion. Charged for fraud but acquitted, he was also banned from banking for the rest of his life. He moved to Aspen, started a mortgage company and was sent to prison for three and one-half years for various infractions. After prison he moved to Florida. On April 8, 2009 he drove to the Tampa airport, parked his car on the top floor of the airport garage, jumped and died in a grove of palm trees.

Switzerland: What do Bank Credit Suisse and auto manufacturer BMW have in common? Swiss citizen Heig Sgarbi and German heiress Susanne Klatten. He worked for the bank; she inherited a fortune from BMW stock. She lent him millions of euros after he threatened to release messages recorded during their trysts. They had met at a spa near Innsbruck, Austria, in 2007. He was sentenced to six years in prison.

Saddlebrook, New Jersey: Juergen Homann pleaded guilty to tax evasion. The dual citizen of Germany and the United States failed to file a form called "F-bar," which advises the IRS of foreign holdings. Mr. Homann deliberately shielded money in the Swiss USB Bank by forming a foundation in the country of Liechtenstein, which is well known for its tax havens. Mr. Homann was one of 285 names turned over to the IRS by the Swiss Bank, identifying secret foreign accounts. The Justice Department is examining the secret-until-now accounts for violations. Mr. Homann will be fined.

New York, New York: A former salesman for Lehman Brothers, Mr. Frederick Bower pleaded guilty to federal charges of conspiracy and securities fraud. It was claimed he prospered from secret stock tips passed on to him by a colleague's wife. He could face up to eighteen months in prison and be fined the huge sum of $12,000. Talk about a mild slap on the wrist! Crime appears to pay—sometimes.

Ligonier, Pennsylvania: A recent federal grand jury accused Mr. Gregory Podlucky of perpetrating a grand bank fraud in the amount of $806 million. He provided the bank and equipment suppliers with "dramatically false financial statements" to obtain leases and loans for the Latrobe, Pennsylvania firm, Le-Nature, Inc. Most of the money went to Mr. Podlucky and his father. Le-Nature is a now-defunct soft drink maker. No potluck for Mr. Podlucky.

Vienna, Austria: Julius Meinl V, the present representative of one of Austria's most noble families, has been charged with a $4 billion bank fraud. He raised a bail of $135 million, owns a private Falcon jet and has a dual Austrian and British citizenship—raising the specter of his fleeing the country. When lawyers for Mr. Meinl posted the large bail in cash, Mr. Meinl was held by the court overnight to be sure that the bank didn't fail to honor or somehow negate the cash draft paid for bail.

The family company dates back to 1862 and is famous for its exotic coffees, pastries and tortes (all hand made) and fancy grocery items. The Meinl Bank, of which Mr. Julius Meinl V is chairman, is one of Europe's largest banks. Vienna has a street named Julius Meinl Gasse. In the middle of this scandal is the family's Meinl European Land, Ltd. based in the Isle of Jersey and controlled by Mr. Julius Meinl. It's been rumored the Meinls lost about $2 billion in the Madoff Ponzi scam.

SUMMARY

Greed and fraud go hand in hand most of the time. The reason? Money.

The lure of supposedly easy money catches those unaware of pitfalls and makes for easy "scores" by scoundrels. Perhaps some of the examples of greed and fraud in this book will help the unaware be more cautious and more informed with their investments. If you have money, need money or desire more money, you're an easy target of the greedy. Beware!

GREEDSTERS PONZI SCHEMES

Chapter 3 – Synopsis

"Classic Frauds"

It seems as if Ponzi schemes are in fashion—we see them written up nearly every time we pick up a newspaper or magazine. Italian-born Charles Ponzi perpetrated not the first but certainly the most famous early fraud of this kind in his adopted country, the United States of America. The "pyramid" scheme now commonly bears his name.

This deceptive investment operation depends upon greed and fraud. In order to divert an investor's money into his pockets, the scoundrel must invent a plausible but fraudulent investment opportunity. But to fund the fraud, gullible investors must be motivated by their own greed for unrealistically high returns.

The two most notorious offenders of modern times, Bernard L. Madoff and R. Allen Stanford, created Ponzi schemes that defrauded investors of billions of dollars. These two greedsters are detailed in their own chapters later in this book, but there are hundreds, if not thousands, of lesser Ponzi schemes. Some of their stories are described in this chapter.

Chapter 3

GREEDSTERS PONZI SCHEMES

The word "Ponzi" hit headlines with the disclosure of the Madoff scandal, which was quickly followed by the Stanford scandal, both of them Ponzi schemes of the highest magnitude. These two dreams of ill-gotten glory will be treated in detail in later chapters of this book. But why is the pyramid scheme called a Ponzi, and why does it work?

The Madoff scheme broke open on December 10, 2008, and the Stanford scheme in January 2009. Both had been simmering with rumors and accusations of insolvency for months prior to their disclosures. Both investigations were back burnered for nearly six months of 2009 while the wheels of justice turned slowly and carefully to gather evidence from authorities and the principal participants.

Madoff and Stanford's combined losses to investors initially were estimated at more than $75 billion—an enormous number. As trustees continue their efforts to recover assets, the figure may come down, but truthfully no one will ever be able to assess the magnitude of the actual losses in both monetary and human terms.

The revelations about these two giant scams created doubts with other investors around the country and revealed many smaller Ponzi schemes.

This chapter deals with twenty less well-known Ponzi schemes that for the most part occurred in the last few years and amounted to multi-millions, if not billions, of dollars of losses for their investors.

A Ponzi scheme is sometimes called a pyramid scheme. The scam is simple: have a plausible investment opportunity providing unusually high returns on the investment, raise "new" money to pay for the promised returns on the first or "old" investments, then run the string out until there is not enough "new" investment monies available to fund the interest payments—let alone to repay even part of investors' original principal investments. A few who remove their money from the scheme early on may make the promised returns, but the greedy, the majority of the investors at the bottom of the pyramid, lose their original investment and any promised returns on that capital.

The Ponzi scheme is built upon the classic principles of greed. The perpetrator must be:
- Highly-intelligent and unscrupulous
- Well-educated
- Gregarious, charming and charismatic
- Credible with a reputation for financial expertise or personal wealth
- Patient while the scheme develops
- Glib and articulate in order to market the product
- Punctual with early payments and redemptions
- Believable at creating excuses for delays and broken promises
- Arrogant and convinced the Ponzi scheme can go on forever

The victim must be greedy, gullible and willing to suspend disbelief because of the hope of quick riches. A mob mentality takes over the many who fear that they will miss the opportunity for huge profits. In the middle of a successful Ponzi ruse, the greedy are begging to be allowed into the scheme. According to Paul H. Luehr of the Federal Trade Commission's Internet Coordinating Committee, up to 95 percent of those investing in Ponzi schemes lose all their investment. The con artist alone gets rich—but only until the scheme unravels.

The twenty Ponzi schemes that follow are a smattering of scams tried by dozens of operators. Total amounts of money lost by investors vary, promised rates of returns on investments vary, the lengths of time a Ponzi survives vary, but *all* Ponzi's fail sooner or later. That's the one sure thing about a Ponzi scheme.

THE FIRST PONZI SCHEMES

Sara Howe has the distinction of floating the first modern Ponzi scheme, in Boston in 1880. She collected money from women only, called it a "Ladies Deposit" and promised an 8 percent return on each sum collected. The scheme came to a conclusion when Ms. Howe took what money she had collected and disappeared.

In 1899, a Mr. William F. "520 Percent" Miller, a bookkeeper from Brooklyn, New York, came up with a Ponzi scheme that promised investors a 520 percent annual return on their invested money. He and his investors apparently failed after he spent most of the money on himself, burning through a million dollars in very short order.

CARLO GIOVANNI PONZI

Charles Ponzi designed the first major Ponzi. He was born on March 3, 1882, in Lugo, Italy, and his full birth name was Carlo Pietro Giovanni Guglielmo Tebaldo Ponzi. He is regarded as one of the most famous swindlers in American history.

He attended the University of Rome la Sapienza, an institution that had a reputation for being a four-year vacation. On November 15, 1903, at the age of twenty-one, he sailed on the S. S. Vancouver to Boston. He later stated that he landed with "$2.50 in cash and $1 million in hopes and those hopes never left me." [Mary Darby, *Smithsonian*, December 1998; reprinted December 19, 2009].

After working for four years in Boston as a waiter and floor-sweeper in a restaurant while he learned English, he was fired for short-changing customers and stealing from the restaurant. He traveled to Montreal in 1907 and became an assistant teller in a newly opened Canadian bank owned by another Italian, Luigi Zarossi.

Advertising by the new bank declared a return of "6 percent interest on deposits," which was double what other financial institutions were paying at the time. Deposit money poured in. Ponzi became bank manager only to find that the bank was in trouble from bad real estate loans and that owner Zarossi had been paying the high interest rate to depositors using the deposits from new customers.

The bank eventually failed of course, and Zarossi skipped to Mexico with what cash the bank had on hand at the time. Ponzi was out of a job and had no personal money. He called on a former customer of the bank, found nobody in the office, and wrote himself a check for several hundred dollars by forging the signature of the company's director. That theft and forgery earned him three years in a Montreal prison.

Upon his release from prison he wanted to return to the States but unfortunately was caught helping illegal Italian immigrants to cross the Canadian-U.S.A. border. He spent two years in an Atlanta prison. While there Ponzi learned the basic elements of a pyramid scheme from Charles W. Morse, who was a successful Wall Street speculator. Morse was in prison for stock manipulations but faked a medical emergency by eating soap shavings in order to poison himself temporarily. He received an early release.

In 1918 Ponzi returned to Boston, married a stenographer and bounced from one job to another. The key to his future came in the mail: a letter from Spain, which included an International Postal Reply Coupon (IRC). Inflation after World War I made it possible to buy an Italian IRC that could be exchanged for American postage stamps of a higher value. When the U.S. postage was redeemed, Ponzi could net a profit for the difference. He formed a company, named it the Securities Exchange Company, raised some money from friends and was off and running with a true pyramid scheme.

The word spread about Ponzi's company giving returns on investments as high as 400 percent annually, doubling investments in ninety days. In February 1920 his company showed a profit of $5,000 (multiply by 10.8 for equivalence to today's dollars). In March, the profit jumped to $30,000. By May 1920 he was clearing $420,000. In July 1920 he showed a profit of millions of dollars. Ponzi was living high on the hog while investors cashed in their life savings and mortgaged their homes to get in on the profits.

Many questions were being raised however: How could a new company be making so much money in so short a time? How could Mr. Ponzi buy a mansion in Lexington, Massachusetts, with a heated swimming pool? How could he afford to bring his mother to the States from Italy via a first-class ship? Why did he maintain accounts in several banks across New England? No answers were forthcoming.

On July 24, 1920 the *Boston Globe* ran a favorable story, stating that Mr. Ponzi was clearing $250,000 per day. However, the *Boston Post* and others continued to have grave suspicions. *Barron's* newsletter examined the records of Ponzi's company and reported there would have to be 160 million postal reply coupons to match the investments of the company, whereas only 27,000 were in circulation. The United States Postal Service confirmed these figures.

Further doubts were raised. The *Post* stated it seemed as if Ponzi was "robbing Peter to pay Paul." On August 2, 1920, the *Post* stated that Ponzi was hopelessly insolvent. That started a massive run on the company's cash, and bank examiners watched Ponzi's account be drained. On August 11, 1920, the roof fell in on him when he was no longer able to return invested money. On August 12 he surrendered, and federal charges of mail fraud were filed against him and the company.

State and federal charges required three separate trials, and they were delayed for an extended time when it was found that Ponzi had never obtained American citizenship and also was a convicted felon in Italy. Trials in the United States resulted in convictions with prison sentences, but these were challenged and he was temporarily freed on bail. While at large, he formed a new company in Florida named Charpon (a contraction of his name) Land Syndicate. In September 1925 he sold small tracts of land to investors, promising returns of 200 percent in sixty days. The land was found to be underwater and he was convicted by a Dade County grand jury for violations of Florida securities and trust laws. Sentenced to a year in jail, he appealed and again abused his bail; he shaved his head, grew a mustache and signed up for the crew on a merchant ship bound eventually for Italy. When the ship docked at the Port of New Orleans, he was apprehended, arrested and returned to Massachusetts to serve his previous sentences there.

Out of prison by 1934, he was immediately deported to his native Italy at the age of fifty-two. In Rome he became a translator of Italian into English. Benito Mussolini gave him a job with Italy's new airline, and from 1939 to 1942, he was a branch manager of the airline in Rio de Janeiro, Brazil. Mr. Ponzi found that several airline personnel were smuggling currency via the airline and blew the whistle on them to the Brazilian Government. The airline failed after the racket was discovered.

Ponzi remained in Brazil "collecting Brazilian unemployment insurance or giving English lessons." On January 18, 1949, at sixty-one years of age, Mr. Ponzi died a charity case in a Rio hospital with barely the $75 needed to pay for his burial.

It is clear Mr. Ponzi was fundamentally a crook from the start of his mature life. He was driven by ambition and fired by greed. In addition to his real name he used innumerable aliases, such as Charles Ponei, Charles P. Bianchi and just plain Carlo. Mr. Ponzi searched for and worked hard toward an illegitimate success that always eluded him. While seeking fame and fortune, he repeatedly lost the latter and gained his place in history as a con artist whose name epitomizes criminal deceit.

WILBUR BURTON FOSHAY
Builder and Utilities Master

The Foshay Tower used to be the tallest and grandest office building in downtown Minneapolis. Surrounding structures now dwarf the building—in much the same way as its builder's grandiosity was cut down to size. The Foshay Company stood tall and proud until the crash of 1929 destroyed it and sent its founder to prison.

Mr. Wilbur Foshay was born in Ossining, New York, on December 12, 1881. His grandfather, Joseph B. Fouché (or Fouchée), accompanied General Lafayette when the latter came to the United States to help liberate the English colonies. Another ancestor purportedly served as Chief of Police under Emperor Napoleon Bonaparte in France.

With a great talent and interest in art, Mr. Wilbur Foshay enrolled in Columbia University but was forced to drop out when his father's business failed. A further educational stint at the Mount Pleasant Military Academy preceded working for four years with the New York Central Railroad. He studied electrical engineering for a time at the Massachusetts Institute of Technology and then settled into a job with Electric Bond and Share Co. Mr. Foshay gained experience in public utilities by working in Wichita, Kansas, and San Francisco.

At the age of thirty-six Wilbur Foshay "walked into Minneapolis, independent, with little money, but with a shrewd knowledge and liking for public utilities," according to *Time* magazine's issue of November 11, 1929. His plan was to own and operate public utilities companies, financing new ventures and gaining working capital by selling Foshay Company securities to the public.

Within one year he owned public utilities in Minnesota, South Dakota, Kansas and Nebraska—and was making money. After eight years his holdings were valued at $10 million, and he sold his assets to buyers from the East Coast. Wasting no time, Mr. Foshay started a new chain of utilities that, by 1927, was appraised at $25 million. This second chain was also sold to Eastern interests.

According to *Time* his third chain of utilities "operated in twelve states and five countries (Canada, United States, Nicaragua, Honduras and Mexico)." The Foshay Company also owned "three Twin City banks, and owned such enterprises as retail and wholesale drugs, hotel companies, textile and shoe factories, rubber plants, flour mills and retail furniture stores in thirty states." All of this was in the years leading up to the stock market crash of 1929.

The stock market crisis didn't do him in. Over-expansion and depreciation of real estate holdings pulled him down. Foshay securities had financed his holdings, and they were sold primarily to employees or businessmen in his districts of business. *Time* magazine printed, "The failure was chiefly remarkable for two things: it was the largest failure in the history of the Northwest, and the man who failed had thrice made fortunes and might make a fourth."

Mr. Foshay struggled to save his empire at the time of the 1929 crash, but a contracting economy is the worst of times to raise money. He went into receivership in November 1929. He continued to sell securities in Foshay Company, however, insisting all was well. He paid out exorbitant interest to some investors, apparently to attract newly raised money to appease the restless older investors. These tactics were brought to the attention of federal authorities and he was charged in federal court with fraud for using a Ponzi-scheme operation. He was convicted and sentenced to the Leavenworth Federal Penitentiary, but was released after three years when President Franklin Roosevelt commuted his remaining sentence. The President commented at the time, "Mr. Foshay was more fool than fraud—a bungler brought down by his own towering ambitions." President Harry Truman gave him a complete and unconditional pardon in 1947.

After being released from prison in the 1930s, little was noted as to his whereabouts. He did move to Salida, Colorado, where he probably became mayor for a short time. He contacted *The Minneapolis Journal* stating, "You may think it's cold in Minnesota—but, here in Colorado, it's so cold at times the fish wear fur coats." He enclosed a picture of a trout wrapped in fur.

Death claimed Mr. Foshay in 1957. He left behind him two legacies: a prison record for fraud and the Foshay Tower in downtown Minneapolis. Constructed in 1928 and finished just before the 1929 crash, the Tower cost $3.7 million. A three-day opening celebration was held with 25,000 invited guests that included many notable personages.

As a side note, Mr. Foshay commissioned a stirring musical march by the famous composer John Philip Sousa for the occasion of the Tower's opening. It was titled "Foshay Tower – Washington Memorial March." The Tower had been patterned after the Washington Monument in our nation's capital. Mr. Foshay heard the march played once, at the dedication. His $20,000 check to Mr. Sousa bounced, and Sousa withdrew the March from the public until 1988 when a group of Foshay sympathizers paid off the debt to Mr. Sousa's estate and the march was placed in the public domain.

The Foshay Tower was, and is, a dramatic building. At its crown, ten-feet-high letters are inset into the four sides of the tower; readable by day and backlit by night, "FOSHAY TOWER" is emblazoned for all to see. Standing 447 feet tall with eighty-two stories, the Indiana limestone-clad exterior recently was given a name for its new status as a four-star hotel: The W Minneapolis—The Foshay.

Until 1971, it was the highest concrete and steel structure west of the Empire State Building in New York City. Today, instead of dominating the skyline of Minneapolis, the Foshay Tower is lost among several taller buildings. It still stands as a landmark and a tribute to Mr. Wilbur B. Foshay, who must have been a remarkable and energetic personality. Did he resort to a Ponzi out of expediency during what he hoped was a short-term economic downturn? It's a shame that a Ponzi scheme has blighted his record.

MARC S. DREIER
"I am a crook"

Marc S. Dreier did it all alone, in spite of the 250 lawyers employed by his Manhattan law firm. On March 17, 2009, Lev L. Dassin, Acting United States Attorney for the Southern District of New York, announced a superseding indictment against Mr. Dreier, increasing the dollar amount of fictitious promissory notes to $700 million and adding further assets to forfeit because of a previous indictment for fraud. A lawyer at the firm, Vincent Pitta, said, "The news of Mr. Dreier's arrest has had a neutron-bomb effect on the firm, Dreier L.L.P." All at the firm will bear the taint of association to this scoundrel.

Mr. Dreier had been a well-known and successful lawyer in New York City by the time he founded the law firm Dreier L.L.P. in 1996 and expanded it to five branch offices by 2009. He was well educated with an undergraduate degree at Yale and a law school degree from Harvard. He staffed his law offices with accomplished lawyers, offering lavish salaries and perquisites to attract the best and the brightest. Mr. Dreier's home office, designed by I. M. Pei, had a prestigious location at 499 Park Avenue.

The fraud perpetrated by Dreier was the selling of up to $700 million dollars of fake promissory notes primarily to hedge funds and prominent businessmen. The notes were especially attractive: Their term was of medium duration, they had generous interest rates and they carried signatures by well-known individuals and companies—all of which were forgeries.

Mr. Dreier's law office on Park Avenue boasted a $40 million art collection touted as "a first rate art museum" by a member of the firm. Works displayed were by the giants of modern art, from Matisse and Picasso to Warhol. He maintained a 121-foot Heesen motor yacht moored either in Manhattan or St. Maarten, with an on-board Jacuzzi spa and a crew of ten. His cars included a Mercedes 500 in New York and an Aston Martin in California. After his divorce, Mr. Dreier surrounded himself with a crowd of attractive young women and celebrities at parties—many of which were aboard his yacht "*Seascape.*" He was a *bon vivant,* throwing lots of money around and living large at a breathtaking pace.

The SEC found that $700 million dollars of fake promissory-note proceeds were missing, along with $35 million dollars in escrow accounts held by the firm. Mr. Dreier handled all financial matters for the law firm, and the investigation after his arrest revealed that many bills had not been paid for months, the firm's health and malpractice insurance was in default and there wasn't enough cash to meet the current payroll.

Mr. Dreier can be classed as a brazen swindler for his giant Ponzi scam, selling new fake promissory notes to raise money to pay interest and principal on old notes, all the while skimming off huge sums of money for his personal use.

It was clear, even to Mr. Dreier, what he had become. He said, "I am a crook." About that, he did not lie.

SERGEI PANTELEEVICH MAVRODI
The Largest Pre-Madoff Ponzi

Mr. Charles Ponzi was Italian and Mr. Sergei Mavrodi was Russian, but these two men spoke the same financial language.

Sergei Panteleevich Mavrodi, his brother Vyacheslav Mavrodi and his brother's future wife, Marina Muravyeva, established MMM as a Russian company (not to be confused with the American corporation 3M) in 1989.

Sergei was the main character in a business fraud that was once described as the world's largest Ponzi scheme (at least before the Madoff and Stanford scandals).

Apparently MMM started as a legitimate importer of office equipment, including computers and related software. A subsidiary, MMM-Bank, was accused by Russian tax police of tax evasion and was shut down, crippling MMM and MMM-Bank operations. A new company, MMM-Invest, was created and became a "successful" Ponzi scheme. In February 1994 MMM promised returns as high as 1,000 percent annually on investments in MMM-Invest stock. By 1994 there were as many as 5,000,000 investors. Mavrodi formed many similar entities—one offered a return of 30,000 percent annually on investments. These companies were advertised widely for their high rate of return.

On July 22, 1994, tax police shut down MMM for tax evasion. One subsidiary, MMM-Invest-Consulting, owed $26 million in back taxes, and MMM alone owed billions of dollars to investors. Fifty investors committed suicide when they learned they had lost everything.

Mr. Mavrodi was arrested in August 1994 for tax evasion. He insisted it was the government's fault that people lost their money. Shortly thereafter, Mavrodi was elected to the Russian State Duma, which gave him immunity from lawsuits. This immunity was cancelled in October 1995 but that didn't deter him from running for Russia's presidency in 1996—an election he lost. MMM declared bankruptcy on December 22, 1997. Mavrodi was again arrested in 2003 after being on the run for six years.

While in custody, he was given until January 31, 2006, to read and prepare a rebuttal to 650 volumes of evidence against him, each volume averaging 260 pages (over 169,000 pages in total).

As reported in the April 27, 2007, edition of *The St. Petersburg Times*, Mavrodi was convicted of fraud on April 24, 2007, sentenced to four-and-a-half years in prison less time served while awaiting trial. He was to be released on May 22, 2007.

He was also fined a magnificent sum equivalent to $350.

Believe it or not, Mr. Mavrodi's brother Vyacheslav, a former partner in MMM, was arrested in 1998 for tax evasion after forming another Ponzi scheme with a company by the name of MMM-96. These blood brothers were obviously born with the same greed gene.

RICHARD S. PICCOLI
Fleeced His Flock

Richard S. Piccoli's Ponzi scheme caused investors to lose "only" $17 million, but the means by which he collected money from investors sets him apart from the norm. Mr. Piccoli preyed on the Roman Catholic Church, its parishioners, its priests and even its cemetery funds. Targeting and committing a fraud against a specific group having the same interests, such as a religion, nationality or even members of the same country club, is called an affinity crime—fleecing your own kind. Mr. Piccoli did it for nearly five years.

For several years, Mr. Piccoli ran advertisements in Catholic newspapers, such as *Western New York Catholic*, making such statements as "serving seniors and retirees since 1975" and listing the names of several priests who had invested in his company. Investigations showed he made no such investments in real estate mortgages as claimed, but instead had several accounts into which he deposited investors' money and then withdrew various amounts to underwrite an extravagant lifestyle.

The *Buffalo News* reported that in the 1970s, Richard S. Piccoli used the name Richard Rhodes to execute a scheme to solicit mortgages for individuals. He then forced them to set up a corporation so he could underwrite the mortgages and place them through his company, Gen-See. The underwriting signature was Richard Rhodes.

Mr. Piccoli was a member of the Knights of Columbus and used his membership to solicit investors in Gen-See, stating that the company had held mortgages for thirty-three years that were safe, suburban mortgages and none had ever lost a dime. Mr. Piccoli showed a potential investor, a fellow Knights of Columbus member, a check from Danny Wegman (a well-known supermarket owner) for $50,000. This so impressed his fellow member that a $35,000 check was promptly handed over. Later, Mr. Wegman denied the check was his and that he had ever invested with Mr. Piccoli.

Victims said that once Piccoli had convinced them to invest, he asked them for names of friends whom he also persuaded to join the scheme.

On January 8, 2009, the SEC filed an enforcement action against Gen-See Capital Corporation a/k/a Gen Unlimited and owner Richard Piccoli to halt ongoing affinity fraud and Ponzi schemes. Assisting the SEC in continuing investigations were the United States Attorney's Office for the Western District of New York and the United States Postal Inspection Service.

These are some heavy hitters pitted against a long-time Ponzi schemer. On October ·21, 2009, Richard Piccoli, age eighty-three, was sentenced to twenty years in prison. Restitution efforts for his victims are ongoing, but clearly there are not enough remaining assets to reimburse them for their losses. As victim Lu Tracy, age sixty-nine, said in court, pointing at Mr. Piccoli:

> There is [sic] two things I will never forget in my life, and that's 9-11 and you Richard Piccoli. He's nothing but a common terrorist. That's what he has done, he has terrorized too many individuals...

All in the name of religion.

LOUIS JAY PEARLMAN
Leaves $300 Million in Debts

Lou Pearlman was known as "Big Poppa," a manager of boy bands from 1993 to 2006. On May 21, 2008, Mr. Pearlman was sentenced to twenty-five years in federal prison, and he is known now only by a prisoner number.

Mr. Pearlman flew high as a major manager of rock and roll bands, grouped as "boy bands" because of the members' young ages. Included in his roster of bands were the Backstreet Boys, O-Town, *NSYNC, US5, C-Note and Smilez & Southstar. Mr. Pearlman founded Trans Continental Records by finding five unknown young boys in a nationwide talent search for the record label's first act. These five winners became the Backstreet Boys and were a major hit, selling 100 million albums worldwide and going gold and platinum in forty-five different countries. Later on, the band *NSYNC sold more than fifty-six million records.

These two huge successes enabled Mr. Pearlman to become a music mogul. He owned an entertainment complex in Florida, a recording studio called Trans Continental Studios, and a dance studio near Disney World named O-Town. Every band but one eventually sued Pearlman over royalties, but Big Poppa wasn't deterred.

Lou Pearlman was born in 1954 in Flushing, New York. His father had a dry-cleaning business and his mother was a school lunchroom aide, according to *The St. Petersburg Times* [Helen Huntley, October 21, 2007]. He was raised in apartments near the Flushing Airport from where Mr. Pearlman could watch blimps take off and land. He was fascinated with them from childhood on. In his teens, he got interested in the music business—Art Garfunkel was a first cousin—and managed a rock band with little success. In 1970 he used his interest in aviation to start a helicopter commuter service.

At that time he was befriended by a German "blimper," Theodor Wüllenkemper, who trained him on blimps in his airship works in Germany. Upon his return to the United States, Mr. Pearlman formed

Airship International, Ltd., went public and sold stock at a penny a share. He leased a blimp and borrowed funds to construct a second blimp, which crashed. He then raised $3 million to purchase additional blimps and signed up Met Life and Sea World for blimp advertising. In July 1991 he moved his company along with several blimps to Florida, lost one major client and suffered crashes of three of his airships. The penny stock in Airship International dropped from a high of $6.00 to 3 cents per share. The airship company was a total loss.

In September 2002 Mr. Pearlman bought a company that went through several name changes and accounting problems. Formerly known as E-Model, it was founded as an Internet business model for talent scouting, by Ayman el Difrawi a/k/a Alec Defrawy, a convicted felon for fraud. An intense period of suits and counter-suits resulted, and Mr. Pearlman declared bankruptcy.

In 2006 investigators found that Mr. Pearlman had "perpetrated a long running Ponzi that had defrauded investors out of $300 million." He had recruited investors for an Employee Investment Savings Account for two companies, Trans Continental Airlines Travel Services, Inc. and Trans Continental Airlines, Inc., which after twenty years existed only on paper. Mr. Pearlman used falsified FDIC, AIG and Lloyd's of London documents to promote investor confidence in his Ponzi and used fake financial statements created by a fictitious accounting firm, Cohen and Siegel, to secure bank loans. In February 2007 regulators declared the savings accounts "a massive fraud," and the State of Florida repossessed the two companies.

Mr. Pearlman took flight at this point but was apprehended in Indonesia on June 14, 2007. On June 27 Mr. Pearlman was indicted by a federal grand jury and charged with bank fraud, mail fraud and wire fraud. On May 21, 2008, he was sentenced to twenty-five years in federal prison on further charges of conspiracy, money laundering and making false statements during bankruptcy proceedings.

An unusual angle to the sentence was that Mr. Pearlman was given the chance to reduce his prison term by one month for every million dollars he helped the bankruptcy trustee recover for individual investors. *The New York Daily News* has reported that he is trying to organize from prison a reality television show featuring another boys' band called Biteboy. Under statutes legislated in the 1970s (known as "Son of Sam Laws"), autobiographies or documentaries by inmates are permissible if the proceeds are used to reimburse losses to victims. If successful, Pearlman could earn the $300 million needed for restitution to his victims and be a free man.

ROBERT P. COPELAND
Cannot Cope with Ponzi Failure

Mr. Robert P. Copeland is all but wiped out at the age of forty-eight, undone by his own hand.

As a lawyer owning his own law firm, Robert P. Copeland, P.C., and several businesses under the names Axiom Development Group, Inc., We Buy, Inc., and HBV Services, Mr. Copeland ran a Ponzi-type scheme offering 15 to 18 percent annual returns on real estate investments. He promised that invested capital was backed by real estate developments, mortgages, bridge loans and promissory notes.

It all sounded good—except he was commingling investors' money with his own in four or more bank accounts; money was being used for personal items; and promissory notes were signed with fraudulent names. Little or no invested money was ever put into any real estate deal on behalf of any investor, and all returns paid out utilized money taken from new investments in the classic Ponzi manner.

On April 9, 2009, the SEC filed a complaint against Mr. Copeland and his companies stating he had fraudulently raised over $35 million from more than 140 investors in Georgia and several other states. According to the complaint he had misappropriated millions of dollars for his own use, including his personal residence, vehicles and expensive works of art.

On the day he was charged the United States had already seized or frozen numerous assets relating to Copeland's scheme, including twelve real estate properties, bank accounts, artwork, jewelry and automobiles.

The SEC complaint went on to state, "Comparatively few assets derived from the raised funds are left to pay the millions of dollars still owed to the remaining investors."

Ironically, it appears that the majority of his victims for the Ponzi came from attendees at several instructive seminars and conferences on investing and finance held by Mr. Copeland. On April 21, 2009, he admitted to authorities his "investment business was all a scam, engaged in little if any real estate development or other profit-making activities with investors' funds."

A Department of Justice press release dated April 9, 2009, quotes United States Attorney David Nahmias as follows: "This is yet another tragic case in which dozens and dozens of victims lost their hard-earned money in what turned out to be a massive and long-running investment fraud scheme. This case is particularly disturbing because the defendant was a lawyer and many of the victims were senior citizens some of whom lost their entire life savings."

Something all of us should know: "Any third party that assisted Mr. Copeland in his scheme or failed to alert authorities or investors, or prevent him from perpetrating his fraud when they had the duty to do so, may be held liable for investor losses," according to Mr. John S. Chapman, a securities attorney.

It's best to remember the Latin term *caveat emptor*—"let the buyer beware"—when it comes to investing hard-earned assets that you need to support your family for the rest of your life. Don't fear to be a whistleblower if at all unsure about the validity of a project or claim in a prospectus or investment plan. If a proposal promises returns too good to be true, it probably is just that—not true.

SHAWN R. MERRIMAN
Preying from the Pulpit

Mr. Shawn Merriman hunted and killed black rhinos in Africa, but it was pure bull he kept shooting to his investors. He developed a smooth delivery as a spiritual counselor and lay bishop of The Church of Jesus Christ of Latter-Day Saints, but he used it to help himself rather than his fellow man.

Operating out of Denver, Mr. Merriman perpetrated a Ponzi scheme in the states of Utah, Minnesota and Colorado through his company, Market Street Advisors. He told potential investors that he would be investing their money in stocks and bonds and stated that he had received "consistent and impressive" annual returns on his portfolio. The SEC states that was not true after his first year of trading.

The head of the SEC's Denver office said, "Our complaint alleges that Merriman repeatedly deceived investors, many of whom considered him a personal friend, by sending them fictitious account statements showing annual rates of return of seven to twenty percent." Another SEC attorney wrote, "Contrary to representations, however, Merriman has admitted that instead of investing in securities, he used investors' proceeds to pay for withdrawals by other investors and to pay for personal expenses and to support his lavish lifestyle."

According to *The Denver Post*, officials of The Church of Jesus Christ of the Latter-Day Saints in Salt Lake City excommunicated Mr. Merriman from the LDS church in late March 2009 for "conduct unbecoming a member." The practice of swindlers like Mr. Merriman using their religious or ethnic status as a selling tool is an affinity fraud. As with any financial scam, the key to a successful affinity fraud is the trust of fellow members.

One Mormon investor said, "The way he, Merriman, talked about his faith, I was enthralled with the whole thing [the investment]. He seemed a righteous religious fellow."

Al Lewis of *Dow Jones* wrote, "Mr. Merriman, as a former stock broker, apparently didn't like reporting his investment losses, but he sure seemed to like going on expensive hunting trips, buying toys and collecting art." The SEC reported, "Among other things, Merriman used investors' money to purchase classic cars, a cabin in

Idaho, and a fine art collection that included works by Rembrandt worth millions of dollars."

As a big-game hunter, Mr. Merriman was unapologetic about gunning down black rhinos. "If a black rhino bull that is past breeding age and is therefore of no use in perpetuating the species dies in the field—he's fertilizer."

Mr. Merriman apparently didn't think far enough ahead to realize he may be in prison long enough to become fertilizer, too.

JAMES G. OSSIE
Currency Trading Ponzi

On January 25, 2009, the U. S. District Court for the Northern District of Georgia filed a complaint against the CRE Corporation of Alpharetta, Georgia, and James G. Ossie, its President and CEO. He was indicted in March 2009 on fifteen counts of wire fraud, and on May 21, 2009, Mr. Ossie pleaded guilty in Federal District Court in Atlanta to a Ponzi scheme that defrauded more than 100 victims out of more than $25 million dollars in nine months. He was sentenced to eighty-two months in prison and ordered to pay $18 million in restitution.

Using the CRE Corporation as the scheme base, investors were told their money would be invested in a fund focused on option contracts in foreign currencies. The SEC investigated the operations of Mr. Ossie and shut down the fund in January 2009.

Investment contracts were offered to investors in increments of $100,000, and a return of 10 percent interest starting within thirty days was guaranteed. Investors were assured that a reserve account had been set up to insure return of capital and accrued interest at any investor's request. By the end of 2008 clients had invested $23 million with CRE. Representations had been made to potential investors through "salespersons known as correspondents, through the CRE website, and in numerous mass conference calls involving groups of investors and prospective investors," according to the files of the Department of Justice.

Sound appealing? It did to investors, but there was one big problem: The representations were all lies. The Department of Justice records state:

> Instead of making profits sufficient to pay 10% monthly returns and fund a "reserve account," Mr. Ossie and CRE lost millions of dollars. Indeed, during CRE's life span, the firm lost over $12 million in foreign currency trading accounts, and there was no "reserve account" established. By the end of 2008, Mr. Ossie owed more than $23 million in pending investment contracts but had only $2 million in all of his bank and trading accounts combined.

Although CRE hired outside accountants for some of the funding projects, Mr. Ossie disallowed any access to the records of the trading accounts that would have revealed the substantial losses.

CRE had planned to launch a $100 million stock offering in early 2009 by selling 50 million shares at $2 per share. Mr. Ossie claimed an independent firm had valued the stock at $40-$45 per share. The court opined that these statements were false. CRE was already insolvent at that time.

THOMAS J. PETTERS
A Minnesota Ponzi

Thomas J. Petters was born in St. Cloud, Minnesota, on July 11, 1957, a long stone's throw south of Little Falls, the birthplace of "Lucky Lindy" Charles Lindbergh. Mr. Petter's father was a fur and fabric tailor.

His boyhood was spent in St. Cloud with his six brothers and sisters. He graduated from Cathedral High School in 1975. His college education was comprised of one quarter at St. Cloud State University in the fall semester after high school.

He was an early entrepreneur, according to a news story in the magazine *CEO WORLD*. In 1973 as a high school sophomore, he started the first of his many companies—Ear Electronics—a mail-order firm concentrating on stereo products.

The business base for a future grand Ponzi scheme was laid in 1980, when he was working as a regional manager for a Colorado chain of electronic stores. The business declared bankruptcy and Mr. Petters was on hand to buy five of the distressed stores in Kansas and Colorado. In 1988 The Petters Company came into existence and Petters Warehouse Direct was created to sell discounted merchandise.

Using product label "Red Tag," he had two Internet websites, redtagbiz.com and Redtag.com. In 2000 he sold four of his Colorado warehouses. In 2001 he teamed up with marketing expert Ted Deikel, former chairman of Fingerhut Companies. For the year 2000 redtagbiz.com reported sales of $1 billion. Mr. Petters was forty-three years old.

In June 2002 Mr. Petters (with Mr. Deikel) bought Fingerhut and four of its buildings. Mr. Deikel was named head of Fingerhut. In April 2003 the Petters Group bought uBid.com.

Son John Petters was tragically stabbed to death in Florence, Italy, in March 2004. A press release by the Petters family in late June 2009 stated that a native Italian, Alfio Raugel, thought John Petters was an intruder on his property when he killed him. Mr. Raugel was convicted of manslaughter and sentenced to three years in prison. The court sentence was light because John Petters "wandered" onto private property by mistake. Mr. Petters later testified that he was both distracted and impaired by the circumstances and trauma of his son's death.

In late fall 2004 Mr. Deikel sold his interest in Fingerhut. In January 2005 Petters Group Worldwide bought Polaroid Holding

Company for $426 million. In 2006 Petters Group Worldwide bought Sun Country Airlines. Mr. Petters now had more than twenty business entities.

From 2004 through 2007 Mr. Petters made donations to Miami University in the amount of $10 million; Cathedral High School, $750,000; and to the College of St. Benedict, $5.3 million.

In July 2008 Petters Group Wholesale acquired several trade magazines.

On September 24, 2008, federal agents raided the home and businesses of Mr. Petters. A few days later, Thomas Petters resigned as CEO of Petters Group Wholesale.

On October 3, 2008, Mr. Petters was arrested at his Wayzata, Minnesota, home. A U. S. District Attorney charged Mr. Petters with twenty counts of wire and mail fraud, money laundering and obstruction of justice. Mr. Petters's Ponzi world was starting to unravel.

On December 1, 2008, a federal grand jury indicted Mr. Petters for masterminding a Ponzi scheme and conspiracy. The total losses to investors are estimated to be $3.5 billion.

On December 3, 2008, Mr. Petters pleaded not guilty. In December a condo project, The Village on the Cannon River, in Northfield, Minnesota, and a second condo project, University Village of Winona in Winona, Minnesota, owed $5.5 million to Home Federal Savings Bank in Rochester, Minnesota, and a third of the units remained empty. That same month, investment banker Houligan Lokey testified that the value of Polaroid was unknown, but 2008 losses were "substantial" in spite of receiving a $21 million settlement in a patent-infringement suit.

On December 22, 2008, court documents were filed showing James Wehmhoff, an Executive Vice President of Petters Group Wholesale (PGW), had possibly hidden as much as $60 million and had acknowledged that Petters told him to prepare false statements to investors. Mr. Wehmhoff also stated, "When I got to PGW, I lost my way." His conduct is estimated to have cost the government as much as $20 million in lost taxes.

Douglas Kelley, court-appointed receiver and trustee for the creditors of Petters's enterprises, reported to the court on assets such as a "vast portfolio of real estate holdings in Minnesota, North Dakota and Florida, as well as homes in Costa Rica, Nevada, cabins in northern Minnesota, jewelry, coins and collectibles, motorcycles, watercraft and automobiles (including a Bentley sold for $138,000, a 2004 Ferrari and a slightly damaged 2005 Porsche), various stock holdings, bank ownership interests, and accounts in up to ten financial institutions." Petters and several executives of PGW owned this property.

Hundreds of millions of dollars of investors' money were drained away from the intended and promised ventures that were to be the purchase, reconditioning and re-sell of used equipment for juicy profit margins. Nothing remotely like that ever occurred. The investors had been duped.

Mr. Petters has forfeited all funds in his banking accounts and all his real property in Wayzata, Minnesota, and Colorado, Florida and Wisconsin— including a house on beautiful Lake Minnetonka just south of Plymouth, Minnesota, where this book is being written. The Petters's home has a waterfront location on sparkling Wayzata Bay that reflects peace and beauty on a summer's day. But on the summer day of June 29, 2009, Mr. Bernard Madoff stood before Judge Chin in federal court way to the east of Lake Minnetonka and heard his consecutive sentences of 150 years in prison read out to condemn him for ruining the lives of so many.

If Mr. Thomas Petters was watching and listening on that day, his heart must have nearly stopped as he absorbed the enormity of Mr. Madoff's sentence. The penalty would extend beyond life expectancy itself.

Judge Richard H. Kyle, United States District Court, St. Paul, Minnesota, on April 8, 2010 sentenced Mr. Petters to fifty years in prison. The prosecution had asked for a statutory sentence of 335 years. The judge stated that he believed "fifty years fair and just. Mr. Petters was Captain of the ship."

According to *The Wall Street Journal,* a fifty-year sentence was not unduly long. Mr. Madoff received a 150-year sentence for *his* Ponzi scheme. In 2000 Mr. Sholam Weiss received an 845-year sentence for fraud, and in 2008 Norman Schmidt was given a 330-year sentence for investment fraud.

A final federal sentence is not subject to parole. At his sentencing, Mr. Petters pledged "to work the balance of my life to try to repair, replace or repay what has been lost. I'm filled with pain and anguish."

He reaffirmed his plans to appeal the sentence.

JACOB EZRA MERKIN
"Too Much Money"

How can a man who has been born to an esteemed and prominent family, has made hundreds of millions of dollars, has graduated from Columbia University *magna cum laude,* has passed through Harvard with honors, has served as director on innumerable boards of companies and has served as trustee for philanthropic organizations—how could such a man then commit fraud and abrogate his fiduciary responsibilities by establishing a long-running Ponzi scheme?

Yet one man did: J. Ezra Merkin. Some investment managers have stated Mr. Merkin's successes had gone to his head, dulling his eye for details. A friend of his sent him an e-mail when he heard Mr. Merkin had been arrested for fraud, stating, "I guess you did such a good job in fooling a lot of people, you ultimately fooled yourself."

Born fifty-five years ago in 1954, the son of Ursula and Hermann Merkin (a well-known banker, author and respected philanthropist), Ezra Merkin attended Ramaz Modern Orthodox prep school on the Upper East Side of New York City, two yeshivas in Israel, Columbia University for his undergraduate Bachelor of Arts and Harvard Law School for his law degree.

He and his wife, Lauren, have four children. They lived well, with a multi-million dollar house in Atlantic Beach, New York, expensive property in Eagle, Colorado (just west of Vail), and an eighteen-room duplex at 740 Park Avenue, the "world's richest apartment building" according to author Michael Gross, who penned a biography about that exclusive address. The duplex cost $11 million in 1995. The Park Avenue building was the childhood home of Jacqueline and Lee Bouvier and has housed Rockefellers, Chryslers and Vanderbilts in its eighty-year history. Inside the duplex, Mr. Merkin had on display the largest private collection of Mark Rothko paintings in the world—valued at $150 million.

Mr. Merkin worked for and with a succession of businesses, starting with the prestigious New York law firm, Milbank Tweed, for three years, then three years with an investment company and finally joining his father in Wall Street finance. In 1985 he founded and co-managed hedge funds called Gotham Capital LP and Ariel Capital LP with Joel Greenblatt. Three years later, Mr. Merkin formed a new company, Gabriel Capital, and later on, Ascot Partners, all of which became very popular with money managers. The finder's fee for funneling money into investment funds like Bernard L. Madoff Investment Securities was 1 to 1.5 percent, and by 2005 Mr. Merkin was "earning" $35 million a year in finder's fees from various hedge funds.

Jacob Ezra Merkin sat on a number of educational and philanthropic boards that provided him the opportunity to direct investments. Yeshiva University, the Fifth Avenue Synagogue and others trusted Mr. Merkin based on the credibility and integrity of his father, Hermann Merkin. Individuals and organizations that did not quite trust Bernard Madoff relied on the reputation of the Merkin family, little realizing that Ezra Merkin was handing over their capital to none other than Bernard Madoff.

On December 11, 2008, Mr. Merkin's reputation and the viability of his funds came to a screeching halt when Mr. Madoff's sons, Andrew and Mark, blew the whistle on their father. Several investors, including New York University, New York University Law School, Mortimer Zuckerman, and the Calibre Fund, have brought lawsuits against Mr. Merkin and his investment funds. The State of New York brought criminal charges asserting that Merkin steered assets to Madoff in exchange for $470 million in fees. Andrew Cuomo, Attorney General of the State of New York, filed a complaint on April 6, 2009, in Manhattan. On February 17, 2010, Merkin's petition for dismissal was denied. New York State Supreme Court Justice Richard B. Lowe wrote in his decision as follows:

> Here, the wrongs alleged include Merkin's misrepresentations and omissions regarding what the investors were investing in, and what his role would be in managing the funds, his affirmative misrepresentations to investors after he had already delegated all authority and discretion to Madoff and his failure to perform due diligence and ignoring signs of fraud...

More than thirty Jewish charities lost billions of dollars. Members of Manhattan's prestigious Fifth Avenue Synagogue "suffered a two-billion-dollar bloodbath." [*Huffington Post*, December 21, 2008]. Untold numbers of individuals, organizations, foundations and trusts lost fortunes—along with their trust in Mr. Merkin and his family.

The UJA-Federation of New York was protected by a conflict of interest prohibition in its bylaws that prevented Mr. Merkin from directing any investments to funds in which he had participation. Through the years there had been some criticism that, due to this clause, UJA was not experiencing the gains that other organizations were.

Mr. Merkin has now resigned his committee memberships, trustee positions and directorships at Yeshiva University, Carnegie Hall, Fifth Avenue Synagogue, GMAC, Beyeler Foundation, Bard College, Ramaz School of New York City and Columbia College.

In all the twelve years of the life of his companies, Mr. Merkin showed losses in only four months—an improbable record by a legitimate company. But he lost billions in one day—December 11, 2008.

Mr. Irving Picard, the court-appointed bankruptcy trustee assigned to recover many of Mr. Merkin's assets for the benefit of the victims of Bernard Madoff's Ponzi scheme, is suing J. Ezra Merkin for monies withdrawn during the height of the Ponzi scheme. An unnamed client invested more than a billion dollars in Madoff companies through Mr. Merkin and withdrew a billion dollars from his account while receiving returns of 40 to 300 percent a year. Mr. Picard also claims that the same investor directed that losses be fabricated in his account to avoid paying income taxes.

It will take many years to expose the layers of intrigue and shady dealings that are hidden in thousands of transactions—and that is assuming that there were any legitimate transactions at all.

The Ponzi scheme attached to Jacob Ezra Merkin is unusual because Mr. Merkin's Ponzi scheme was feeding Mr. Madoff's Ponzi scheme. They kept this façade of respectability going for many years, until the recession of 2008-2009 brought them all down.

The SEC barred Victor Teicher, who was jailed in 1994 in an insider trading scandal, from the securities industry in 2000. But he served as money manager for Mr. Merkin up to that time and continued to have a relationship with him until the scandal broke. He wrote in e-mail to Mr. Merkin the day after Madoff's arrest:

> The Madoff news is hilarious; hope you negotiate out of this mess as well as possible…I'm yours to help in any way I can; unfortunately, you've paid a big price for a lesson on the cost of being greedy.

JOSEPH S. FORTE
A $122 Million Ponzi Loss

Mr. Joseph S. Forte can blame Bernard L. Madoff for the blow-up of *his* Ponzi scheme.

Since December 11, 2008 (when Mr. Madoff confessed to authorities his $50-billion-plus operation was all a scam), many investors have started to question the status of their investments in securities or other assets that have paid or promised to pay unusually high rates of return. If too many investors demand their money, the basic elements of a Ponzi scheme come to light; there simply aren't enough assets to redeem the investments.

This was the case of the company Joseph Forte, L.P. Mr. Forte, as CEO, told future investors his company would trade in securities futures contracts, such as foreign currency futures, metal futures and futures of the Standard & Poor's 500 stock index. He stated that he would give an investor an annual return on his money of 18.52 to 36.19 percent.

On January 7, 2009, the Commodities Futures Trading Commission and the Securities and Exchange Commission filed charges against Mr. Forte. Before being charged, Mr. Forte admitted that he had obtained as much as $50 million from as many as eighty investors.

Investigations have shown that despite his assertion the fund's value was as high as $154 million, the actual value on September 30, 2008, was $146,814. According to the SEC, "Mr. Forte has no money to pay anyone." Where did the $153,853,186 go? Mr. Forte confessed to raking off up to $12 million for himself and spent up to $20 million of new money to pay off old investors. That sum accounts for up to $32 million, so $122 million must be written off as a loss to his investors.

According to Mr. Daniel M. Hawks, Director of the Regional Office of the SEC, "It wasn't until he realized that he wasn't going to be able to continue to honor redemption requests" that he gave up on his Ponzi scheme.

It turns out Mr. Forte wasn't registered to be a commodity pool operator, and from October 2002 until February 2007, did little trading on behalf of his investors. He has been specifically charged with solicitation fraud, misappropriation of pool funds and sending customers false account statements.

More than one of his customers tried to retrieve his investment from Mr. Forte's company, and repayment continued to be delayed. That put some of his clients on a "watch basis" and eventually brought him down.

An element of greed is the belief by the perpetrator that the Ponzi scheme can go undetected—forever.

HEARD, MOORE AND HELFGOTT
Promised 10 Percent a Month

It is not hard to find three Ponzi schemes, but it is rare to find three people involved in one Ponzi scheme. It is accepted knowledge that if you are going to commit a crime: do it by yourself. If two are doing it, the odds of being caught are quadrupled. If three are doing it, DON'T.

A ten-page Ponzi indictment of three men was filed in the United States District Court for the Northern District of Ohio, Eastern Division, and put before a grand jury. The three had their respective financial affairs bundled together.

That grand jury will never forget the complications of a group of human beings who did concoct and attempt to pull off a conspiracy involving a Ponzi scheme combined with other overt acts that included securities fraud, wire fraud and mail fraud. Reading the indictment with its complexities is a test of anybody's patience.

Mr. Leon S. Heard, age seventy-two, lived in Cleveland Heights, Ohio, and was a business associate of Mr. Moore. He was not registered with the SEC and the State of Ohio and was not licensed to sell securities. He was a disbarred attorney.

Mr. Darryl G. Moore, age forty-one, lived in Solon, Ohio, and was a business partner of Mr. Heard in Alice's International Salon and Spa, a beauty salon in Cleveland, Ohio. Mr. Heard and Mr. Moore were co-signers on common bank accounts in the names of various entities, such as D-MO Investors, LLC. They also shared a bank account with Steven L. Helfgott.

Mr. Steven Helfgott, age fifty-four, lived in Cleveland Heights, Ohio, and while he was licensed to practice law in Ohio, was not registered with the SEC and the State of Ohio, nor licensed to sell securities. Helfgott opened a bank account in the name of D-MO Group, Inc. c/o Steven J. Helfgott. Through this account, money was deposited and paid out for a Ponzi scheme.

The United States prosecutor in U. S. District Court charged: "From June 1999 to at least May 30, 2002, Heard, Moore and Helfgott unlawfully, willfully and knowingly did combine, conspire, confederate and agree together and with each other to violate the laws of the United States, to wit: To commit (a) mail fraud, in violation of Title 18, United States Code, Section 1341; (b) wire fraud, in violation of Title 18, Section 1343; and (c) securities fraud, in violation of Title 15, United States Code, Sections 78j(b) and 78ff, and Title 17, Code of Federal Regulations, Section 240 10 (b)-5."

Heard and Moore ran the Ponzi scheme soliciting investors to purchase securities and other investments, purportedly exclusive, in so-called medium-term notes, offshore investments with a Swiss bank, or currency trading. The duo knew there were no such investments.

Investors were promised a high rate of return on their investment, as high as 10 percent per month, and interest would be paid monthly. The investors didn't know their money was, in fact, diverted to the trio's own use and there were no investments made. Money used for interest was from new investor deposits or existing investors adding to their investment. It was the classic "rob Peter to pay Paul" scenario.

To sound legitimate, the trio represented that the investor's money would go to a "hot-shot broker" named "Steve," who "worked for Merrill Lynch." "Steve" was Steve Thorn, stepson of Mr. Heard, a business associate of Mr. Moore and a former licensed broker dismissed by Merrill Lynch. Behind the scenes, Mr. Thorn was running his own Ponzi scheme, and Heard, Moore and Helfgott were selling investments similar to those Thorn was independently selling in his own Ponzi scheme.

Some of the trio's investors' money went directly to Thorn for his personal use and expenses. When this was exposed, the District Court froze all of Thorn's bank accounts. In violation of the Court order, the trio continued to send investors' money to Thorn for his expenses. There is no record in this particular court order that Thorn was ever charged with any crime.

One of the trio, Mr. Helfgott, opened an account at Key Bank in the name of D-MO Group, and received and paid out monies from and to investors. A second Key Bank account was opened named D-MO Investors, LLC. These two accounts became a fountain of money for the trio.

While their investors lost millions of dollars, the trio also lost the stolen millions as their currency dealings went awry. All three took severe hits. Mr. Heard declared bankruptcy.

On June 1, 2007, the grand jury indicted Mr. Heard and Mr. Helfgott for their part in the Ponzi scheme. The sentence given Mr. Heard was severe. He had been disbarred but represented himself as a licensed lawyer and committed acts as a current member of the Bar. At the time of sentencing, Heard said to the judge, "Your Honor, I apologize for my amoral and antisocial behavior; it has ruined my life and that of my family. I beg the court, as an elderly, remorseful man in poor health and lacking a moral compass, for leniency and compassion." After this statement, the judge responded, "Adios, amigo...thirty years (read "life" in your case) in the slammer. Those who emulate you will now have second thoughts about committing crime."

That is the last heard from Mr. Leon S. Heard.

BRYANT ISMAIL RODRIGUEZ
Christian Evangelical Church Ponzi

On December 23, 2008, the Acting United States Attorney for the Southern District of New York, Lev Dassin, and Ronald Verrochio, Inspector-in-Charge of the New York office of the United States Postal Inspection Service, announced the arrest of Bryant Ismail Rodriguez, also known as Bryant Rodriguez, also known as Rubin Rodriguez, also known as Salvador Rodriguez, also known as Robert Rodriguez, or, lastly, as Ismail Rodriguez, for mail fraud involving a Ponzi scheme. If convicted, the charges could carry a maximum prison term of twenty years.

Mr. Rodriguez has had a felony conviction for impersonating a United States Immigration Officer.

The El Camino Church is a small Christian Evangelical Church at Audubon Avenue and 172nd Street in Washington Heights, New York. Mr. Rodriguez showed up for baptism classes in 2007 and insinuated himself into the church congregation. Soon, he began soliciting the parishioners to entrust some of their money to him. He promised a 30 percent return on their money every two weeks and did provide such payments to the early investors. Money poured in.

His Ponzi scheme was, according to the *New York Times*, a classic one. Investors were encouraged to give him their money, and he stated that he would invest it in his company, C & E, which sold wholesale electronics to such retailers as Best Buy and P. C. Richards and Son. In the early stage of the Ponzi, Rodriguez promised a "$10,000 bonus for every $5,000 invested." At least $1.1 million was invested with him.

Early investors did receive high interest rates on their money, and a few received all or part of their principal investment back. But most received nothing. The church's pastor, Reverend Miguel Amadis, and his family lost $300,000. A Mr. McAllister, lawyer for Mr. Rodriguez, blamed the pastor for losses to members of the congregation. Mr. Amadis, referring to Mr. Rodriguez, said, "He's trying to say I had something to do with it, but that's just not true. He came to us like anyone else comes to the church. When I met this guy, he convinced me he was a true Christian. Man, this guy could talk. He could convince anybody."

Mr. Rodriguez told parishioners he "wanted a blessing for a blessing" by providing Jews and Christians with the opportunity to invest in his company. A spokesman for the United States Postal Inspection Service, Mr. Allan Weissman, said, "These investors obviously weren't billionaires, but it's all relative. Money lost means a lot to them—life savings, in many cases—and they are devastated."

Yes, it *is* relative—a few dollars to some is a lot of money. Ponzi schemes tear the fabric of trust between people.

J. V. "JUNIOR VILLAIN" HUFFMAN
Big House, Big Cars, Big Spender

On November 14, 2008, J. V. Huffman, Jr., of Conover, North Carolina, confessed to bilking hundreds of neighbors, church associates and even the elderly out of millions of dollars—more than $35 million. Not so much money when compared with the billions lost by Madoff, Stanford or perhaps a host of other big frauds, but when you have lost all you have, including your trust in your fellow man, it is a major loss.

When Mr. Huffman confessed his crimes, he also admitted he had never invested any investor's money in mutual funds, as he had promised to do, or in other people's mortgages to buy and sell them at big profits. After authorities did a search of his home, the SEC stated that he used some funds from new clients investing in his company, Biltmore Financial Group, to pay profits to old investors. Some funds were used to buy a new Aston Martin convertible and a $1 million recreational vehicle, and to pay for home renovations, vacations and rental properties.

A gentleman who stated he had known the Huffman family his whole life proclaimed the entire family had been living high on the hog, and that "it doesn't take a brain surgeon to figure out that a man can't have all that money and possessions that J. V. had by staying home every day not having a real job... and get rich that fast."

Mr. Huffman tasted money, his appetite grew for it and he passed over the line into greed. It showed in his "come-on" figures. He advertised that an investment with him and his company would give returns that were "guaranteed never to drop below 0.0 percent." [*Hickory Daily Record,* November 18, 2008, Sarah Williamson.] Theoretically, investors would be paying Huffman to hold their money at 0.0%! Investors were told that they could withdraw their money without penalty within thirty days, and the money would be invested in mutual funds. In another instance, an investor questioned what would happen as the sub-prime mortgage crisis took the country into recession and relates Huffman's response:

> He said he only dealt in five- to seven-year mortgages and the competition is tough, but there was still money to be made. He said he may have to reduce the five- to seven-year mortgages to two- to three-year mortgages, but it would be okay. He had an answer for anything I asked.

A dossier released by Biltmore Financial Group to investors stated interest rates paid to investors ranged from 8.025 percent to as high as 16.65 percent in 2007. In Biltmore's first year, 1991, the interest rate paid was 10.15 percent.

Mr. Huffman confessed to authorities he never invested any monies received from investors, that only newly invested money was used to pay interest to the earlier investors.

He received five consecutive sixty-month sentences (or twenty-five years) as the minimum punishment for his crimes. His victims were in court to insure that the courtroom could see the faces of the real people he had harmed.

JOHN G. BENNETT, JR.
A Christian Businessman

It all began in 1989, and it came to an end in March 1995 when Mr. Bennett was convicted of wire, mail and bank fraud, carrying a sentence of twelve years in prison.

Partially under the guise of Christianity, Mr. Bennett operated the largest Ponzi scheme ever by a non-profit enterprise. Over the six-year period, he fleeced "180 organizations and over 150 financially-savvy philanthropists in America, who fell victim to the largest fraud ever to occur in the non-profit sector."

The sales pitch was a simple one: Invest in "New Era Philanthropy" and within three months, New Era would match the investment and pay double the amount to a designated charity. It seemed like a sure way to double-up on a charitable gift.

It was actually a Ponzi scheme. New Era would take the "contribution" in the amount of $5,000, and in the required three-months period, pay a 100 percent return with a matching contribution. Mr. Bennett claimed his New Era philanthropy would place the money in a quasi-escrow account with the Prudential Insurance Company, which would be investing the money in treasury bills to generate the income required to double the contributed amount. He also bought various bonds to show prospective "clients" as evidence of values in New Era, but he showed the same bonds time and again, professing they were part of a portfolio of many bonds that were constantly changing. They weren't.

Suspicions were raised regarding a possible Ponzi scheme as early as 1993, but the Attorney General could not find a dissatisfied investor and gave New Era a clean bill of health. Success made it possible to increase the minimum amount to $25,000 from $5,000. Spring Arbor College had invested $1 million with New Era in spite of warnings by its bookkeeper. In March 1995 the bookkeeper launched a full-scale investigation of New Era's books and found earnings of only $34,000 on deposited funds that should have been earning as much as $1 million in annual interest.

The bookkeeper contacted the SEC, IRS and the State's Attorney General's Office, all of whom contacted Prudential regarding the $60 million in treasury bills supposedly held by them in New Era's account. They were there all right, but Prudential discovered Bennett had borrowed $52 million on margin, had repaid only $7.1 million and couldn't account for the missing $44,900,000. Bennett was given twenty-four hours to repay the money; he couldn't do it. On Friday, May 12, 1995, Prudential Securities liquidated $44,900,000 of the account.

A run on the balance of $8 million in the account for New Era precipitated the death of the company. On May 15, 1995, New Era declared bankruptcy with "assets" of $80 million and liabilities of $551 million. Mr. Bennett had enriched himself to the tune of at least $135 million while losses were distributed among 1,100 donors to New Era.

In court, Mr. Bennett faced charges of eighty-two federal counts of money laundering, and wire, mail and bank fraud. He could have been sentenced to up to twenty-seven years in prison but the judge gave him only twelve years.

A wide variety of colleges and organizations were taken in by the Bennett Ponzi scheme. The following is just a partial list of losers with their respective losses:

- Academy of Natural Sciences, Philadelphia, PA—$2.7 million
- Biblical Theological Seminary, Hatfield, PA—$5.8 million
- Covenant College, Lookout Mountain, GA—$5 million
- Detroit Institute of Arts, Detroit, MI—$4 million
- Houghton College, Houghton, NY—$4 million
- John Brown University, Siloam Springs, AR—$4 million
- International Missions, Reading, PA—$5 million
- King College, Bristol, TN—$5 million
- University of Pennsylvania, Philadelphia, PA—$2.1 million
- Buford Television, Inc., Dallas, TX—$3 million
- Amelior Foundation, Morristown, NJ—$1.9 million

Contributions to New Era Philanthropy totaled $400 million in 1994. Mr. Bennett boasted, "We give more money away than the Carnegies, Mellons and Rockefellers."

It might be added, "But they didn't go to jail for being Ponzi crooks."

NORMAN YUNG YUEN HSU
Targeting the Apparel Industry

A magnetic personality? A scoundrel of the first water is more like it. When reading accounts of Mr. Hsu, it is clear that he was an opportunist and a social climber, but he was also armed with the charm of a first-rate con artist.

Born in Hong Kong, China, in October 1951, Hsu has ethnic roots in Shanghai, according to a college and business friend, Pedro Woo. Hsu was raised in Hong Kong and moved to the United States, where he received a Social Security card in 1969. Sometime between 1969 and 1984 he became an American citizen.

Piecing together his personal business life between the period of 1969 and 2009 is like assembling a jigsaw puzzle with several pieces missing. He did attend the University of California at Berkeley and graduated in 1973 with a Bachelor of Arts degree in Computer Science. He was married in 1974, and in 1976 received a California real estate license to buy and sell property. How successful he was in the ensuing few years is unknown.

In 1981 he graduated with a Master of Business Administration degree from the Wharton School of Business at the University of Pennsylvania—no mean feat.

By 1982 he had formed several sportswear companies. One named "Laveno" was in partnership with several Hong Kong partners. It went bankrupt in 1984. Other businesses were called "Wear This", "Base" and "Foreign Exchange." The fates of these three companies are unknown, as well as several clothing stores and restaurants with which he was engaged during the 1982 to 1988 period.

In 1989 he started a business to buy and sell latex gloves and eventually sold other clothing. He raised more than a million dollars, some of it through restaurateur August Wu. Another investor, Alvin Chau, an accountant, said that Hsu had a very good business reputation. The Deputy Attorney General of California called the latex-glove venture "a classic pyramid (Ponzi) scheme." In 1990 several investors sued Hsu after no profits were paid out and no products surfaced. Hsu filed for bankruptcy protection.

Whether related or not, in September 1990 Hsu claimed he was kidnapped by San Francisco Triad society gang leader Raymond Kwok Chow. When they ran a red light in Foster City, California, police arrested several men who admitted to being part of an Asian gang. Hsu was released.

In February 1991 Hsu agreed to serve three years in prison and pay a $10,000 fine to settle one count of grand theft for his latex-glove Ponzi scheme. He failed to appear for official sentencing and a warrant was issued for his arrest.

It turned out Hsu had fled to Hong Kong where he resided from 1992 to 1996. He started at least two new companies there "with vague charters." He apparently prospered but dissolved his companies in 1997 and 1998 when a Hong Kong court declared him insolvent and bankrupt.

Hsu showed up back in the United States in the late 1990s, had several San Francisco and Los Angeles addresses, was an investor in Silicon Valley enterprises and real estate in the Bay area and had a business in the garment industry. Soon he appeared in New York City, living in a fancy SoHo apartment and flying around in chartered jets. He was again involved in the apparel game.

In 2003 Hsu began donating large sums of money to political campaigns, became a Trustee of The New School in New York (donating a $100,000 scholarship) and became known as someone who could raise major sums of money quickly. By 2007 he was classed as a "HillRaiser" for Hillary Clinton's 2008 presidential campaign.

In August 2007 a *Wall Street Journal* article about Hsu started a long decline in his fortunes. Among other disclosures, the article pegged his association with the Paw Family of Daly City, California. A campaign-finance filing listed Hsu's residence as that of the Paws. Mr. Paw, a mailman, owned with his family a gift shop, lived in a 1,280-square-foot house and had recently refinanced a mortgage for $270,000. The U. S. Justice Department started an investigation for possible campaign irregularities, such as building several contributions into one and using the Paw family name as major contributors.

After the August 2007 article in the *Wall Street Journal,* Hsu surrendered in the District Court House of Redwood City, California, and was freed on $2 million bail. The following week, Hsu failed to appear in court to surrender his passport, his bail was revoked and the $2 million forfeited. A "no bail" warrant was issued for his arrest.

On September 6, 2007, the FBI in Grand Junction, Colorado, arrested him when he fell sick on the California Zephyr train headed for Chicago. Prescription pills were found loose in his train compartment, and it later was revealed he had mailed suicide notes to several friends.

A Colorado judge refused to accept the prosecutor's suggestion of a $50 million bail and set bail for Hsu at $5 million (Hsu had $6 million in his checking account). Hsu was returned to California under arrest after being released from the hospital in Grand Junction.

On September 19, 2007, in Manhattan, the U. S. Attorney filed a complaint against Hsu charging fraud by a Ponzi scheme and the breach of campaign finance laws.

The next day, Source Financing Investors, LLC and Joel Rosenman (Woodstock Festival founder) filed suit against Hsu for $20 million because of "false promises" on investments.

An investment group named Briar Wood Investors sued Hsu for fraud and, a day later, for pressuring them to make certain campaign contributions.

By November 27, 2007, a federal grand jury in Manhattan had indicted Hsu for violating campaign finance laws and for a $20 million fraud promising investors a high rate of return on investments in the short term.

An article in the *Wall Street Journal* of May 8, 2009, stated that Hsu pleaded guilty in a New York court to ten counts of mail and wire fraud and of running a multi-million-dollar investment Ponzi fraud.

Hsu was quoted as saying, "I would use later investments to pay off earlier investments, so as to create the impression that my investment strategy was operating properly, when in fact, it was not. I knew what I was doing was illegal."

He will receive a trial by jury at a later date. He could be sentenced to a prison term of up to forty-five years.

NICHOLAS J. COSMO
Another Mini-Madoff Scheme

A mere $380 million may seem like peanuts when compared to Bernard Madoff's $65 billion or Allen Stanford's nearly $8 billion Ponzi schemes, but the Ponzi scheme of Nicholas J. Cosmo has a distinction in the realm of fraud.

In 1997 while a stockbroker for Continental Broker Dealer Company, he was given a twenty-one month federal prison term for a single count of misappropriation of funds. He pleaded guilty and paid restitution, and on August 23, 2000, was released from the federal prison in Allenwood, Pennsylvania.

During his early adult years, Mr. Cosmo received treatment for uncontrolled gambling addiction and risking other people's money.

So with a thorough knowledge of the consequences of fraud and some understanding of his own addiction to risk and speculation, Mr. Cosmo ran a *second* Ponzi scheme involving "bridge loans, promising a yield of 40 to 80 percent on the established $20,000 minimum investment in his company Agape World, Inc." He was CEO of Agape for nine years.

A bridge loan is money borrowed at a high rate of interest for the period of time it takes to secure a long-term loan on an asset. Investors were paid periodic interest from money invested in Agape by new investors who were snagged by the lure of high interest returns on their investment.

On January 26, 2009, Mr. Cosmo was arrested for allegedly defrauding clients who had invested in Agape. Per the FBI and U. S. Postal Inspection Service, little if any of up to $380 million of investors' money was used for bridge loans; most of the money was used for personal expenses.

These expenditures include the purchase of an indoor paintball arena in Hauppauge, New York, which was converted into an indoor athletic field for an additional million dollars; the payment of $212,000 as restitution for previous frauds; $100,000-plus for hotels, jewelry, and limousine rides; and $95,000 to his wife. Beyond interest payments to some "old" friends, it is unclear where the remainder of the money was spent.

Mr. Cosmo was unrepentant regarding his early conviction and prison term. He has stated, "I take full responsibility for my actions then and now. My debt to society and the clients affected have been paid back by a fine and jail time. Today, I owe no apologies to anyone for my actions, which occurred in the past. I have paid for my mistakes in my life; I have lost everything I had. This included my fiancée, an early part of my son's life, but never my family or my true friends."

* * *

How many times is a person allowed to try Ponzi schemes? How could a person fail to learn from experience the high cost of dishonesty? Try a Ponzi scheme once and rack it up as a mistake in judgment. Try it twice—you're a fool and a double criminal.

It must be a basic element of greed that one cannot learn from experience.

GREEDSTER BERNARD L. MADOFF

Chapter 4 – Synopsis

"Setting Records"

Mr. Bernard L. Madoff perpetrated the largest Ponzi fraud in history. Remarkably, the scheme was fueled by billions of dollars invested by thousands of investors and persisted for a period of at least twenty years. Mr. Madoff's firm reported to investors that thousands of trades had been executed—but actually not a single transaction occurred. All trading reports and customer account statements were false.

Excerpts from the actual courtroom transcripts of the Madoff sentencing hearing are included here, and an excerpt from the SEC's report on the fraud is an appendix to this chapter. Mr. Madoff's statement to his victims in court and the closing remarks of Judge Chin lend a sense of actually being present for the sentencing of Bernard L. Madoff to 150 years in prison.

The SEC's report, signed by Inspector General H. David Kotz, tells of six substantive incidents between 1992 and 1996 where the

SEC failed to adequately follow up on reports of irregularities with Bernard L. Madoff Investment Securities, LLC.

The entire Madoff history is one that arouses almost total unbelief. The case is an astounding example of criminal fraud accompanied by the poor oversight of regulatory agencies, financial institutions and greedy investors—all of whom failed to exercise a reasonable skepticism about Mr. Madoff's unrealistic returns on investments.

Chapter 4

GREEDSTER BERNARD L. MADOFF

VICTIMS WERE "BERNED" AS HE "MADE-OFF" WITH THEIR MONEY

On September 11, 2001, the World Trade Center, in the heart of New York City's financial district, collapsed when two Boeing 767 jet airliners were used as tremendous bombs to destroy the north and south towers. In all, seven buildings were lost—as well as 2,605 lives on the ground and in the Twin Towers.

On December 11, 2008, a bomb of a different sort detonated in Manhattan when Bernard "Bern" Madoff's confessions to his two sons on the prior day were made public. He had admitted to Mark and Andrew Madoff that the asset-management arm of Bernard L. Madoff Investment Securities LLC, with *billions* of dollars in trust and under management, was in reality one giant Ponzi scheme. His sons, in turn, turned him into the federal authorities. Mr. Madoff was arrested the next day.

The second event may be the more enduring catastrophe for Wall Street.

As the history of pyramid schemes compiled in Chapter 3 of this book has revealed, the Ponzi scam is not new. This chapter will describe in detail the scope of Madoff's Ponzi because of its magnitude and duration. The reader will learn how a sophisticated scoundrel managed to hoodwink both institutional and individual investors. Always be wary of the crook touting too-good-to-be-true returns on invested money. When the victims' dreams end with the loss of their financial security, that crook couldn't care less.

Over 16,000 claims by account holders have been filed with the Securities Investor Protection Corporation. Many of these claims represent individuals whose life savings were wiped out by Madoff. A total of at least *$65 billion* in investors' money, fictitious trades, withdrawals, interest and other monetary movements was manipulated over the past two decades. The dollar amount of these paper transactions would equal the capital of a company the size of the Walt Disney Company or the Boeing Company.

The man Bernard Madoff is an enigma, hard to penetrate, hard to figure out, and hard to read; "inscrutable" may be the best word to describe the person who caused suicides, crushed the funding of philanthropic institutions and foundations, closed the doors of financial institutions, wiped out personal fortunes and retirement plans and emptied education trusts for the next generation. How could this happen? Because his investors believed this man was magic, that he had a golden touch with money, that he would deliver steady returns at unusually high rates. Did any of the victims look into the mirror and ask, "Was I perhaps the greedy one—as culpable as the Ponzi schemer?"

After the fact, we ask how so many intelligent people could be so lax in monitoring their investments. Greed lets the guard down; the tough questions don't get asked.

Mr. Madoff's operations were scrutinized closely over the years by potential investors, the SEC, hedge funds and financial experts, and even though some questions were raised and some doubts never answered, the Madoff fraud was not unmasked. Through his amazing forty-eight year run since forming Bernard L. Madoff Investment Securities in 1960, Mr. Madoff was able to allay most fears and inquiries without being threatened by any individual, institution or regulatory agency. Billions of dollars in the form of tons of paper changed hands. Transactions were documented, reports were distributed, quarterly and annual statements generated, payments made—BUT in Mr. Madoff's own words:

> *For thirteen years* [in reality more than twenty] *not a single real transaction was actually ever made. It is all a big lie—a giant Ponzi scheme.*

No wonder it shook Wall Street to its foundations to hear this confession from the former Chairman of the NASDAQ stock exchange. As you read this you may be thinking, "No way is this possible." But, it's true. His disclosures to authorities trace the fraud back to 1988 or earlier.

THE AMAZING ASCENT
The American Dream

Bernard Lawrence Madoff, known as "Bern" or "Bernie," was born April 29, 1938, in the borough of Queens, New York City. His family was Jewish. His father, Ralph, a plumber, was the son of a Polish immigrant. His mother, Sylvia, a housewife, was the daughter of Romanian and Austrian immigrants. Ralph and Sylvia married in 1932 at the height of the Great Depression. Bernie was born six years later.

It was apparently tough sledding for the elder Madoffs through the period of the 1930s, '40s and '50s. They had a tax lien of $13,000 on their home from 1956 until the lien was finally satisfied in 1965. Mother Sylvia registered as a broker-dealer in the 1960s and used their home address to form a company, Gibraltar Securities. The SEC forced the company to close, as required reports about its financial condition were never filed. Biography.com has posted, "many suggest that the company was a front for Ralph's 'backhanded dealings'" in its biography of Bern Madoff. [http://www.biography.com/articles/Bernard-Madoff]. Further details were not given.

Son Bernie Madoff went to Far Rockaway High School, where he was a member of the swim team and held a summer job as lifeguard at Silver Point Beach Club, Atlantic Beach, Long Island. After graduation, he spent a year at the University of Alabama. But he transferred to Hofstra University the following year and graduated from there with a degree in political science. A year at Brooklyn Law School concluded his academic education. In 1959 he married his current wife, Ruth Alpern, while she was still in college. Ruth graduated from Queens College and went to work for a stock brokerage firm in Manhattan.

In 1960 with $5,000 savings earned from lifeguarding and installing and servicing lawn sprinklers, plus some help from Ruth's father, Saul Alpern, a retired Certified Public Accountant, Bernie and Ruth Madoff formed the destined-to-be-infamous firm of Bernard L. Madoff Investment Securities, LLC ("BLMIS"), a limited liability company.

Starting with practically no capital, no experience, and no pertinent education, Bern Madoff, with his wife as his partner and her father as his only promoter, launched BLMIS. The firm mushroomed in its forty-eight years to become a major player on Wall Street.

In the beginning, BLMIS was a penny stock trader. Its business was small change. The next step was to make markets (by quoting bid and ask prices) by way of the National Quotation Bureau's listing of stocks on a so-called "pink sheet." Not satisfied with the speed of making trades, the firm initiated a third step—the use of information technology or innovative computerized information. This success led to the establishment of the National Association of Securities Dealers Automated Quotations (NASDAQ). Madoff made his mark by being a third-market provider and bypassing established exchange specialists by executing orders over-the-counter (OTC) from retail brokers. Bern Madoff became the largest market maker at the NASDAQ. By 2008 he was the sixth largest market maker on Wall Street.

Mr. Madoff was well known for the practice of "payment for order flow," where a dealer pays a broker for the right to execute a customer's order. Called a legal "kickback," some dealers question the ethics of such a practice. Madoff defended it by comparing it to a ladies-stocking manufacturer who supplies display racks at no charge to the retail store selling stockings. He said then, "Order flow is an issue that attracted a lot of attention, but is grossly overrated." [McMillan, Alex (May 29, 2000). "Q&A: Madoff Talks Trading". CNN. Retrieved December 11, 2008.]

There has been a huge question about whether the retail investor got the best price possible in these third-market transactions. By choosing a value in the spread between "bid" and "ask" prices favorable to the dealer, market makers could shave a small profit on every transaction. Even after paying brokers for redirecting up to 10 percent of orders from the New York Stock Exchange to BLMIS, Madoff earned record profits throughout the 1990s.

The company prospered as the reputation grew that money invested with BLMIS was producing steady annual returns of 10 percent or more. By the 1980s Madoff's reputation had spread, and the firm was responsible for more than five percent of all trades made on the New York Stock Exchange. Well-known figures and celebrities became steady investors with BLMIS. Names such as director Steven Spielberg, actor Kevin Bacon, musician John Denver, Holocaust survivor and Nobel laureate Elie Wiesel, New Jersey Senator Frank Lautenberg, Hall of Famer Sandy Koufax and many, many others clamored to place their capital with Madoff. The master con artist must have been dumbstruck to have people begging for him to steal their money.

The firm was a family operation. Ruth Madoff worked for BLMIS from its inception. Eventually, Bernie's younger brother Peter and niece Shana joined the firm as Managing Director and Chief Compliance Officer and compliance attorney, respectively. Sons Mark and Andrew worked in the trading section along with Charles Weiner, Bernie's nephew. Shana Madoff later married Eric Swanson, an assistant director in the compliance division of the SEC, who professes that he played no part in the SEC's dealings with BLMIS investigations over the years.

Mark, Andrew, Peter and Shana Madoff combined, drew $80 million in compensation over an eight-year period and "used the bank account at BLMIS like a personal piggy bank," according to the court-appointed bankruptcy trustee, Irving Picard, in an interview with Morley Safer of CBS's *60 Minutes*. [http://www.huffingtonpost.com/2009/09/28/madoff-trustee-irving-pic_n_301637.html].

Peter Madoff withdrew over $16 million from an account in which he had deposited only $14.00 after 1995. Over the years that they were employed in the family business, both Mark and Andrew borrowed millions of dollars from their parents. In a lawsuit filed against Madoff family members, Picard seeks to recover $200 million in assets for the Madoff investors victimized in the fraud.

In the early days Ruth and Bernie first lived in a ranch-style house in Roslyn, New York, but around 1980 they acquired an oceanfront residence in Montauk, Long Island, which had views of the Atlantic Ocean to the south and Block Island to the north. This home was 120 miles from the executive offices of BLMIS at 885 Third Avenue. The distance between work and home may explain why they maintained a magnificent penthouse on the Upper East Side of Manhattan as their primary residence. Bernie chaired that building's co-op board.

BERNARD L. MADOFF INVESTMENT SECURITIES LLC

The firm of Bernard L. Madoff Investment Securities LLC occupied the seventeenth, eighteenth and nineteenth floors at 885 Third Avenue (popularly known as the Lipstick Building) in midtown Manhattan. The seventeenth floor housed Bernie Madoff's private office, and it was from there that the giant Ponzi scheme was hatched and executed.

Like BLMIS, the Lipstick Building is distinctive. The building itself is most unusual in the New York cityscape and contrasts dramatically with the square and rectangular shapes around it. It was designed by Philip Johnson and was the last project before the famous Johnson/Burgee Architects partnership ended. Completed in 1986, it has thirty-four floors and is 453 feet tall. Its nickname comes from its oval shape and red enamel and granite exterior that resemble a tube of red lipstick. Light plays off the exterior's continuous wall of imperial red granite and steel. In between each floor is a small line of enameled red panels. It is a building that commands attention despite its commercially less favorable location on Third Avenue at 53rd Street. All of its exterior offices give the sense of a broad window expanse like a corner office. It is ironic that a building so full of natural light hid so many secrets.

It was the perfect site for a successful business boiling with activity like Madoff's firm. The main activities took place on the eighteenth and nineteenth floors. Few were allowed into the seventeenth floor private sanctum of Bernie Madoff. Only twenty-four trusted employees had access to it. The seventeenth floor of Lipstick will forever be known as the spot where Bernard L. Madoff lost everything he owned and everything that had been entrusted to him by others.

At the height of his "success," according to a March 13, 2009, court filing, Madoff and his wife were worth up to $126 million, plus an estimated $700 million for the value of his business interest in Bernard L. Madoff Investment Securities LLC. Other major assets included securities ($45 million), cash ($17 million), a half-interest in BLM Air Charter ($12 million), a 2006 Leopard yacht ($7 million), jewelry ($2.6 million), a Manhattan apartment ($7 million), a Montauk home ($3 million), Palm Beach home ($11 million), property in Cap d'Antibes, France ($1 million), and furniture, household goods and art ($9.9 million).

Mr. Madoff did spread his wealth around. The political parties were not ignored. From 1991 forward, over $230,000 was donated with 88 percent going to the Democrats and 12 percent going to the Republican Party. Donations to Washington's elected officials included Senator Charles Schumer (who returned about $30,000 to the trustee in the Madoff case) and the Democratic Senatorial Campaign Committee (which returned $100,000 to the trustee).

Washington's lawmakers and regulators were attracted to the Madoff Group because of its activities in leading trade associations. Mr. Madoff became a member of the Board of Directors of the Security Industry Association that merged with the Bond Market Association to become SIFMA, the Securities Industry Financial Market Association. Peter Madoff served two terms as a Director of SIFMA. He stepped down after the December 11, 2008 news broke, but from 2000 to 2008, Peter and Mark Madoff gave $56,000 to the Association in general, and thousands more to help pay the costs of industry meetings. Niece Shana Madoff served on the Executive Committee of SIFMA's Compliance and Legal Division. She too resigned her post after December 11, 2008.

Madoff served on many boards and committees: He was Board Chairman and Treasurer of the Sy Syms School of Business at Yeshiva University (from which he has now resigned); board member of the New York City Center; Member of New York City's Cultural Institutions Group (CIG); on the executive council of the Wall Street division of the UJA Foundation of New York; a board member of the Securities Industry and Markets Association (SIFMA); and last but not least, Founder, Chairman of the Board of Directors and on the Board of Governors of the National Association of Securities Dealers and its exchange, NASDAQ.

When his son Andrew was diagnosed with lymphoma, he contributed $6 million toward lymphoma research. In 2008 Andrew returned to work and became Chairman of the Lymphoma Research Foundation only to resign when the Ponzi scheme broke six months later.

Numerous donations were made to hospitals, theaters, and educational, cultural and health charities such as the Gift of Life Bone Marrow Foundation. After indictment, the Robert I. Lappin Charitable Foundation, the Picower Foundation and the JEHT Foundation were all forced to close—either from lack of continued flow of gifts or to dodge the possibility of "clawbacks" (being forced to give money back to the donor source if the donation monies were declared tainted). They were right to be concerned about clawbacks. Irving Picard, the bankruptcy trustee assigned to liquidate BLMIS and restore as much value as possible to its victims, has said he will use clawback provisions against targeted investors who benefited from the Ponzi scheme by withdrawing money as much as six years before the fraud was discovered—even though these investors experienced net losses at the time of BLMIS's insolvency. Clawbacks are an increasingly common tool for companies to recoup bonuses or other compensation paid to an employee due to an undeserved windfall or bonus.

The Sarbanes-Oxley Act and the Troubled Asset Relief Program ("TARP") legislation both contain measures that allow recovery of compensation from CEOs or CFOs of public companies (and senior executives under TARP) if there has been misconduct, material mistakes in performance or misstatement of financial statements. Use of clawbacks to recover monies previously paid out will be a very costly and complicated legal maneuver, however.

The life of Bernard Lawrence Madoff as a free man came to a screeching halt on December 11, 2008. But Madoff was an intelligent man; he must have known that he was doomed. Ponzi schemes don't last forever, and they consume the perpetrator. He was questioned regarding the extraordinary results he was achieving so many years in a row by many investors, regulators and bankers. Observations such as "unlikely," "impossible," "no way" came from savvy observers.

Yet, his Ponzi scheme survived for all of those years. He remained calm, relied on his reputation and advanced complex explanations as to his processes of trading and investing. These explanations confounded even the sharpest investment minds.

What was Bernard Madoff's investment strategy? Madoff explained his strategy to *The Wall Street Journal* in 1992 as follows:

> Purchase blue chip stocks and then, take options contracts on them, which is sometimes called a split-strike conversion or collar. Typically, a position will consist of the ownership of thirty to thirty-five S & P 100 stocks, most correlated to that index, the sale of out-of-the-money 'calls' on the index and the purchase of out-of-the-money 'puts' on the index. The sale of the 'calls' is designed to increase the rate of return, while allowing upward movement of the stock portfolio to the 'strike' price of the 'calls.' The 'puts,' funded in large part by the sales of the 'calls,' limit the portfolio's downside.

In the 1970s Madoff had marketed the notion that he invested funds in "convertible arbitrage positions in large-cap stocks, with promised returns of 18 percent to 20 percent." In 1982 he began using futures contracts on the stock index. He also placed "puts" on futures during the 1987 stock market crash.

A few analysts performing "due diligence" investigations were unable to replicate the Madoff Funds past returns using historic price data for U. S. stocks and options on the indexes. The criminal complaint against two programmers working for Madoff alleges, "It is doubtful Madoff made any or all of the required trades this strategy dictates, because purported trade volumes appear to far exceed the listed derivative open interest." Rather, *Barron's* in 2001 raised the possibility that Madoff's returns were most likely due to front running his firm's brokerage clients.

What enabled the Ponzi scheme to be perpetrated for so long? The greed of investors to achieve greater annual returns and the botched investigations by the SEC over a period of years made this astonishing scam possible.

"Feeder funds" and wealthy individuals fed investment capital to BLMIS. Feeders were a particularly important source of the new funds necessary to keep a Ponzi scheme alive. The Fairfield Greenwich Group was a major one.

In 1983 Walter M. Noel, Jr. founded an investment firm called the Fairfield Greenwich Group in Greenwich, Connecticut. In 1989 it merged with another small firm whose general partner was Jeffrey Tucker, a lawyer from the Enforcement Division of the SEC. Their main business was feeder distribution of monies received from investors to various operating investment concerns. One was BLMIS, whose success and stability earned their investment funds a top position with Fairfield. Likewise, Fairfield became BLMIS's leading feeder.

Noel and Tucker benefited from Fairfield's success and fed billions to Madoff with major emphasis on foreign money. At one time it was reported that Noel's family fortune was $14 billion. Retained invested money was 95 percent foreign—68 percent from Europe, 6 percent from Asia and 4 percent from the Middle East. Mr. Noel's four daughters, who married internationally, were major forces in gathering investment funds. Fairfield manages $16 billion and claims to have lost at least $7 billion in the Madoff collapse. In 2008 prior to the December revelations by Bernie Madoff to his sons, Mr. Noel told an acquaintance, "Everything I am, I owe to Bernie Madoff."

SEC INVESTIGATION

Serving on boards and committees and being philanthropic was no help in keeping critics at bay regarding performance of Madoff

Securities funds. Beginning in 1992 there were six SEC investigations of various practices and the lack of information regarding high returns on investments. Incompetent SEC staff work accounted for Madoff's Ponzi scheme surviving those investigations.

Then, a financial analyst/whistleblower named Harry Markopolos came along. He figured that to deliver 12 percent annual return to investors, BLMIS would have to earn 16 percent gross revenue in order to pay the 4 percent feeder fund managers their commissions. The feeder funds that were luring new victims were essential for funding the Ponzi. He informed the SEC that the gains reported by BLMIS were legally and mathematically impossible.

The Boston office of the SEC ignored Markopolos's warnings of suspected fraud at BLMIS in 1999, 2001 and 2002. Meaghan Cheung at the New York City office of the SEC ignored more evidence presented by Mr. Markopolos in 2005 and 2007. Markopolos's fraud reports of 2005 and 2007 stated that it was inconceivable that BLMIS's "growing volume could be competently and legitimately serviced by his [Madoff's] accounting/auditing firm, a three-person firm with one active accountant." [Madoff's auditor/accountant, David Friehling, the only active accountant in the accounting firm of Horowitz and Friehling, Certified Public Accountants, informed a CPA association that the firm had not conducted audits in fifteen years.]

The 2005 report by Harry Markopolos was seventeen pages long and specified twenty-nine numbered red flags. This report concluded:

> Bernie Madoff is running the world's largest unregistered hedge fund. He's organized this business as a 'hedge fund of funds' privately labeling their own hedge funds that Bernie Madoff secretly runs for them using a split-strike conversion strategy getting paid only trading commissions which are not disclosed. If this is not a regulatory dodge, I do not know what is.

The SEC's Inspector General, H. David Kotz, discovered six botched investigations of Mr. Madoff and BLMIS by the SEC since 1992. These included Mr. Markopolos's four reports, especially that of 2005. Excerpts from official Executive Summary of the Report of Investigation by the SEC and the Office of Inspector General (H. David Kotz), Case No. OIG-509 that unveil the failure of the SEC to uncover Bernard Madoff's Ponzi scheme are attached as an appendix to this chapter.

THE NIGHTMARE BEGINS
For Some It Will Never End

Bern Madoff got away with it all until May 2008 when one investor wished to withdraw a large cash sum from BLMIS and Mr. Madoff didn't have the cash. He tried desperately to raise it but couldn't.

On December 10, 2008, he called his sons into his office, explained the situation and admitted to them that the past thirteen years (or more accurately twenty years) were a hoax, a lie and a fabrication from start to finish. The sons decided to go to the authorities. On December 11, 2008—the very next day—the Feds moved in and Mr. Madoff was through.

What an amazing end to an amazing business career. What a price he paid. For in addition to the legal consequences of his criminal acts, he destroyed so many lives.

JUDGE DENNY CHIN
He Took the Other Fork in the Road

Because Judge Denny Chin was destined to sit in judgment of Bernard L. Madoff and to make the decision for his sentencing, it is interesting to note some details of his life that parallel Madoff's beginnings. Both men rose to significant heights from humble beginnings.

Denny Chin was born in 1954 in Kowloon, Hong Kong, and was brought to the United States when he was two years old. He grew up in the Times Square area of New York City with four siblings. The family lived above an adult-movie theater near the old Hell's Kitchen neighborhood. In 1971 the judge graduated from Stuyvesant High School, earned his Bachelor's degree, *magna cum laude,* from Princeton University in 1975 and in 1978 graduated from Fordham University School of Law, where he was Managing Editor of the Fordham Law Review.

Professionally, Judge Chin served as a law clerk for the Hon. Henry Werker of the U. S. District Court, Southern District of New York, from 1978 to 1980. He entered private practice for two years, and then became assistant U. S. Attorney for the Southern District of New York for four years. He again entered private practice from 1986 to 1994. On March 14, 1994, President Bill Clinton nominated him to a newly created seat on the United States District Court for the Southern District of New York, and he received Senate confirmation on October 9, 1994. Judge Chin, age 39, was the first Asian American appointed as a U. S. District Judge outside of the Ninth Circuit.

Judge Denny Chin was eventually to fill the spot on the United States Court of Appeals for the Second District (the position vacated by Judge Sonia Sotomayor as she became a Justice of the Supreme Court of the United States).

One wonders what went through Judge Chin's mind as he heard the pleas and testimony of Bernard Madoff in his courtroom. Did he reflect upon the similar beginnings and diametrically opposed outcomes of his own and Mr. Madoff's life?

THE CHRONOLOGY OF INDICTMENT, PLEA AND SENTENCING

The chronology of Bernie Madoff's criminal indictments is as follows:

- ***December 10, 2008*** – Madoff confesses to his two sons that he has conducted a massive Ponzi scheme for the last twenty years or more. [As of this writing, federal prosecutors continue to investigate the Madoff family and associates in the firm, including Peter, Mark (now deceased) and Andrew Madoff. Frank DiPascali, a senior stock analyst for Madoff's trading desk, and David G. Friehling, Madoff's accountant, have pleaded guilty and are cooperating in the investigation of other Madoff family members and associates.]
- ***December 11, 2008*** – Mark and Andrew Madoff contact federal authorities through their own attorneys at Paul, Weiss, Rifkind, Wharton & Garrison LLP and disclose their father's illegal activities. Madoff is arrested, handcuffed and led away from his penthouse apartment at 133 East 64th Street. He is charged with securities fraud, mail fraud, wire fraud, money laundering, false statements, perjury, false filings with the SEC and theft from an employee benefit plan.
- ***December 12, 2008*** – Before U. S. District Judge Denny Chin, Bernard Madoff pleads guilty to eleven felony counts related to the Ponzi scheme and is placed under house arrest, with the ability to walk freely during the daytime hours and confined to his home only at night.
- ***December 19, 2008*** – Bail conditions are modified to limit Madoff's movements and to require twenty-four

hour monitoring of his apartment. Madoff is unable to meet bond conditions that required four people to sign his personal recognizance bond. Only his wife and brother agree to sign.

- *January 6, 2009* – Prosecutors seek to revoke Madoff's bail and send him to jail immediately after he mails packages of valuables to his sons, his brother and friends in violation of the bail agreement, which barred him from disposing of any assets.
- *February 2009* – SEC reaches an agreement with Madoff that bans him from the securities industry for life.
- *March 12, 2009* – Madoff is relocated to Metropolitan Correctional Center, known as 10 South, a miserable facility that has previously housed mobsters and terrorists.
- *March 20, 2009* – Appellate court denies Madoff's appeal to leave jail and return to his apartment awaiting trial.
- *June 26, 2009* – Judge Chin orders Madoff to forfeit $170 million in assets and for his wife to relinquish all of her assets except for $2.5 million. Bankruptcy trustee Irving Picard indicates to the court, "Mr. Madoff has NOT provided meaningful cooperation or assistance."
- *June 29, 2009* – Madoff is sentenced to 150 years in federal prison.

THE VICTIMS SPEAK

Mr. Madoff was brought to Judge Chin's courtroom for sentencing from the Metropolitan Correctional Center in New York, where he had been incarcerated since March 2009.

Excerpts of statements by his *victims* delivered at the Madoff sentencing follow. These nine individuals asked to speak at the hearing. There were 113 Victim Impact Statements submitted to the court. The excerpts that follow are from the official court transcript of <u>United States v. Bernard L. Madoff</u>, 09 Cr. 213 (DC) before the Honorable Denny Chin, U. S. District Court, Southern District of New York. In some cases, some portions of the statements have been omitted due to their length.

```
96TJMAD1                Sentence

UNITED STATES DISTRICT COURT
SOUTHERN DISTRICT OF NEW YORK
------------------------------x

UNITED STATES OF AMERICA,

            v.                          09 CR 213 (DC)

BERNARD L. MADOFF,

            Defendant.

------------------------------x

                                        New York, N.Y.
                                        June 29, 2009
                                        10:00 a.m.


Before:

                    HON. DENNY CHIN,

                                        District Judge
```

SOUTHERN DISTRICT REPORTERS, P.C.
(212) 805-0300

```
96TJMAD1                    Sentence
```

1   (In open court)

2   (Case called)

3   THE COURT: Please be seated. Good morning. Mr.
4   Madoff, would you please stand.

5   Mr. Madoff, you pled guilty on March 12th, 2009 to 11
6   counts of securities fraud, investment advisor fraud, wire and
7   mail fraud, money laundering, making false statements, perjury,
8   filing false documents with the SEC and theft from employee
9   benefit funds. You are here this morning to be sentenced for
10 those crimes.

11   Have you reviewed the presentence report?

12   THE DEFENDANT: Yes, I have, your Honor.

13   THE COURT: Did you discuss it with your lawyers?

14   THE DEFENDANT: I have.

15   THE COURT: Mr. Sorkin, have you reviewed the
16 presentence report and discussed it with your client?

17   MR. SORKIN: Yes, your Honor, we have.

18   THE COURT: Do you or your client have any objections
19 to the factual recitations or the guidelines calculation?

20   MR. SORKIN: We do not, your Honor.

21   THE COURT: Thank you. You can be seated.

22   Ms. Baroni, does the government have any objections to
23 the presentence report?

24   MS. BARONI: No, your Honor.

25   THE COURT: Thank you.

SOUTHERN DISTRICT REPORTERS, P.C.
(212) 805-0300

Accordingly, here the guideline range is not life imprisonment, but 150 years, the maximum sentences for each of the 11 counts added together. Of course, in light of Booker and the case law that followed, the guideline range is advisory only. While I must give the guideline range fair and respectful consideration, I am not bound by it. In fact, the Probation Department recommends a sentence of 50 years. Instead I must make an individualized assessment based on all the facts and circumstances, including the factors set forth in the statute. In the end, I must impose a sentence that is reasonable.

We will proceed as follows:

First we will hear from the victims. Then Mr. Sorkin will speak on behalf of Mr. Madoff. Next Mr. Madoff may speak if he wishes. Finally, I will hear from the government.

First the victims. I have received several hundred written statements from victims including the e-mails and letters submitted back in March. Every victim who made a timed request to speak will be permitted to speak today except in two instances. Two members of the same family asked to speak, and we will permit one person to speak on behalf of the family. Two victims have now withdrawn their request. Accordingly, we will hear from 9 victims today.

First we will hear from Mr. and Mrs. Ambrosino. The Ambrosinos can step up to the microphone. Go ahead. Mr. Ambrosino, go ahead. Come up to the microphone so everyone can hear you.

MR. AMBROSINO: Thank you, your Honor. My name is Dominic Ambrosino and my --

THE COURT: Sir, just keep your voice up.

MR. AMBROSINO: I thank the court for allowing me to speak today. As a retired New York City Correction Officer, I am very familiar with the inside of a courtroom. However, I never in my wildest dreams ever expected to be sitting in one as a victim of an indescribably heinous crime --

THE COURT: Mr. Ambrosino, slow down a touch so our Court Reporter can transcribe what you're saying.

MR. AMBROSINO: That dream came true on March 12th as I watched Bernie Madoff stand and be cuffed. However, the dream really started as a nightmare on December 11th. I can remember the exact second my wife told me the news. I immediately knew all the ramifications, but I don't think she did. The fallout from having your entire life savings drop right out from under your nose is truly like nothing you can ever describe. At first it was the obvious, and how will we pay our bills? How can someone do this to us?

We worked honestly and we worked so hard. This can't be real. We did nothing wrong.

SOUTHERN DISTRICT REPORTERS, P.C.
(212) 805-0300

I don't know if anyone other than another victim can explain what the less obvious effects are, how every decision directly and indirectly hinged on the fact that we had the security of our savings. When I was able to leave the job, we bought a motor home to travel the country. We took out a mortgage since it was better to keep our savings in Madoff. We sold the house my wife lived in for 27 years and also put all those profits -- and they were high -- into our Madoff account. We trusted that the savings and planning would see us through our retirement.

We had ideas of traveling the country. It all stopped abruptly on December 11th. As a result, we are left with no permanent house, a depreciating motor home, we are upside down on the loan and an income from my pension that is our life. This pension used to be perceived as spending money before December 11th, and now although it doesn't cover our monthly expenses, we rely on it fully. It is all we have.

I sustained a 52 percent hearing loss on my job, and at 49 years' old I can't go back to my previous career so I have taken on a job this summer in Arizona as an construction project coordinator. The job will only last until August. Then I don't know what I am going to do.

My wife's foot was run over by a van while in New York City. There was a plea hearing in March. She had a job lined up before the trip. The expenses of the trip were given to us and we had to let it go since she was in a cast for eight weeks. She is now rehabilitating and still feels pain when she stands for long periods of time.

With that background as to who I am, I would like to share some of the specific problems Madoff's crime brought to us. My pension distribution, a one-time decision, and our health insurance plan, also one-time decision, were based on the fact that we had savings and security with Madoff. If I should die, my wife is left without my income or health insurance.

We sold our home in New York with the expectation that someday we would have the finances to purchase another one. We have no credit now and can't get a mortgage. We have been forced to take care of people's homes while they are traveling for the summer, as we used to do prior to December 11th.

We have through the generosity of friends been able to stay rent free on the RV lots of people in the community. This will come to a screeching halt in October when the owners return for the winter season. We don't know where we'll go at that time. We don't have enough income from my pension to pay monthly rent.

The most devastating to us is we lost our freedom. We lost the ability to share our life every day as we explore the country every day. We lost the time to hold hands as we walked. As they say in the commercial, this is priceless.

In closing, I would like to say, Judge Chin, sentencing Bernard L. Madoff to the fullest extent will certainly not eliminate any of the issues I wrote about. It probably won't even gain me satisfaction. As the guard who used to be on the right side of the prison bars, I'll know what Mr. Madoff's experience will be and will know that he is in prison in much the same way he imprisoned us as well as others.

He took from us the freedom that we held so preciously close to our lives, the very thing I always valued and never took for granted. In a sense, I would like someone in the court today to tell me how long is my sentence.

Thank you very much.

THE COURT: Thank you. Next we'll hear from Mr. and Mrs. FitzMaurice.

MS. EBEL: No, Judge Chin. I am next.

THE COURT: I saw the gentleman standing up next and I thought you were Maureen Ebel.

MS. EBEL: Yes, I am. I am here with may brother, William Thomas McDonough.

THE COURT: All right.

MS. EBEL: My name is Maureen Ebel and I am a victim of Bernard L. Madoff.

I have lost all of my life's hard-earned savings. I have lost my life savings because our government has failed me and thousands and thousands of other citizens. There are many levels of government complicity in this crime. The Securities & Exchange Commission, by its total incompetence and criminal negligence, has allowed a psychopath to steal from me and steal from the world.

I am a 61-year-old widow and I am now working full time. I have done many things to survive since December 11th, including selling a lot of my possessions and working three jobs at the same time. I have lost a home that my husband and I had owned for 25 years because of this theft.

I have lost my ability to care for myself in my old age. I have lost the ability to donate to charity, especially the Leukemia & Lymphoma Society. I have lost my ability to donate my time working for that charity as I had done in the past because now I must work full time in order to eat.

I have lost the ability to help future generations of my family get an education. I have lost the ability to help them with their housing needs. It pains my so much to remember my husband getting up in the middle of the night. He was a very fine physician. He would get up in the middle of the night year after year in all kinds of weather to go to the hospital to save someone's life in rain, ice and snow.

He would save someone's life so that Bernie Madoff could buy his wife another party rock. I have lost the ability to move around the world freely at this stage in my life using the money my husband and I have worked so hard to earn. We had

SOUTHERN DISTRICT REPORTERS, P.C.
(212) 805-0300

[Partial omission of Ms. Ebel's testimony. Below is a partial transcription of the testimony of victim Mr. Fitzmaurice.]

1 worked, saved and planned for our old age so that we could
2 leave something behind and not be a burden when we became sick
3 and old.

[Omission of some of Mr. Fitzmaurice's testimony.]

3 My wife and I are not millionaires. He has taken our
4 entire life savings. We have not been overlooked just as many
5 of his other victims. We have worked hard, long and hard for
6 all of our lives to provide for our family and to be in a
7 position to retire someday. I am now forced to work three
8 jobs. My wife is working a full-time job only to make ends
9 meet, to allow us to pay our mortgage and put food on the
10 table.
11 We are 63 years' old. It will be no retirement for us
12 in the next two or three years. There will be no trips to
13 California to visit our one-year-old grandson. There will be
14 no vacations of any type. Again we are too old to recoup the
15 monies that he has taken from us. We can only work as long as
16 our health will hold up and then we will have to sell our home
17 and hope to survive on social security alone.

20 Where will we be able to live? How will we pay our
21 bills? How will we get medical insurance?
22 All of his victims worldwide will be waiting to see
23 that true justice is served. True justice is a maximum
24 sentence in a maximum security prison. I have a quotation from
25 my wife, since only one of us could speak. She wants to say:

```
 1              "I cry every day when I see the look of pain and
 2       despair in my husband's eyes. I cry for the life we once had
 3       before that monster took it away. Our two sons and
 4       daughter-in-law have rallied with constant love and support.
 5       You, on the other hand, Mr. Madoff, have two sons that despise
```

[Omission of all of Ms. Carla Hirschhorn's testimony and Ms. Sharon Lissauer's testimony. The transcript continues with the testimony of Mr. Burt Ross:]

```
 6       you. Your wife, rightfully so, has been vilified and shunned
 7       by her friends in the community. You have left your children a
 8       legacy of shame. I have a marriage made in heaven. You have a
 9       marriage made in hell, and that is where you, Mr. Madoff, are
10       going to return. May God spare you no mercy."
11              THE COURT: Thank you.
```

[Additional omissions from Mr. Ross's testimony.]

```
 4              What Bernard L. Madoff did far transcends the loss of
 5       money. It involves his betrayal of the virtues people hold
 6       dearest -- love, friendship, trust -- and all so he can eat at
 7       the finest restaurants, stay at the most luxurious resorts, and
 8       travel on yachts and private jets. He has truly earned his
 9       reputation for being the most despised person to be in America
10       today.

20              Please Allow me to take a liberty now by speaking for
21       many of those victims who because of frailty, privacy,
22       distance, or other reasons are unable to bear witness today.
23       We urge your Honor to commit Madoff to prison for the remainder
24       of his natural life, and when he leaves this earth virtually
25       unmourned, may Satan grow a forth mouth where Bernard L. Madoff
```

deserves to spend the rest of eternity.

Thank you.

THE COURT: Thank you. Next we'll hear from Michael Schwartz.

MR. SCHWARTZ: Can everyone hear me?

My name is Michael Schwartz. I am 33 years' old. It was my family's trust fund that helped fund the money for Bernard Madoff's organization. Since I was a teenager, I invested into what I thought was a forthright and legitimate investment firm. During this time I made sure I lived well within my means, nothing extravagant. I viewed my investment as a safety net in case I should hit hard times or perhaps face medical issues.

Unfortunately, several months ago, my job was regionalized, eliminated. I was handed a letter of recommendation and sent on my way. It didn't hit me until I got home that the company that you ran had already taken my life savings. At 33, I was wiped out.

I am one of the lucky ones by far. I have my health. I am young, I have great friends, got a loving wife. Unfortunately, the money you took from other members of my family wasn't a minor setback. It was quite a bit more. Your Honor, part of the trust fund wasn't set aside for a house in the Hamptons, a large yacht or box seat to the Mets. No, part of that money was set aside to take care of my twin brother who

is mentally disabled, who at 33, he lives at home with my parents and will need care and supervision for the rest of his life.

19 We'll hear next from Miriam Siegman.
20 MS. SIEGMAN: I was born a few blocks from this
21 courthouse. I still live here. On a cold winter's day just
22 before my 65th birthday, the man sitting in front of me
23 announced to the world that he had stolen everything I had.
24 After that he refused to say another word to his victims. I am
25 here today to bear witness for myself and others, silent

1 victims.
2 The streets of my childhood felt safe. The streets I
3 wander now feel threatening. The man sitting in this courtroom
4 robbed me. In an instant his words and deeds beat me to near
5 senselessness. He discarded me like road kill. Victims became
6 the byproduct of his greed. We are what is left over, the
7 remnants of stunning indifference and that of politicians and
8 bureaucrats.
9 Six months have passed. I manage on food stamps. At
10 the end of the month I sometimes scavage in dumpsters. I
11 cannot afford new eyeglasses. I long to go to a concert, but I
12 never do. Sometimes my heartbeats erratically for lack of
13 medication when I cannot pay for it.

```
14              I shine my shoes each night, afraid they will wear
15    out. My laundry is done by hand in the kitchen sink. I have
16    collected empty cans and dragged them to redemption centers.
17              I do this. People ask how are you? My answer always
18    is I'm fine, but it is not always true. I have lived with
19    fear. It strikes me at all hours. I calculate again and again
20    how long I can hold out.
21              It is only a matter of time. I will be unable to meet
22    my own basic needs, food, shelter, medicine. I feel grief at
23    no longer being able to help support my beloved sister. I feel
24    shame and humiliation asking for help.
25              I also feel overwhelming sadness. I know that another
 1    human being did this to me and to all victims, but I don't know
 2    why. What I do understand frightens me. The man who did this
 3    had deep contempt for his victims.
```

[Omission of some of the testimony of Ms. Seigman. Ms. Seigman closes by addressing Mr. Madoff directly.]

```
17              Face an acknowledge the murderous effects of your
18    life's work. I long for the truth that might become of a trial
19    and hope justice had placed a higher premium on truth and
20    expediency. Forgiveness for now, it will have to come from
21    someone other than me.
22              THE COURT: Thank you. Finally we'll hear from Sheryl
23    Weinstein.
24              MS. WEINSTEIN: Hello, your Honor.
```

[Omission of the beginning of the testimony of Ms. Sheryl Weinstein.]

```
 9          You have read and you appear from many of us, the old,
10     the young, the healthy and infirm about the unimaginable extent
11     of human tragedy and devastation. According to a Time Magazine
12     article, there are over 3 million individuals worldwide who
13     have been directly or indirectly affected. They, the press and
14     the media, speak of us as being greedy and rich. Most of us
15     are just ordinary working people, worker bees, as I like to
16     refer to us.
```

[Omission of some testimony of Ms. Weinstein.]

```
15          Ms. Couric said to me you sound angry, and I said yes,
16     you're right. When someone steals from you, you get angry.
17     That was the beginning of my healing process.
```

[Omission of some testimony of Ms. Weinstein.]

```
 3          We, the victims, are greatly disappointed by those
 4     agencies that were set up to protect us. SIPIC has now
 5     redefined what we are entitled to. The IRS approved their
 6     office request to be a custodian of our IRAs and pension funds
 7     and the SEC appears to have looked the other way on numerous
 8     occasions. This is a human tragedy of historic proportions and
 9     we ask -- no, we implore -- that those whose agencies may have
10     failed us in the past through acts of omissions, step up to the
11     plate, fulfill their responsibilities. I thank your Honor for
12     your indulgence and I feel comfortable you will make sure
13     justice is served.
14          Thank you.
15          THE COURT: Thank you.
16          Thanks to all the victims who spoke today and to all
17     those who wrote. I appreciate hearing your views.
```

[The statement of Mr. Sorkin, Mr. Madoff's attorney, is excerpted below:]

```
25              In closing, your Honor, there is no question that this
 1   case has taken an enormous toll, not only on Mr. Madoff and his
 2   family, but to the victims to be sure. But it has also taken a
 3   toll, your Honor, as Mr. Madoff will say, on the industry that
 4   he helped revolutionize, that he helped grow, and now has
 5   become the object of disrespect and abomination, and that is a
 6   tragedy as well.

 7              We ask only, your Honor, that Mr. Madoff be given
 8   understanding and fairness, within the parameters of our legal
 9   system, and that the sentence that he be given be sufficient,
10   but not greater than necessary, to carry out what this Court
11   must carry out under the rules, statutes and guidelines.
12              Thank you, your Honor.
13              THE COURT: Thank you.
```

The statement of defendant, Bernard Madoff, to the court:

```
14              Mr. Madoff, if you would like to speak, now is the
15   time.
16              THE DEFENDANT: Your Honor, I cannot offer you an
17   excuse for my behavior. How do you excuse betraying thousands
18   of investors who entrusted me with their life savings? How do
19   you excuse deceiving 200 employees who have spent most of their
20   working life working for me? How do you excuse lying to your
21   brother and two sons who spent their whole adult life helping
```

21   People have accused me of being silent and not being
22   sympathetic. That is not true. They have accused my wife of
23   being silent and not being sympathetic. Nothing could be
24   further from the truth. She cries herself to sleep every night
25   knowing of all the pain and suffering I have caused, and I am

[Lines omitted]

1   tormented by that as well. She was advised to not speak
2   publicly until after my sentencing by our attorneys, and she
3   complied with that. Today she will make a statement about how
4   she feels about my crimes. I ask you to listen to that. She
5   is sincere and all I ask you is to listen to her.
6   Apologizing and saying I am sorry, that's not enough.
7   Nothing I can say will correct the things that I have done. I
8   feel terrible that an industry I spent my life trying to
9   improve is being criticized terribly now, that regulators who I
10   helped work with over the years are being criticized by what I
11   have done. That is a horrible guilt to live with. There is
12   nothing I can do that will make anyone feel better for the pain
13   and suffering I caused them, but I will live with this pain,
14   with this torment for the rest of my life.
15   I apologize to my victims. I will turn and face you.
16   I am sorry. I know that doesn't help you.
17   Your Honor, thank you for listening to me.
18   THE COURT: Thank you.

2   I will hear from the government.

3   MS. BARONI: This defendant carried out a fraud of
4   unprecedented proportion over the course of more than a
5   generation. For more than 20 years he stole ruthlessly and
6   without remorse. Thousands of people placed their trust in him
7   and he lied repeatedly to all of them. And as the Court heard
8   from all of the victims, in their words and in the letters, he
9   destroyed a lifetime of hard work of thousands of victims. And
10   he used that victims' money to enrich himself and his family,
11   with an opulent lifestyle, homes around the world, yachts,
12   private jets, and tens of millions of dollars of loans to his
13   family, loans of investors' money that has never been repaid.
14   The guideline sentence in this case, as your Honor
15   knows, is 150 years and the government respectfully submits
16   that a sentence of 150 years or a substantial term of
17   imprisonment that will ensure that he spends the rest of his
18   life in jail is appropriate in this case.

[The Court then hears from Ms. Baroni representing the government:]

19   This was not a crime born of any financial distress or
20   market pressures. It was a calculated, well orchestrated,
21   long-term fraud, that this defendant carried out month after
22   month, year after year, decade after decade. He created
23   literally hundreds and hundreds of thousands of fake documents
24   every year. Every time he told his clients that he was making
25   trades for them he sent them trade confirmations filled with

lies. At every month end he sent them account statements that were nothing but lies. And the defendant knew that his clients made critically important life decisions, as your Honor heard today, based on these lies. Decisions about their children's education, their retirement, how to care for elderly relatives, and how to provide for their families. He knew this, and he stole from them anyway.

In doing so, he drove charities, companies, pension plans and families to economic ruin. And even on the most dispassionate view of the evidence, the scale of the fraud, which is at a conservative estimate, your Honor, $13 billion, when you look at the duration of the fraud, which is more than 20 years, when you look at the fact that the defendant could have stopped this fraud and saved the victims' losses, all of these facts justify a guideline sentence of 150 years.

THE COURT: Thank you.

I take into account what I have read in the presentence report, the parties' sentencing submissions, and the e-mails and letters from victims. I take into account what I have heard today. I also consider the statutory factors as well as all the facts and circumstances in the case.

In his initial letter on behalf of Mr. Madoff, Mr. Sorkin argues that the unified tone of the victims' letters suggests a desire for mob vengeance. He also writes that Mr. Madoff seeks neither mercy nor sympathy, but justice and objectivity.

[Finally, Judge Chin speaks:]

            Moreover, as many of the victims have pointed out,
this is not just a matter of money. The breach of trust was
massive. Investors -- individuals, charities, pension funds,
institutional clients -- were repeatedly lied to, as they were
told their moneys would be invested in stocks when they were
not. Clients were sent these millions of pages of account
statements that the government just alluded to confirming
trades that were never made, attesting to balances that did not
exist. As the victims' letters and e-mails demonstrate, as the
statements today demonstrate, investors made important life
decisions based on these fictitious account statements -- when
to retire, how to care for elderly parents, whether to buy a
car or sell a house, how to save for their children's college
tuition. Charitable organizations and pension funds made
important decisions based on false information about fictitious
accounts. Mr. Madoff also repeatedly lied to the SEC and the
regulators, in writing and in sworn testimony, by withholding
material information, by creating false documents to cover up
his scheme.

[Judge Chin continues:]

5   I received letters, and we have heard from, for
 6   example, a retired forest worker, a corrections officer, an
 7   auto mechanic, a physical therapist, a retired New York City
 8   school secretary, who is now 86 years old and widowed, who must
 9   deal with the loss of her retirement funds. Their money is
10   gone, leaving only a sense of betrayal.
11   I was particularly struck by one story that I read in
12   the letters. A man invested his family's life savings with
13   Mr. Madoff. Tragically, he died of a heart attack just two
14   weeks later. The widow eventually went in to see Mr. Madoff.
15   He put his arm around her, as she describes it, and in a kindly
16   manner told her not to worry, the money is safe with me. And
17   so not only did the widow leave the money with him, she
18   eventually deposited more funds with him, her 401(k), her
19   pension funds. Now, all the money is gone. She will have to
20   sell her home, and she will not be able to keep her promise to
21   help her granddaughter pay for college.

[A part of Judge Chin's remarks is omitted.]

 7   I do not agree that the victims are succumbing to the
 8   temptation of mob vengeance. Rather, they are doing what they
 9   are supposed to be doing -- placing their trust in our system
10   of justice. A substantial sentence, the knowledge that
11   Mr. Madoff has been punished to the fullest extent of the law,
12   may, in some small measure, help these victims in their healing
13   process.
14   Mr. Madoff, please stand.
15   It is the judgment of this Court that the defendant,
16   Bernard L. Madoff, shall be and hereby is sentenced to a term
17   of imprisonment of 150 years, consisting of 20 years on each of

[Lines omitted.]

```
18  Counts 1, 3, 4, 5, 6, and 10, 5 years on each of Counts 2, 8,
19  9, and 11, and 10 years on Count 7, all to run consecutively to
20  each other. As a technical matter, the sentence must be
21  expressed on the judgment in months. 150 years is equivalent
22  to 1,800 months.
23          Although it is academic, for technical reasons, I must
24  also impose supervised release. I impose a term of supervised
25  release of 3 years on each count, all to run concurrently. The
 1  pronounce it as part of the sentence.
 2          THE COURT: The forfeiture order is hereby
 3  incorporated.
 4          MS. BARONI: Special assessment.
 5          THE DEFENDANT: I did the special assessment of
 6  $1,100.
 7          MS. BARONI: Thank you.
 8          THE COURT: Mr. Madoff, please stand one more time.
 9          Mr. Madoff, you have the right to appeal at least
10  certain aspects of this judgment and conviction. If you wish
11  to appeal, you must do so within ten days. If you cannot
12  afford an attorney, the court will appoint one for you.
13          We are adjourned.
14          (Adjourned)
```

"A MEASURE OF JUSTICE"

Judge Chin sentenced Madoff to 150 years in prison, as follows:

- Forty years for two counts of international money laundering
- Twenty years for securities fraud
- Twenty years for mail fraud
- Twenty years for wire fraud
- Twenty years for false filing with the SEC
- Ten years for money laundering
- Five years for investment advisor fraud
- Five years for false statements
- Five years for perjury
- Five years for theft from an employee benefit plan

Judge Chin acknowledged that any sentence beyond a dozen years or so would be largely symbolic for Mr. Madoff, who is seventy-one years old and has a life expectancy of about thirteen years. But Judge Chin set forth the following reasoning for the consecutive sentence of 150 years as just for the self-confessed criminal Bernard L. Madoff:

> Symbolism is important for three reasons: The need for retribution, the need for deterrence and a measure of justice for the victims…
>
> The message must be sent that Mr. Madoff's crimes were extraordinarily evil and that this kind of irresponsible manipulation of the system is not merely a bloodless financial crime that takes place just on paper, but that it is…one that takes a staggering human toll…

Chin added that Madoff had not been fully cooperative with authorities.

Immediately after sentencing, as prisoner #61727-054, he was moved to the U. S. Penitentiary in Atlanta, Georgia, for the night, and then moved to Butner Federal Correctional Complex in North Carolina—his home for the rest of his life. The Butner Complex has five prisons housing 4,875 inmates. Madoff is in one of the medium-security prisons with 725 inmates. He is assigned sixteen visiting points per month. Visits on weekdays count as one point; weekends and holidays count as four points. Visits are limited to three adults at a time. If cleared to work, Madoff will work in the prison seven hours per day. There has been one report from former Butner inmates that Mr. Madoff took a severe beating from another inmate and was treated for a broken nose and several cracked ribs. The prison authorities said they were unaware of the incident.

POSTSCRIPT

On the second anniversary of Bernard Madoff's arrest, his older son Mark took his own life. Despair and disgrace had overwhelmed him as he watched friends and colleagues ruined by the loss of their invested assets with BLMIS. Just two days earlier civil suits had been filed to recover monies from him, his wife and his young children. The continuing threat of personal criminal investigation and indictment loomed before him. He confided to friends that he had come to understand that every asset he had would be subject to clawbacks and that he was entirely unemployable for the remainder of his life. He lived with universal condemnation by society. Whether or not he and his brother Andrew were truly duped by their father—we may never know.

Prison officials denied Bernard L. Madoff the permission to attend his son's funeral. One wonders if those mourning Mark would have wished to have Mr. Madoff among them.

Mark Madoff is not the only casualty—Thierry Magon de La Villehuchet, chief executive officer of Access International Advisors took his own life in December 2008 after learning of his firm's losses on investments made with Bernard Madoff.

Another casualty of the scandal, billionaire Jeffry Picower drowned in his swimming pool in October 2009 after an apparent heart attack. His death followed just weeks after he was sued for clawback of monies withdrawn from BLMIS over many years. His wife ultimately settled with federal prosecutors and trustee Irving Picard by returning every cent of the $7.2 billion that Picower had withdrawn from BLMIS based on his original $619 million investment. Mr. Picard believed that Picower had to know he was in a Ponzi scheme since he had experienced an implausible and staggering 950 percent return on his capital in some years.

Recovered monies will be distributed only to Madoff investors that lost all their original capital investment. Investors who received distributions of more cash than they originally invested are not expected to be eligible to share in the recovery. Court appeals on the distribution qualifications are also pending.

On September 11, 2009, the U. S. Government commenced the selling of Mr. Madoff's real estate.

- The duplex home of the Madoff's in New York City was listed for $9.9 million.
- The Long Island "retreat" was listed for $8.75 million. On Labor Day, 2009, seventy brokers arrived to preview the property and twenty-three detailed showings were made.
- The Palm Beach winter residence was listed for $8.5 million.

Sales of these assets and auctions of personal possessions have yielded millions of dollars to the restitution funds.

The Madoff feeder fund called Fairfield Greenwich Advisors agreed to pay $8 million to settle fraud charges by the State of Massachusetts. Fairfield had $6.9 BILLION of its clients' $14 billion of assets invested with BLMIS.

On September 1, 2009, Irving Picard stated that he would pursue clawbacks from charities that benefited from Mr. Madoff's donations.

As of October 29, 2009, Mr. Picard announced 15,974 claims for losses had been filed with his office. There were 8,095 confirmed customer accounts.

The net loss valuation: $21.2 BILLION.

The net assets recovered by February 2011: Over $10 BILLION and growing.

In another strange twist in this ongoing travesty, professional investors have been buying up the valid claims of victims that have been approved by the trustee at a discount to their face value. In recent months, Madoff victims have been offered 20 to 34.5 cents on the dollar for their claims. These claims may ultimately be valued at more than 50 cents on the dollar — a nice profit for the speculators. The victims, some of whom are experiencing dire financial difficulties, are easy prey for an immediate payout.

Trustee Picard made news again in February 2011 when he announced that he would bring a lawsuit against BLMIS' primary bank, JP Morgan Chase, and the Wilpon family, owners of the New York Mets. The lawsuit against JP Morgan Chase cites internal e-mails within the bank that document awareness of something amiss with BLMIS—eighteen months or more before the scandal broke. JP Morgan Chase had been the only major bank that had weathered the current financial debacle with its reputation remarkably intact.

Bernard Madoff's first interview since his incarceration was granted to Diana B. Henriques and reported in *The New York Times* on February 16, 2011. Ms. Henriques commented on Madoff's conviction that his bank and others had to have been aware of the Ponzi scheme:

> In many ways, however, Mr. Madoff seemed unchanged. He spoke with great intensity and fluency about his dealings with various banks and hedge funds, pointing to their "willful blindness" and their failure to examine discrepancies between his regulatory filings and other information available to them.

"They had to know," Mr. Madoff said. "But the attitude was sort of, 'If you're doing something wrong, we don't want to know.' "

Hundreds of millions of victims worldwide have been defrauded as well by bankers, investment bankers and financial institutions in the Great Recession and its aftermath. But regulatory authorities and the Department of Justice have failed to convict a single miscreant of criminal fraud. So far, Bernard L. Madoff, a "second tier" player in Wall Street who pleaded guilty to his crimes, is the only greedster who has seen prison time for his fraud.

Although not without controversy, Trustee Irving Picard has zealously and aggressively made it his mission to recover as much value as possible for Madoff's victims—far more than ever considered possible. No champion has entered the field in behalf of the ordinary investor and shareholder fleeced by the financial institutions and their greedy minions.

Mr. Madoff is undoubtedly ruing the day he became entranced with the almighty dollar—for due to his greed he will be a slave for the rest of his life. His family has been ostracized and condemned.

His son has taken his own life. Those he loved and all those who trusted him have suffered disaster at his hands. The name of Bernard L. Madoff will forever be associated with arrogance and greed.

[EXCERPT FROM THE PUBLIC VERSION OF THE SEC REPORT CITED]

UNITED STATES SECURITIES AND EXCHANGE COMMISSION OFFICE OF INSPECTOR GENERAL

Case No. OIG-509

Investigation of Failure of the SEC To Uncover Bernard Madoff's Ponzi Scheme

Executive Summary

The OIG investigation did not find evidence that any SEC personnel who worked on an SEC examination or investigation of Bernard L. Madoff Investment Securities, LLC (BMIS) had any financial or other inappropriate connection with Bernard Madoff or the Madoff family that influenced the conduct of their examination or investigatory work. The OIG also did not find that former SEC Assistant Director Eric Swanson's romantic relationship with Bernard Madoff's niece, Shana Madoff, influenced the conduct of the SEC examinations of Madoff and his firm. We also did not find that senior officials at the SEC directly attempted to influence examinations or investigations of Madoff or the Madoff firm, nor was there evidence any senior SEC official interfered with the staff's ability to perform its work.

The OIG investigation did find, however, that the SEC received more than ample information in the form of detailed and substantive complaints over the years to warrant a rough and comprehensive examination and/or investigation of Bernard Madoff and BMIS for operating a Ponzi scheme, and that despite three examinations and two investigations being conducted, a thorough and competent investigation or examination was never performed. The OIG found that between June 1992 and December 2008 when Madoff confessed, the SEC received six[10] substantive complaints that raised significant red flags concerning Madoff's hedge fund operations and should have led to questions about whether Madoff was actually engaged in trading. Finally, the SEC was also aware of two articles regarding Madoff's investment operations that appeared in reputable publications in 2001 and questioned Madoff's unusually consistent returns.

The first complaint, brought to the SEC's attention in 1992, related to allegations that an unregistered investment company was offering "100%" safe investments with high and extremely consistent rates of return over significant periods of time to "special" customers. The SEC actually suspected the investment company was operating a Ponzi scheme and learned in their investigation that all of the investments were placed entirely through Madoff and consistent returns were claimed to have been achieved for numerous years without a single loss.

The second complaint was very specific and different versions were provided to the SEC in May 2000, March 2001 and October 2005. The complaint submitted in 2005 was entitled "The World's Largest Hedge Fund is a Fraud" and detailed approximately 30 red flags indicating that Madoff was operating a Ponzi scheme, a scenario it described as "highly likely." The red flags included the impossibil-

---

[10] There were arguably eight complaints, since as described in greater detail below, three versions of one of these six complaints were actually brought to the SEC's attention, with the first two versions being dismissed entirely, and an investigation not opened until the third version was submitted.

* After the OIG issued the ROI to the Chairman of the SEC, at the SEC's request, the OIG prepared a modified public version of the ROI which redacted the identities of certain individuals because of privacy concerns as well as additional language at the request of the U.S. Department of Justice.

ity of Madoff's returns, particularly the consistency of those returns and the unrealistic volume of options Madoff represented to have traded.

In May 2003, the SEC received a third complaint from a respected Hedge Fund Manager identifying numerous concerns about Madoff's strategy and purported returns, questioning whether Madoff was actually trading options in the volume he claimed, noting that Madoff's strategy and purported returns were not duplicable by anyone else, and stating Madoff's strategy had no correlation to the overall equity markets in over 10 years. According to an SEC manager, the Hedge Fund Manager's complaint laid out issues that were "indicia of a Ponzi scheme."

The fourth complaint was part of a series of internal e-mails of another registrant that the SEC discovered in April 2004. The e-mails described the red flags that a registrant's employees had identified while performing due diligence on their own Madoff investment using publicly-available information. The red flags identified included Madoff's incredible and highly unusual fills for equity trades, his misrepresentation of his options trading and his unusually consistent, non-volatile returns over several years. One of the internal e-mails provided a step-by-step analysis of why Madoff must be misrepresenting his options trading. The e-mail clearly explained that Madoff could not be trading on an options exchange because of insufficient volume and could not be trading options over-the-counter because it was inconceivable that he could find a counterparty for the trading. The SEC examiners who initially discovered the e-mails viewed them as indicating "some suspicion as to whether Madoff is trading at all."

The fifth complaint was received by the SEC in October 2005 from an anonymous informant and stated, "I know that Madoff [sic] company is very secretive about their operations and they refuse to disclose anything. If my suspicions are true, then they are running a highly sophisticated scheme on a massive scale. And they have been doing it for a long time." The informant also stated, "After a short period of time, I decided to withdraw all my money (over $5 million)."

The sixth complaint was sent to the SEC by a "concerned citizen" in December 2006, advising the SEC to look into Madoff and his firm as follows:

> Your attention is directed to a scandal of major proportion which was executed by the investment firm Bernard L. Madoff . . . . Assets well in excess of $10 Billion owned by the late [investor], an ultra-wealthy long time client of the Madoff firm have been "co-mingled" with funds controlled by the Madoff company with gains thereon retained by Madoff.

In March 2008, the SEC Chairman's office received a second copy of the previous complaint, with additional information from the same source regarding Madoff's involvement with the investor's money, as follows:

> It may be of interest to you to that Mr. Bernard Madoff keeps two (2) sets of records. The most interesting of which is on his computer which is always on his person.

The two 2001 journal articles also raised significant questions about Madoff's unusually consistent returns. One of the articles noted his "astonishing ability to time the market and move to cash in the underlying securities before market conditions turn negative and the related ability to buy and sell the underlying stocks without noticeably affecting the market." This article also described that "experts ask why no one has been able to duplicate similar returns using [Madoff's] strategy." The second article quoted a former Madoff investor as saying, "Anybody who's a seasoned hedge-fund investor knows the split-strike conversion is not the whole story. To take it at face value is a bit naïve."

The complaints all contained specific information and could not have been fully and adequately resolved without thoroughly examining and investigating Madoff for operating a Ponzi scheme. The journal articles should have reinforced the concerns about how Madoff could have been achieving his returns.

The OIG retained an expert in accordance with its investigation in order to both analyze the information the SEC received regarding Madoff and the examination work conducted. According to the OIG's expert, the most critical step in examining or investigating a potential Ponzi scheme is to verify the subject's trading through an independent third party.

The OIG investigation found the SEC conducted two investigations and three examinations related to Madoff's investment advisory business based upon the detailed and credible complaints that raised the possibility that Madoff was misrepresenting his trading and could have been operating a Ponzi scheme. Yet, at no time did the SEC ever verify Madoff's trading through an independent third-party, and in fact, never actually conducted a Ponzi scheme examination or investigation of Madoff.

The first examination and first Enforcement investigation were conducted in 1992 after the SEC received information that led it to suspect that a Madoff associate had been conducting a Ponzi scheme. Yet, the SEC focused its efforts on Madoff's associate and never thoroughly scrutinized Madoff's operations even after learning that the investment decisions were made by Madoff and being apprised of the remarkably consistent returns over a period of numerous years that Madoff had achieved with a basic trading strategy. While the SEC ensured that all of Madoff's associate's customers received their money back, they took no steps to investigate Madoff. The SEC focused its investigation too narrowly and seemed not to have considered the possibility that Madoff could have taken the money that was used to pay back his associate's customers from other clients for which Madoff may have had held discretionary brokerage accounts. In the examination of Madoff, the SEC did not seek Depository Trust Company (DTC) (an independent third-party) records, but sought copies of such records from Madoff himself. Had they sought records from DTC, there is an excellent chance that they would have uncovered Madoff's Ponzi scheme in 1992.[11]

In 2004 and 2005, the SEC's examination unit, OCIE, conducted two parallel cause examinations of Madoff based upon the Hedge Fund Manager's complaint and the series of internal e-mails that the SEC discovered. The examinations were remarkably similar. There were initial significant delays in the commencement of the examinations, notwithstanding the urgency of the complaints. The teams assembled were relatively inexperienced, and there was insufficient planning for the examinations. The scopes of the examination were in both cases too narrowly focused on the possibility of front-running, with no significant attempts made to analyze the numerous red flags about Madoff's trading and returns.

During the course of both these examinations, the examination teams discovered suspicious information and evidence and caught Madoff in contradictions and inconsistencies. However, they either disregarded these concerns or simply asked Madoff about them. Even when Madoff's answers were seemingly implausible, the SEC examiners accepted them at face value.

In both examinations, the examiners made the surprising discovery that Madoff's mysterious hedge fund business was making significantly more money than his well-known market-making operation. However, no one identified this revelation as a cause for concern.

Astoundingly, both examinations were open at the same time in different offices without either knowing the other one was conducting an identical examination. In fact, it was Madoff himself who informed one of the examination teams that the other examination team had already received the information they were seeking from him.

---

[1] As discussed in the body of the Report of Investigation, this is premised upon the assumption that Madoff had been operating his Ponzi scheme in 1992, which most of the evidence seems to support.

In the first of the two OCIE examinations, the examiners drafted a letter to the National Association of Securities Dealers (NASD) (another independent third-party) seeking independent trade data, but they never sent the letter, claiming that it would have been too time-consuming to review the data they would have obtained. The OIG's expert opined that had the letter to the NASD been sent, the data would have provided the information necessary to reveal the Ponzi scheme. In the second examination, the OCIE Assistant Director sent a document request to a financial institution that Madoff claimed he used to clear his trades, requesting trading done by or on behalf of particular Madoff feeder funds during a specific time period, and received a response that there was no transaction activity in Madoff's account for that period. However, the Assistant Director did not determine that the response required any follow-up and the examiners testified that the response was not shared with them.

Both examinations concluded with numerous unresolved questions and without any significant attempt to examine the possibility that Madoff was misrepresenting his trading and operating a Ponzi scheme.

The investigation that arose from the most detailed complaint provided to the SEC, which explicitly stated it was "highly likely" that "Madoff was operating a Ponzi scheme," never really investigated the possibility of a Ponzi scheme. The relatively inexperienced Enforcement staff failed to appreciate the significance of the analysis in the complaint, and almost immediately expressed skepticism and disbelief. Most of their investigation was directed at determining whether Madoff should register as an investment adviser or whether Madoff's hedge fund investors' disclosures were adequate.

As with the examinations, the Enforcement staff almost immediately caught Madoff in lies and misrepresentations, but failed to follow up on inconsistencies. They rebuffed offers of additional evidence from the complainant, and were confused about certain critical and fundamental aspects of Madoff's operations. When Madoff provided evasive or contradictory answers to important questions in testimony, they simply accepted as plausible his explanations.

Although the Enforcement staff made attempts to seek information from independent third-parties, they failed to follow up on these requests. They reached out to the NASD and asked for information on whether Madoff had options positions on a certain date, but when they received a report that there were in fact no options positions on that date, they did not take any further steps. An Enforcement staff attorney made several attempts to obtain documentation from European counterparties (another independent third-party), and although a letter was drafted, the Enforcement staff decided not to send it. Had any of these efforts been fully executed, they would have led to Madoff's Ponzi scheme being uncovered.

The OIG also found that numerous private entities conducted basic due diligence of Madoff's operations and, without regulatory authority to compel information, came to the conclusion that an investment with Madoff was unwise. Specifically, Madoff's description of both his equity and options trading practices immediately led to suspicions about Madoff's operations. With respect to his purported trading strategy, many simply did not believe that it was possible for Madoff to achieve his returns using a strategy described by some industry leaders as common and unsophisticated. In addition, there was a great deal of suspicion about Madoff's purported options trading, with several entities not believing that Madoff could be trading options in such high volumes where there was no evidence that any counterparties had been trading options with Madoff. The private entities' conclusions were drawn from the same "red flags" in Madoff's operations that the SEC considered in its examinations and investigations, but ultimately dismissed.

We also found that investors who may have been uncertain about whether to invest with Madoff were reassured by the fact that the SEC had investigated and/or examined Madoff, or entities that did business with Madoff, and found no evidence of fraud. Moreover, we found that Madoff proactively informed potential investors that the SEC had examined his operations. When potential investors expressed hesitation about investing with Madoff, he cited the prior

SEC examinations to establish credibility and allay suspicions or investor doubts that may have arisen while due diligence was being conducted. Thus, the fact the SEC had conducted examinations and investigations and did not detect the fraud, lent credibility to Madoff's operations and had the effect of encouraging additional individuals and entities to invest with him.

A more detailed description of the circumstances surrounding the five major investigations and examinations that the SEC conducted of Madoff and his firm is provided below. In June 1992, several customers of an investment firm known as Avellino & Bienes approached the SEC conveying concerns about investments they had made. The SEC was provided with several documents that Avellino & Bienes created that indicated that they were offering "100%" safe investments, which they characterized as loans, with high and extremely consistent rates of return over significant periods of time. Not everyone could invest with Avellino & Bienes, as this was a "special" and exclusive club, with some special investors getting higher returns than others.

As the SEC began investigating the matter, they learned that Madoff had complete control over all of Avellino & Bienes' customer funds and made all investment decisions for them, and, according to Avellino, Madoff had achieved these consistent returns for them for numerous years without a single loss. [Text omitted.]

As the foregoing demonstrates, despite numerous credible and detailed complaints, the SEC never properly examined or investigated Madoff's trading and never took the necessary, but basic, steps to determine if Madoff was operating a Ponzi scheme. Had these efforts been made with appropriate follow-up at any time beginning in June of 1992 until December 2008, the SEC could have uncovered the Ponzi scheme well before Madoff confessed.

SIGNATURE PAGE OF SEC REPORT

SEC Office of Inspector General Report of Investigation – Case No. OIG-509
EXECUTIVE SUMMARY

selling by hedge fund, fund of funds as they face investor redemptions." His e-mail was ignored.

After Madoff was forced to register as an investment adviser, the Enforcement investigation was inactive for 18 months before being officially closed in January 2008. A couple of months later, in March 2008, the Chairman's office received additional information regarding Madoff's involvement with the investor's money from the same source. The previous complaint was re-sent, and included the following information:

> It may be of interest to you to that Mr. Bernard Madoff keeps two (2) sets of records.[5] The most interesting of which is on his computer which is always on his person.

This updated complaint was forwarded to the Enforcement staff who had worked on the Madoff investigation, but immediately sent back, with a note stating, in pertinent part, "[W]e will not be pursuing the allegations in it."

As the foregoing demonstrates, despite numerous credible and detailed complaints, the SEC never properly examined or investigated Madoff's trading and never took the necessary, but basic, steps to determine if Madoff was operating a Ponzi scheme. Had these efforts been made with appropriate follow-up at any time beginning in June of 1992 until December 2008, the SEC could have uncovered the Ponzi scheme well before Madoff confessed.

Submitted: _____ Date: Aug. 31, 2009
H. David Kotz, Inspector General

---

[5] The allegation that Madoff kept two sets of records also turned out to be true.

GREEDSTER STANFORD'S PONZI

Chapter 5 – Synopsis

"On and Offshore"

Mr. R. Allen Stanford isn't as well known as Mr. Madoff, but his Ponzi crime has cost investors billions of dollars in losses.

The island of Antigua in the West Indies, where he was knighted and called "Sir Allen," was Mr. Stanford's offshore base for a classic Ponzi scheme.

From a United States base in Houston, Texas, he parlayed the sales of high-yield certificates of deposits by his international bank into millions and billions of dollars to fund a pyramid scheme. Mr. Stanford lived a lavish lifestyle with a luxury yacht and grandiose offices in Houston and Antigua. He even owned a professional West Indies cricket team that he dreamed would dominate the world of competitive cricket.

Since 2009 he has been languishing in prison awaiting trial wearing the orange uniform of an inmate. His associates have pleaded guilty to a Ponzi fraud, but Mr. Stanford maintains his innocence.

That's one of the elements of greed—the perpetrator can remain in denial about his fraudulent behavior.

Mr. Stanford may soon realize that fraud will be punished—especially now that Mr. Madoff has received 150 years in prison for running his Ponzi scheme. Mr. Stanford's mature life has run the gamut from owning yachts, jets and a cricket team (from wealth gained by bilking billions of dollars from innocent people) to being badly beaten by fellow prison inmates. Does he understand criminal greed yet?

Chapter 5

GREEDSTER STANFORD'S PONZI

Sir James Carlisle, Governor-General of the tiny British Commonwealth islands of Antigua and Barbuda, granted Robert Allen Stanford a knighthood in 2006, and he became a Knight Commander of the Order of the British Empire. Thereafter, he was entitled to be called Sir Allen—and although the knighting of the Texas billionaire was not without controversy—he made sure that all knew that was what he wanted to be called. His path to knighthood and his fall from grace lead to an engrossing tale of Texas-sized greed.

A SAFE HARBOR

Some 500 years ago, Columbus encountered the small island of Antigua (on his second voyage in 1493) and named it for Santa Maria la Antigua, a saint known for the miracles she performed in Spain. Antigua is located in the Leeward Island chain and lies about seventeen degrees north of the equator. It is strategically positioned at the entrance to the eastern Caribbean Sea and ideally located for access to North, South and Central America. Pirates flourished in the vicinity for most of Antigua's history—and Mr. Stanford is only the most recent swindler to use it for modern-day financial piracy.

In 1632 the British colonized Antigua and soon thereafter included tiny Barbuda in their empire. African slaves were imported in the seventeenth century to do the work of sugar plantations, and that industry prospered for a time. Admiral Horatio Nelson found St. John's secure harbor convenient for the British fleet in the Caribbean to enforce commercial shipping laws, but by the late nineteenth century, the sugar economy had faded and the small islands of Antigua and Barbuda were severely economically depressed.

Sir Allen Stanford had a different safe harbor in mind for Antigua. This small nation—primarily relying on tourism to support its population—welcomed him.

ROBERT ALLEN STANFORD
Magnum Cum Fraudie

It is hard to understand how R. Allen Stanford, a lanky fifth-generation Texan standing tall at six feet four inches, could become a political and financial force in a small Caribbean island nation populated by fewer than 100,000 people. Seemingly, his physical presence and a great deal of money overpowered Antigua and its statesmen.

Mr. Stanford was born in 1950 in the small town of Mexia, Texas. He graduated from high school in Fort Worth, and then earned a Bachelor of Arts degree in finance from Baylor University in 1974.

His father, James, is a former mayor of Mexia and a board member of the Stanford Financial Group. Mr. Stanford has falsely stated on the company's website that his grandfather started Stanford Financial Group in 1932. Mr. Stanford created that bit of history to add credence to a company begun in the 1980s and wholly owned by him and his father, James.

R. Allen Stanford has also implied that he shares ancestry with Leland Stanford, a railroad magnate, governor of California and founder of Stanford University. In 2001 Sacramento news sources documented that an unknown man claiming to be a distant relative of Leland Stanford drove up in a stretch limousine to Leland Stanford's mansion and wrote a check for $2 million to complete the renovation of the historic home. Governor Gray Davis's office issued a press release announcing the donation by R. Allen Stanford, a relative of Leland Stanford. Stanford University asserted that there was no family connection. In 2006 the university brought a trademark infringement suit to prohibit the use of the school's name by Mr. R. Allen Stanford.

The real history of Mr. Stanford is that he became an entrepreneur while he was still at Baylor. His first venture was a bodybuilding gym in Waco, Texas. At age twenty-four he experienced his first business failure. He switched into real estate, and with his father, bought distressed Houston properties whose values had tumbled during the bust of the energy bubble of the early 1980s. They made a fortune as real estate values rose again in the boom cycle of the late '80s. R. Allen Stanford gained complete control of the company when his father retired in 1993. The company had grown to about 500 employees by that time.

Sometime in the 1980s Mr. Stanford moved to the Caribbean island of Montserrat. He used a company named Stanford Financial Services as the vehicle to organize Guardian International Bank. A move to Antigua was necessary when the British cracked down on the offshore banking industry. He renamed the bank Stanford International Bank ("SIB") and made it an affiliate of Stanford Group Company in Houston.

Mr. Stanford has resided in St. Croix (American Virgin Islands), Houston, Texas, and St. John's City, the capital of Antigua. In Antigua he lived primarily on his 112-foot luxury yacht *Sea Eagle,* which was anchored hard by his linchpin bank, Stanford International. An emblem of an eagle was incorporated in the Stanford Group's logos, the company magazine and on the yacht.

He has dual citizenship in Antigua and the United States. Antigua is known for legal gambling and as an offshore financial haven for "tax residency." Mr. Stanford thrived under these conditions, and using his dual citizenship status even pushed for establishment of a tracking station on the north coast of Antigua for the U. S. Air Force.

THE STANFORD FINANCIAL EMPIRE

Mr. Stanford blazed a complicated trail of questionable deeds and misdeeds for almost three decades, culminating in 2009 with a variety of legal entanglements. He manipulated his financial "empire" between his base of power in tiny Antigua and his American presence in Houston, Memphis and Tupelo, Mississippi. Unfortunately for several of the Antiguan principals of his companies, Antigua and Barbuda both recognize extradition proceedings with the United States.

Stanford Group Company in Houston provided the foundation for the rapid growth of SIB in Antigua. The core of the SIB banking business was soliciting and harvesting certificates of deposit by offering higher interest rates than other area banks, and guaranteeing instant availability of the money without the usual penalties for cashing CDs before their maturity. This was the base for a massive Ponzi scheme. Mr. Stanford and his bank claimed his CDs were as safe as FDIC-insured accounts. Money poured in from Antiguans and from surrounding countries in both Central and South America. Eventually, the Stanford Financial Group had investors in 131 countries.

As Mr. Stanford added to his empire over the years, the Stanford Financial Group set up affiliates in Colombia, Ecuador, Panama, Peru and Venezuela. On Antigua, Stanford not only owned the major bank, but also an airline, restaurants, a newspaper, a sports club and the cricket stadium. He had a finger in almost every aspect of the island's commerce. Detractors in Antigua have said, "He has a lien on our whole country."

At the fullest extent of operations before the crash of the Stanford Empire, he had fifty-two worldwide offices with associates actively soliciting investors with the primary sales incentives being the abnormally high interest rates for CDs without early redemption penalties.

Employees referred to Antigua as "Stanford Land" and were told that Mr. Stanford would build the largest financial company in the world there. They proudly wore the company logo—a Golden Eagle—which Mr. Stanford described as his knight's shield and required all his employees to wear. Mr. Stanford cultivated his friendship with Prime Minister Lester Bird of Antigua and Barbuda. At Prime Minister Bird's request, he formed and joined a banking advisory board after American regulators questioned banking operations in Antigua in 1998. Mr. Stanford was now in a position to regulate his own operations. In 1999 Antigua was placed on a watch list of questionable banking operations.

KNIGHT OR ROBBER BARON?

Alec Wilkinson wrote a lengthy profile of Sir Allen Stanford in *The New Yorker* on March 9, 2009, titled "Not Quite Cricket," in which he notes that author Jamaica Kincaid refused to shake Stanford's hand after the ceremony where they were both knighted, saying, "Your honor demeans my own." She commented further to Mr. Wilkinson:

> He's always been a crook, and everybody knows it. Stanford is a standing scandal in Antigua—he's both a joke and a benefactor. In Antigua, there's always a man—a person who comes in from the rest of the world—a pirate. Piracy is very close to Antiguan history. They've been coming and hiding money and stealing for hundreds of years. This man comes to Antigua and corrupts the place, and everybody's happy because they're making money.

You could almost conclude that Ms. Kincaid didn't like Allen Stanford. But many others of her countrymen did like him and participated in the increased prosperity he generated.

DOMESTIC BLISS
Money CAN Buy You Love

Mr. Stanford is known by now as one of the biggest scoundrels of business history, but he lived extremely well for twenty-five years on other people's money. His lavish lifestyle included estates in Texas, Florida, St. Croix, and Antigua. He owned a fleet of vehicles, two jet planes and the luxury yacht *Sea Eagle*.

Mr. Stanford's six children were also well taken care of during his glory days. His domestic entanglements are too byzantine to unravel—he managed liaisons with three women in addition to his relationship with a wife. He has a total of six children by his wife, Susan, and three other "outside" women. Each has received extremely generous child-support payments and financial settlements over the years. Since 2007 Mr. Stanford has been involved in a divorce action with Susan Stanford from whom he has been separated for over a decade. But it was a paternity suit over support of the two children he had with Ms. Louise Sage that began the unraveling of Stanford's financial empire. Ms. Sage disputed Mr. Stanford's reported $5 million annual income. Discovery for that lawsuit unmasked a lifestyle supported by far more than $5 million a year.

PHILANTHROPY AND POLITICS
"Brash, Cash, and a Dash of Flash"
—*The Houston Chronicle,* February 21, 2009

After his downfall, Reuters News was given an exclusive tour of the Stanford Financial Group headquarters in Houston. The reporter, gawking at the grandeur of the massive office appointed in marble and mahogany, commented, "[it] once boasted a five-star dining room, movie theater, professional kitchen and wine bar." A private bathroom was a chamber of black granite and mahogany paneling with an enormous mirror and luxury appointments. On a wall hung a framed letter on White House stationery dated January 25, 2006, and signed by then President George Walker Bush.

In addition to the money spent energizing the economy of Antigua and living a life of opulence at home and at work, Mr. Stanford had a reputation for philanthropy. In 2008 he wrote in the company magazine that Stanford Financial Group had raised over $15 million for St. Jude Children's Research Hospital. [St. Jude's has disputed this figure and said they had received $8 million over a two-year period.] He was a benefactor of the University of Houston's Bauer College of Business and had planned to endow a building. He was a patron of the arts in Houston as well.

The company's website and the 2008 edition of the glossy company magazine "The Stanford Eagle" crowed, "Sir Allen supports charitable, cultural, educational, social and sporting events and organizations throughout the world." Stanford's investors, who actually funded his philanthropy, probably would have preferred to make their own gifts and take their own tax deductions.

Neither did Mr. Stanford neglect the political arena. Campaign contributions to both parties and to lobbyists amounted to more than $5 million since the year 2000. Beginning in 1999 the Stanford Group expended a great amount of effort lobbying Congress and the Clinton White House not to impose more stringent controls on offshore financial havens and money laundering activities.

Anti-money-laundering legislation quickly passed through the House Banking Committee in 2000, but a final vote was blocked as powerful GOP congressmen and senators such as then-House Majority Leader Dick Armey, then-House Majority Whip Tom DeLay and then-Senate Banking Committee chair Phil Gramm stopped the bill's passage through Congress.

DeLay was particularly targeted for generous donations. "DeLay's committees paid for flights on Stanford's jets at least sixteen times since 2003, including on Oct. 20, the day the former House majority leader was indicted in a Houston courthouse on money-laundering charges," according to Bloomberg News.

In addition Stanford Financial or its employees contributed to the legal defense funds of three lawmakers charged with ethical violations: Texas Republican Tom DeLay, Democratic Senator Robert Torricelli, and Republican Bob Ney.

Mr. Stanford contributed $100,000 to the George W. Bush Inaugural Committee in late 2000. According to *Public Citizen,* a nonprofit public consumer advocacy organization, the Treasury Department loosened its controls for reporting requirements and changed tax shelter regulations to "ease tax administration" in 2001.

In the 2008 election cycle the Stanford Financial Group continued to make generous bi-partisan donations, including contributions to House Majority Leader Harry Reid, Senate Minority Leader Mitch McConnell and several others. Lobbyists were paid $2.2 million in 2008 alone to lobby Congress on topics that might affect the Stanford Group.

GOD AND CRICKET
An Unusual Religious Conversion

Mr. Stanford had some serious eccentricities that would appear in contradiction to his business practices. For instance—a miraculous religiosity is part of his complicated personality. He related to many people that in the 1980s he had experienced a religious "happening." He somehow encountered a Catholic priest who needed medical attention. Mr. Stanford flew him to the United States to have wounds on the priest's hands and feet treated. Mr. Stanford believed that the priest had experienced a miraculous duplication of the *stigmata* on his hands and feet—bleeding wounds similar to those received by Jesus Christ during his crucifixion. By the time he returned to Antigua, Mr. Stanford was a changed man. To this day Mr. Stanford maintains that he carries with him wherever he goes a bottle containing the congealed blood from one of the wounds on the priest's feet.

The other unusual aspect of Mr. Stanford's persona was his obsession with cricket. On this subject he concurred with the populace of Antigua, for whom cricket is a national preoccupation. He spent well over $50 million in the West Indies to establish the new game of Twenty20, a variation on traditional Test Cricket that has tremendous appeal to modern fans.

Conventional cricket is called Test Cricket because of the severe strain on professional players who may have to play steadily for as long as five consecutive days. In both Test and Twenty20 cricket, a bowler throws a series of six balls at a batter. The batter tries to hit each ball, and the bowler and his team try to put the batter out by returning each batted ball to the wicket (home plate) before the batter can run the course. The bowler is attempting to knock down wickets; the batter is protecting the wickets. Playing six balls is a "series" or an "over." Test cricket can average about 450 overs per match.

Twenty20 cricket is played on the same size field, but a match ends after each side has had twenty overs. Balls can be thrown up to ninety miles an hour and can bounce en route to the batter to add difficult variations to protecting the wicket. The game has a very complicated set of rules.

The cricket team of the West Indies represents up to fifteen nations and territories and is a member of the "Test Cricket League." The team has had a distinguished history but experienced a thirty-year decline from its championship teams of the 1970s. The aging heroes of those years of West Indian dominance of the sport are still remembered in Antigua. Mr. Stanford set out to return the West Indies team to world-class status—but in the new Twenty20 form. He was engrossed by the intensity of the compressed three-hour-long match and believed that Twenty20 would attract legions of fans as an exciting new international sport. He spent at least $75 million to buy the West Indies cricket franchise and for the team to become a serious contender in the sport.

THE STANFORD SUPERSTARS

Mr. Stanford renamed the team "The Stanford Superstars," built his own stadium on Antigua and contracted with top players worldwide to form a competitive Twenty20 team. The *coup de grace* was the establishment of a $20 million purse for each of five annual matches to be played between England and the West Indies.

The England and Wales Cricket Board (E.C.B.) was not happy about doing business with a flamboyant Texas billionaire, but they made the deal to gain his patronage and the $20 million prize. Stanford immediately embarrassed them by landing a helicopter on the hallowed Lord's Cricket Ground to deliver a clear Plexiglas trunk full of American dollars and gain publicity for the agreement. One observer commented, "Mr. Stanford has done more than almost anyone to damage a noble game."

In October 2008 the first of the five planned Stanford Championship Cricket Tournaments was played in Antigua. The Stanford Superstars, designed and recruited to be a "dream" team of talent, crushed the English team. The fans in Antigua were elated; the English chagrined. Mr. Stanford made all the English newspapers in an offensive photo posed with the English players' pretty wives and girlfriends on and around his lap.

That day was to be the first and last celebration of its kind for Sir Allen Stanford. After the fraud charges were made public some four months after the first match, the E.C.B. canceled further annual matches and negated their Master Agreement with R. Allen Stanford, who became known as "The Dark Knight."

A sad footnote: Each of the "Stanford Superstars" received $1 million for winning the match against England. It is feared some may have promptly deposited their cash in the Stanford International Bank to secure their retirement. Lennox Cush, the only American on the team, was given $160,000 even though he was injured and couldn't play. He told Alec Wilkinson that he had left his money in the Stanford bank in Antigua. "He [Mr. Stanford] told us he will keep it safe until we need it."

FADING GLORY

In the final months of late 2008 and early 2009 examiners investigating the Stanford banks began to find gross irregularities, including a $1.6 billion loan to a shareholder—R. Allen Stanford. His twenty-five-year Ponzi scheme had run *its* course as surely as the Stanford Superstars had seen their final day of glory.

Although small in comparison to the legal difficulties Mr. Stanford is now experiencing, he was no stranger to lawsuits. In 1983 Mr. Stanford received a default judgment for $31,800 back rent owed on the premises of that first venture, the health club in Waco. Then in 1990 Mr. Stanford and his wife, Susan, were sued in United States

Tax Court for under-reporting U.S. federal taxes of $423,531.36, and public records showed they owed hundreds of millions of dollars in taxes for other years.

Mr. Stanford had been under scrutiny by federal examiners in mid-2008 when two former Stanford brokers had filed a wrongful termination lawsuit against Stanford Financial Group. They claimed that Stanford "overstated the asset value of individuals in order to mislead potential investors, didn't file mandatory forms disclosing its clients' offshore accounts and purged electronic data from its computers in response to an SEC investigation." They felt they might be implicated in the various "unethical and illegal business practices" that they had observed as employees.

Stanford Financial counter-sued and asserted, "These allegations were made by disgruntled employees and are totally without merit." Apparently, this suit and the counter suit reached a quiet out-of-court settlement.

The details of this wrongful termination suit were much publicized in England after the cricket match debacle. Citing the allegations contained in that complaint, officials with the E.C.B. were denounced for failure to do due diligence on the legitimacy of Mr. Stanford before signing the Twenty20 five-year contract with him.

During the last three months of his life as a free man, Mr. Stanford began to show the signs of extreme emotional duress. *The Miami Herald* ran a story by Michael Sallah and Rob Barry on December 6, 2009, which describes the desperation of the Texas tycoon prior to his arrest in February 2009. Everywhere he turned he was met with reversals of fortune—many of them caused by his own folly.

During 2008 Mr. Stanford had been caught between the stock market contraction and the massive redemptions of CDs that occurred when investors saw the value of their equity investments diminishing precipitously. The bank had no reserves; new investment had dried up. His lavish spending on cricket and his costly lifestyle caused him to draw more heavily from SIB, and the financial group was hemorrhaging cash. But, he had a few new schemes that he thought could buy time until the economy recovered.

SIB had proposed to back a luxury development in Antigua selling lots for estates with private airplane hangars and beachfront access that would attract affluent buyers and "new" cash. But, by the end of 2008, it was clear that the Antiguan government had refused to approve the plans and grant permits for the development. Mr. Stanford had alienated his Antiguan friends in high places. He was enraged by their disregard for him.

He invested $63.5 million in two small islands and inflated their value fifty times over in just a six-month period by flipping their ownership among different entities owned by him. His hope was to create a real estate asset on the corporate financial statements that would reassure investors that the bank was sound and stop the redemptions. This scheme also failed.

For a few months he thought that a massive infusion of capital from the country of Libya might forestall the dissolution of his Ponzi scheme. Libya had already placed approximately $140 million with the Stanford investment funds. Hoping to get another injection of new capital, Mr. Stanford flew his private jet to Libya twice to meet with government officials in Tripoli—but the Libyans didn't bite.

Meanwhile Stanford's heavy drinking and erratic behavior were beginning to trouble his staff. Always known for a quick temper, he lashed out at various individuals. He blamed his CFO James Davis in particular for the collapse of the companies. Everyone was told that Mr. Stanford's whereabouts should be kept secret—even from one another. His behavior was unpredictable and often violent. As his fortunes tanked, he often drank up to four bottles of liquor per day. He did $45,000 worth of damage to the mahogany paneling on his luxury yacht *Sea Eagle,* breaking bottles and beating the walls with his fists in fits of impotent rage.

During the same period Mr. Stanford had two palatial homes completely razed. The two mansions, located in Florida and in the U. S. Virgin Islands, had been recently renovated at great expense and were valued at $20 million. His baffled employees asked themselves what could possibly motivate this deranged and senseless destruction?

Messrs. Sallah and Barry write in the *Miami Herald* article, "By the end of the year, his businesses were losing $33.3 million a month in operating costs alone, records show. With dwindling cash, staff members were forced to put expenses on their personal credit cards." At one point the bank in Antigua had scarcely more than $800,000 operating cash on hand. CFO James Davis wired $6 million from the Houston office to keep the bank open.

On September 1, 2009, it was revealed that on February 17, 2009, the U. S. District Court had ordered Stanford employees to freeze all files and preserve all records. About February 21 of that year, a Stanford employee, Thomas Raffanello, ordered another employee to contact a local shredding company to come and shred a ninety-five gallon bin of documents.

As the feds were closing in on him, Mr. Stanford is described as personally carrying financial records to a mountaintop on his Mount Welcome property in the U. S. Virgin Islands and torching them with gasoline in a steel drum. Employees were directed to continue to shred and destroy documents in Florida and Antigua.

To stall the investigation Mr. Stanford decided to send two company officers to meet with the authorities. The false information communicated by SIG's Chief Investment Officer, Ms. Laura Pendergest-Holt, in those interviews held in January 2009 has resulted in her being charged with obstruction of justice in addition to other charges of criminal fraud. Her testimony convinced the regulators that a massive fraud had been perpetrated on investors.

He probably wasn't aware of the significance of it, but Friday the 13th, February 2009, was destined to be a very unlucky day for Mr. Stanford. Behind the scenes, both the SEC and the FBI were very busy with a final review of documents gathered over several months pertaining to Mr. Stanford, his actions and those of his various companies. Both agencies had been examining documents and interviewing personnel in Houston and on Antigua regarding the bank's high-yielding certificates of deposit. The decision was taken to bring criminal fraud charges against Mr. Stanford.

By February 17, 2009, the roof really started to fall in on Stanford. On this day, the SEC applied for and requested "emergency preliminary relief" for the Stanford case that was immediately granted by Judge Reed O'Connor, a federal judge in the Northern District of Texas. This prompt action was probably due to the criticism of the SEC's inaction in the Madoff scandal.

The restraining order issued was aimed at Robert Allen Stanford (and the feds didn't grace him with the title of "Sir"), three of his companies, Stanford International Bank, Stanford Group Company and Stanford Capital Management; Chief Financial Officer James Davis of SIB; and Chief Investment Officer Laura Pendergest-Holt of Stanford Investment Group. The SEC sought to freeze all assets inside or outside the United States and effect the disgorgement of ill-gotten gains to settle penalties and interest. The SEC charged Mr. Stanford and the other principals of the companies with criminal fraud.

Although he has denied that he intended to flee the United States, Mr. Stanford tried to rent a private jet with a credit card in order to fly to Antigua. He failed since the jet charter would only accept a bank wire transfer, and even his own banks could not comply due to the freezing of their assets. On February 19th, Stanford was peacefully apprehended at his girlfriend's house in Virginia. His assets were completely frozen: Sir Allen Stanford couldn't so much as write a check or use a credit card.

SEC INVESTIGATIONS

The New York Times printed details relating to the fraud charges cited in the SEC's restraining order on February 18, 2009. The article stated that there had been raised eyebrows among American authorities "as far back as a decade ago," as regulators were searching for the procedures whereby Stanford's banks could pay higher rates on CDs "because of the consistently higher returns they made on investors' assets."

The Stanford Financial Group had claimed to have a monitoring team of more than twenty analysts and yearly audits of the investments by regulators in Antigua. The SEC found that none of those assertions were true. The offices of the Stanford banks' auditors were deserted and appeared to be almost a stage set of new office furniture and equipment that had never been occupied. Even though several of the big four international accounting firms have a presence in Antigua, Stanford had chosen a small firm completely inadequate to the audit of a financial network of this size and complexity.

How had Mr. Stanford manipulated the reporting to the SEC that required disclosures that should have betrayed the irregularities? He did it through a key individual acting as a double agent. Mr. Leroy King, formerly a vice-president of Bank of America, had moved to Antigua to serve as its chief regulator. The SEC had secretly solicited King, the head of Antigua's financial services regulatory commission, to help them investigate SIB. But Mr. Stanford had gotten to King first. Mr. King had been bribed with over $100,000 to submit inaccurate audits and to reassure all investors and government authorities that SIB's operations were in accordance with banking regulations. Even after February 18, 2009, Mr. King had told Antiguan authorities, "I'm absolutely sure my banking system is clean."

Because of sensitivities regarding the Madoff case, the SEC reopened examinations of Mr. Stanford's offshore banking activities back to the 1998 probe, when no charges were brought against him. The current SEC charges result from an investigation opened in October 2006 following a routine exam of the Stanford Group. Nothing was done about the results of the examinations, at the request of another federal agency (unnamed), but the suspended investigation resumed in December 2008.

As the news broke of the SEC investigations of the Stanford Group, *The Houston Chronicle* began an almost daily report on the scandal that they called "Stanford Watch." On February 19, 2009, it reported a breakdown of twenty-one criminal indictment counts, ranging from conspiracy to commit mail, wire and securities fraud to obstruction of justice and money laundering against Stanford, Pendergest-Holt, Gilberto Lopez (the Houston-based chief accounting officer) and Mark Kuhrt (the Houston-based global controller). Lopez and Kuhrt were not indicted for obstruction of justice. Bruce Perraud was indicted in Miami with a lesser charge for document shredding.

Mr. James M. Davis, SIB's CFO and Allen Stanford's Baylor roommate and lifelong friend, was a soft-spoken, religious man who led prayers before business meetings. He must be spending a good deal of time now pondering how his own behavior veered to criminality. Mr. Davis became a government informant and reached a plea bargain. In July 2009 Mr. Davis agreed to plead guilty to fraud and conspiracy and to cooperate with authorities in their investigation. He admitted that the Stanford group of companies had bilked investors for nearly two decades and had invested in bogus real estate transactions and other risky assets in total contradiction of the information disclosed to investors. He could receive a sentence of up to thirty years in prison, but he hopes for a lighter sentence due to his cooperation with the court.

The government is seeking extradition of Leroy King from Antigua. The SEC requested his assistance to investigate SIB's operations on February 20, 2009. He replied, "My agency has no authority to act in the manner requested and would itself be a breach of the law if I were to accede to your request." After Mr. Stanford's arrest, Mr. King began a series of wire transfers to Antigua totaling $560,000 from his personal accounts in the United States. Federal examinations of his bank accounts in eight East Coast cities showed that he had made regular deposits of thousands of dollars from 2005 to 2009. Use of the Stanford jet and tickets to the Super Bowl had rounded out the package of bribes received from Mr. Stanford.

In June 2009 the Antiguan government fired Mr. King. The regulatory commission's board had been investigating Leroy King for several weeks, and "after giving him a final opportunity to provide an explanation for his questionable conduct," they kicked him out.

"While Mr. Stanford quarterbacked his massive Ponzi scheme, he paid the referee [Mr. King] to spy on the huddles and provide an insider's play-by-play of the SEC investigations," said Robert Khuzami, the SEC's enforcement director.

THE DARK KNIGHT

As for R. Allen Stanford, he has remained in custody continuously since his apprehension in February 2009. Due to his "motive, means and opportunity to leave the United States before trial" and the probability that he would spend the rest of his years in prison, the U. S. Attorney filed in court to have Mr. Stanford held in custody until his criminal trial. The document also revealed that Mr. Stanford was seeking treatment for his heavy drinking.

Mr. Stanford just didn't seem to understand his life of privilege had ended. As his net worth evaporated, he couldn't even hire an attorney, and court-appointed public defenders took over his case for a time. Kent Schaffer was initially assigned by the court to work with Stanford to prepare to defend himself. Mr. Schaffer noted, "I will charge only the public defender rate of $110 an hour, which is less than a fifth of my standard billing rate." (A directors' and officers' liability insurance policy supplied funds for Mr. Stanford to hire private attorneys for a time, but Lloyds of London won its appeal to deny him access to such funds. Stanford is now represented once again by court-appointed defenders.)

"Sir" Allen complained bitterly about cell conditions in the Joe Corley Unit located in Conroe, Texas, where he was housed with as many as ten others in the same room and without air conditioning in the oppressive summer heat of south Texas.

On at least two occasions, Mr. Stanford was taken to a hospital from that federal detention facility, once for his heart racing faster than 300 beats per minute and once as the result of a prison brawl where he suffered a broken nose, severe facial bruising and a concussion. At a pre-trial hearing, a gaunt, thinner version of Mr. Stanford showed up bruised and spitting blood.

Due to changes in counsel, the massive number of documents entered in discovery for the trial and Mr. Stanford's mental incompetence due to drug dependency, he was again moved in early 2011—this time to the Butner facility in North Carolina where Bernard Madoff is incarcerated.

STANFORD'S LEGACY

As all the charges became public and the details of the investigation were released, terrified investors began to panic. Bank statements issued by SIB had been completely fictional. Brett Zagone, a Houston technology saleswoman, entered a Stanford Group sales office to find out what had happened to her investments with the firm. *Time* magazine quoted her: "I am extremely concerned," she said. "On a scale of 1 to 10—infinity." Over 30,000 clients in 131 countries were defrauded of over $8 billion of their savings in this second-worst pyramid scheme in business history.

Meanwhile, on November 11, 2009, Mr. Danny Boger, former President of Stanford Financial Group of North America, wrote a book about the company that stated it was "deeply rooted in values of teamwork: respect, accountability, integrity and trust." He certainly didn't learn those values from Robert Allen Stanford.

And in little Antigua, Sir Allen, now stripped of his title, is referred to as the Dark Knight. We think "Stir" Allen more appropriate to his station while residing in a detention facility.

WHERE DID THE $7 BILLION GO?

The court-appointed receiver, Ralph Janvey of Dallas, is a former employee of the Comptroller of the Currency. He has been notable for his aggressive pursuit of the international assets of the fallen Stanford financial interests and for initiating clawback litigation to recover monies paid out to charities and political campaigns. Investors who managed to get redemptions before the scandal broke are also at risk for the clawbacks. Some estimate that the receiver may require more than a decade to complete the recovery of assets due to the international scope of the Stanford Ponzi—second only to the Madoff scheme in magnitude.

But Janvey himself must have caught the contagion and developed the appetite for greed. His firm has petitioned the court for payment of fees and expenses already totaling more than $20 million, and he stands to rake off a third or more of the available remaining assets of approximately $80 million.

* * *

On March 6, 2012, Mr. Stanford was convicted on thirteen of fourteen counts of conspiracy, fraud and obstruction of justice in federal court at Houston, Texas. A jury of four women and eight men voted for his conviction.

The defense had claimed that Mr. Stanford was unfit to stand trial due to a loss of memory. He had been severely beaten in prison. He declined to testify.

Not all people think he is guilty, however. A taxi driver in Antigua has stated: "Mr. Stanford is a bloody good man." Lawyers for Mr. Stanford have said, "Of course we're going to appeal."

Allen Stanford will need a miracle from Santa Maria la Antigua to save him from spending his remaining days incarcerated in a Texas prison hotter than the hinges of Hell.

GREEDSTER BANKS

Chapter 6 – Synopsis

"Over-Reaching"

Banks are behaving like spoiled brats—they live by the U. S. government and yet complain about the government's regulation; when the chips are down and hard times arrive, they turn to that same government with hands out for billions of dollars in loans at low interest rates. How cheap can they get? Their problems are severe but mostly of their own making.

During the most recent melt down (2007 through 2012 at this writing), the United States government made available huge chunks of money in troubled asset relief for major banks that were "too big to fail." How did they achieve that status? They had loaded up with junk bonds and sub-prime mortgages to pump up profits, and they had created all sorts of exotic instruments that carried high rates of return because of their high risk. "Toxic" lending to unqualified borrowers meant Uncle Sam had to help—and that's why our present system is being labeled "paternalism" instead of capitalism. This modification of our economy suits the greedster banks very well.

Greed altered the way bankers were compensated. Fat salaries based on commissions with additional profit-sharing and stock option plans, retention bonuses and performance bonuses for special employees were all based upon the banks' calculated paper values. When the economy tanked and those toxic assets couldn't be digested, banks grew very sick indeed. But the inflated salaries and bonuses to bankers continued.

Strong banks are needed. Let's see them admit their mistakes and return to financing healthy businesses and individuals with the ability to repay their loans. Let them thrive with profits based on reasonable interest rates and responsible lending. Greed is terminal, even though some greedsters don't think so.

Chapter 6

GREEDSTER BANKS

"The Autumn of 1929 was, perhaps, the first occasion when men succeeded on a large scale of swindling themselves." *The Great Crash,* 1929, John Kenneth Galbraith. What would he say of today?

IT TAKES ONE TO KNOW ONE

BANK \'baŋk\• *(noun):* An organization, usually a corporation, chartered and regulated by the state or federal government, that receives demand deposits and time deposits; honors checks and other instruments drawn on those deposits; pays interest on interest-accruing accounts; discounts notes; makes loans; and invests in securities; collects checks, drafts, and notes; issues certified checks; and issues drafts and cashier's checks.

How would modern life be possible without the complex technology of a banking system that has all those functions and gives us international twenty-four hour access to our funds—in the local currency—wherever we are?

We've come a long way, baby. The ancient Egyptians used a system of weights and measures to exchange value for value based on the purity and weight of precious metals. Use of precious metals for monetary exchange led to the earliest "banker"—a moneychanger in ancient Hellenic society. Greek coins were first minted to be consistent in size and value. The moneylenders of the Roman Empire did business in courtyards from a long table called a "bancu"—the word "bank" was derived from this practice.

Gold, silver and copper have traditionally been the predominant monetary metals due to their relative scarcity and beauty. As a result, goldsmiths and silversmiths were early bankers in medieval times. The populace began to use the smiths for safekeeping of precious-metal wealth. In return, the smiths would give the depositor a handwritten receipt. It soon became customary to pay creditors with the smiths' receipts rather than by recovering the actual gold or silver to give to the creditor. Creditors became willing to accept the receipts as payment once they were assured that the receipts could be redeemed for gold or silver on demand.

These receipts were the first bank notes. That system of bank notes written against precious metal reserves was known as the gold exchange standard and continued in a modified form in the United States into the early 1970s. Today it is no longer possible to demand gold or silver to redeem paper currency because actual precious metal reserves no longer back our outstanding U.S. dollar notes.

The medieval goldsmith and silversmith banks made another discovery. They realized that only a small quantity of the precious metals was withdrawn for exchange, and that new deposits continuously matched this amount. Therefore, a great deal of the precious metals was sitting idle. Loans could be made based on that value, interest income earned on those loans and adequate reserves still retained to cover withdrawals.

Today, banking can be classified in two main categories: Investment banking and commercial banking. There are many sub-classes to the two categories such as credit unions, savings and loans, offshore banks, private banks and even Islamic banks [these banks are organized to be consistent with the Islamic law, which prohibits charging interest or lending to businesses that offer goods and services prohibited by the Koran].

The rules and regulations for organizing and operating banks vary considerably worldwide. The United States of America has some 7,500 banks that conduct business through 75,000 branches (although these numbers may have diminished due to the recession of 2008-09 and its painful aftermath). If supplied with adequate capital, it is not difficult for individuals or corporations to organize a bank. Both urban and rural landscapes are dotted with friendly neighborhood banking.

Very simply, if an organization has sufficient capital it can apply to state or federal banking authorities for a charter as a state, national or thrift bank. Shares may be sold in a public offering or through private placement to accredited investors. An application must be made to the Federal Deposit Insurance Corporation (FDIC) for protection for deposits up to $250,000. Either the Comptroller of the Currency or a state banking authority must grant an application to form a new or "*de novo*" bank. The Comptroller of the Currency will ultimately play a role in regulating the new bank's operations. There are other requirements—ultimately 140 pounds of paper may be necessary to submit all the required information to the proper authorities.

As the new bank takes on deposits and sells certificates of deposit (CDs), and as it borrows money from the government at the attractive discount rate, it will soon have large sums of money to lend. You must pay interest out on the CDs you sell and on those Federal Reserve borrowings, but you will lend money at several times your cost—which is known as "making your spread." Your return on invested capital is practically assured, and your profits will be determined by the degree of risk you assume in your lending practices.

Under most circumstances, your friendly neighborhood banker serves your financial needs and makes money while doing it. Short of having the financial system fall apart as happened in the 2007-2012 financial crisis, the banking business is a safe and rewarding venture. The recent bank failures were the result of greedy banks lending to borrowers who were a poor credit risk in order to achieve higher interest rate returns.

The large banking organizations that dominate our financial system are conglomerates that are national and international in scope. They deploy thousands of branches and employees and have capital in the billions of dollars in order to make very large loans to service the financial needs of modern global corporations.

Traditionally, these organizations were very stable and grew with their geographic market to offer a broad range of full-service banking, financing, real estate lending, asset management, risk management and investing functions for individuals, small capital business, medium capital and larger corporations. Now the large banks have become veritable goliaths of financial services. They have an array of options to satisfy all customer needs: Trust services, investment banking, underwriting, risk insurance, broker and market maker of securities, pension accounts, payroll systems—almost anything that involves money, time and goods can be arranged for the largest and most desirable accounts. Many, if not all, of these services and products can be monitored online through the Internet.

Banks, both large and small, are essential to local, national and global commerce. But in a global community, regulatory monitoring of loan portfolios, ratios of capital and assets to loan portfolio values and validation of reserves can be a very difficult responsibility.

Because of the complexity of our modern financial systems, the trust that individuals and corporations placed in the largest banks was based in part on the sheer size of their assets under management. The public relied on the expertise of a bank's network of lending committees and lender qualifying research to make sound lending decisions. The tables were turned with the advent of so-called toxic assets, credit default swaps and sub-prime mortgages.

The resulting losses and bailouts of banks have dealt a punishing blow to the safety of the largest banks in the United States. In fact, in the *Global Finance* ratings system of the world's safest banks for 2009, the United States had only five banks in the top fifty listed, *and none in the top thirty*: The Bank of New York Mellon Corporation was in thirty-second place. The remaining four U. S. banks are ranked in the bottom eleven on the list. In 2004 Citigroup was ranked number one—and it is no longer even on the list of the top fifty banks. [The 2009 rankings are included as an appendix to this chapter.]

The 100 largest banks in the world had these average operating percentages in 2004:

Assets:	15% Liquid
	37% Other Assets
	48% Loans, Net
Operating Income:	52% Net Interest Revenue
	48% Other Operating Income
Overhead:	61%
Loan Loss Provision:	8%
Profit Before Tax:	29%
Tax:	9%
Net Income:	20%

There is no need to pity the business of big banks: A 20 percent net income is a fine profit and it is no wonder that banks have grown to their present size when they can generate profits of that magnitude.

How do bankers structure loans for such lucrative gains? As an example, a bank borrows $200,000 from the Federal Reserve Bank (the "Fed") at 1 percent interest and lends it to a borrower at the rate of 5 percent. The bank has a spread of 4 percent income from that loan. But because federal banking regulations require only a ratio of 1:5 reserves to lending capital, the bank can lend $1 million with the $200,000 borrowed from the Federal Reserve held as its reserves. So the bank has made a profit of 5 percent on $1 million and paid the Federal Reserve only 1 percent on $200,000. The bank in this scenario pays a total of $2,000 in annual interest on $200,000 borrowed but realizes a profit of $48,000, or 2,400 percent! The usual transaction isn't quite that simple nor the spread quite that lucrative, but it is easy to see what a high percentage of profit is possible.

To continue this hypothetical bank's lending history, let us suppose that the next loan is made to a borrower with less than stellar credit so that the interest charged is 2 percent over the prime lending rate of 5 percent due to the risk. Now the spread is 6 percent, and the net gain is $68,000 against the $2,000 interest paid to the Fed. The assumption of the higher risk has paid off handsomely. When the economy is strong, these types of loans flourish because business is expanding, and the risk of companies failing to service their loans is lower.

Then the steam goes out of the economic engine and loans are due. Borrowers' revenues have contracted and they are unable to pay interest on their loans on time or perhaps not at all. The bank must now account for the loan in the "non-revenue" category of its financial statements and call for repayment of the principal amount. If the borrower cannot liquidate assets or generate revenue to pay off the principal, the bank must reverse its projected profits into losses. Even though banks are required to keep loan loss reserves to cover for a certain percentage of their loans going bad, a bank can fail if it has a large portfolio of bad loans.

The Great Recession of 2007 to 2009 created this negative banking scenario. Even the biggest banks were at the brink of failure. Big banks *can* fail even though we hear the phrase "too large to fail." Many believe that an insolvent organization *should* fail. As the long recovery continues into 2012, the issue is unresolved.

When a bank of any size has so many bad loans that there is not enough capital in the bank to cover the losses, there are four possibilities:

- Find a private source to inject more capital (which dilutes the ownership of the original shareholders)
- Ask for government assistance and possibly turn over control to the government
- Merge with a stronger banking organization that can assume the losses but will pay only a small amount to shareholders for the bank's performing assets
- Close the bank with the consequence of complete loss of capital and shareholder value

Prudent leadership steers clear of ultra-high risks, but the price of that caution is often lower profits than those of the competition. Analysts may deem such a bank a "loser" in good times and "lucky" in bad times. This mentality makes taking risks very tempting—especially if you are not a stakeholder. When the economy is surging with growth, obscene bonuses may be paid, annual salaries increase and retention bonuses for the largest producers are paid. The bank's financial statements look great, and both management and shareholders are happy. Aggressive bankers look smart, and the cautious decision-makers look out-of-step. Stable earnings and low loan losses are sacrificed to achieve high ratings from analysts and the concomitant rise in share values. Expectations are elevated to unsustainable heights, and the fall back to earth can be lethal.

With the benefit of 20/20 hindsight, it appears that the banking system and the Federal Reserve gushed money for growth during the recent expansion (funds at "discount window" borrowing by banks reached loan rates as low as 1/3 of 1 percent or .0033 percent), and then made loans with very few restrictions on borrowers. Certainly, a few people were in a position to reap huge compensation from the profits that resulted, but the majority of us not associated with banking did not receive lavish raises or bonuses. Regulators and legislators must determine whether permitting this boom/bust cycle in the economy is to the betterment of most people when an average of four to five years of the inflated bubble or boom economy is followed by several years of an extremely painful bust of that bubble.

It is not just our country that is affected: as the pundits often say, "when Uncle Sam sneezes, the world catches a cold." In 2008 when the U. S. economy slowed precipitously, the ensuing collapse of financial markets, home mortgages and banks was a worldwide catastrophe. Pension funds around the world now buy a variety of instruments from many different sources. Imagine the surprise of a schoolteacher in Scandinavia who learns that his pension fund has collapsed due to the mortgage defaults in Middle America. Account holders in the United Kingdom were at risk for the loss of £6.5 billion (nearly US $13 billion) when the banks of Iceland collapsed in 2008.

It would seem that the lax standards of lending during the boom are too destructive to repeat in the future. Loss of jobs, loss of homes and loss of life savings and retirement funds have harmed a very large number of individuals and families—and they may never recover financially during their lifetimes from these financial reversals.

Perhaps you have noticed in the previous pages that not one word has been written about bankers—the decision-makers, the owners and the day-by-day beat of the heart that throbs behind the scenes of these monumental edifices. The bankers are the machines that drive the dollars down the drain or to accumulated wealth in assets. They are those same moneychangers of old with many generations of innovation behind them.

One innovation is that one doesn't have to *be* a banker to *act* like one. There was a reason to give this chapter the subtitle "It takes one to know one." Chief Executive Officers, Chief Financial Officers and corporate treasurers—all are really bankers when you think about it. They take in money as revenue, spend it on personnel and hard assets and create products or services that then produce earnings for shareholders. They strive to placate the media, investors and analysts by delivering better quarterly earnings than the competition. The greater good for society is unaddressed by them, and corporate entities, whether banks or ordinary commercial enterprises, are unapologetic for that fact.

Competition is so severe that there is a "slug fest" going on. General Motors coined the recent slogan "May the Best Car Win," almost as if their car is wearing boxing gloves in the marketplace. To carry the analogy a step further, one can envision the Chief Executive Officer with his arm raised in victory before the consumer audience.

This brings us to the controversial subject of compensation for bankers. Executive staff is very important to the success of any banking organization. They lure borrowers, negotiate and execute lending agreements, create new products and plan for continued growth. They lead employees under their supervision, identify problems and risk and have their thumbs on the pulse of their customers and other businesses.

But, big deals now generate big fees and commissions, so a shift in title and compensation has occurred in recent years. Individuals managing profit centers, sections and departments are now given the title of Managing Director instead of the traditional appellations of Vice President, Senior Vice President, and Executive Vice President. This title change is consistent with the corporate governance scheme of titles in the United Kingdom and is increasing in U. S. firms. The creation of managing directors who are at the executive officer level also facilitated a shift from a salary-based compensation model to a commission-based model.

Operating on a commission-based compensation model usually means a more modest base salary with the larger part of the compensation package meted out in the form of an annual bonus and possibly stock options. While the public finds the current level of executive compensation for bankers unconscionable, there is a concern that government-mandated annual salaries may force the best and the brightest talent to seek positions with private firms or foreign entities that are not subject to such guidelines. Particularly for those who have had performance-based compensation models, the annual flat salary may now be unacceptable. There is some evidence that a brain drain occurred in Japanese banks where executives had job security but relatively low incomes.

The question becomes, what is the cost to the taxpayers who must bail out banks when the innovators and whiz kids of the financial world design products and lending practices that fail to properly assess risk factors or, worse yet, ignore them?

There is a sense of public outrage that the very managers who ran the bank portfolios that accrued losses so large the banks' survival was threatened are now receiving raises and generous bonuses just to retain their services. The turmoil in financial markets has caused many experts to call for more government regulation of financial products and compensation despite any consequences.

The fear among the largest banks is that the most talented employees will only use the major U.S. banks as stepping-stones into the ranks of firms not subject to U.S. banking regulations. Giving foreign banks such a competitive edge would mean that U.S. banks would be relegated to less lucrative deals and would lose the ability to compete effectively. Ultimately, U.S. banks would be diminished in size and rank relative to private and foreign banks.

The Obama administration has responded to public criticism of greedy salaries by trying to curb executive compensation. In June 2009 the President appointed Kenneth Feinberg to oversee executive compensation at firms that received government bailouts, such as AIG, Bank of America, Citigroup, General Motors and Chrysler. AIG alone has received $180 billion in taxpayer assistance and yet wished to pay out $165 million in bonuses.

While it is safe to say that government intervention typically restrains corporate innovation, we may well ask if we want our banks experimenting with innovative products that risk the solvency of our financial system? Innovation by definition implies that there are no experience-based projections that can be relied upon. Risk that call for the return of same stock if certain performance figures aren't met. If the stock price goes up over five years, the employee profits from the gains.

As of 2010 Goldman Sachs employs 35,700 people. It has a private investment arm where partners make large private commitments. The targeted areas are energy, casinos, media, hotels, insurance and finance, plastics and rubber, meat processing, healthcare, and others. Diversification is the rule. [Harper, Christine (Dec. 10, 2009). "Goldman Sachs's Top Managers to Get All-Stock Bonuses". Bloomberg.com.]

The firm is a good neighbor and makes significant contributions worldwide. Goldman is making a great deal of money and is therefore liberal with bonuses and gives much away through its foundation. It is prospering due to wide spreads between the cost of money and interest and dividends earned on that money. Companies abound that need the expertise of the Goldman team (and others like them) to direct the most advantageous strategy to borrow money or to sell their companies. Fat fees are paid for such advice. Home runs are common; such is the financial game in the big leagues—and greed is the name of the game.

WELLS FARGO
John G. Stumpf and Howard I. Atkins
Joint Chief Executive Officers

Wells Fargo is chartered in Sioux Falls, South Dakota, but is headquartered in San Francisco. The present company is the result of at least twenty-eight mergers, acquisitions and name changes over the years since 1852. A major change occurred when Wells Fargo Bank merged with the Norwest Corporation of Minneapolis in 1998 and retained the name of Wells Fargo and the use of the famous Wells Fargo stagecoach trademark.

On October 3, 2008, the new Wells Fargo acquired Wachovia Corporation for $14.8 billion in an all-stock transaction. Wachovia Bank had become well known, especially on the eastern seaboard of the United States. On September 4, 2001, First Union Corporation had merged with Wachovia with Wachovia surviving as the name of the merged bank. Citigroup had its eye on Wachovia as well, but the Wells Fargo offer for Wachovia was almost seven times that offered by Citigroup.

Wells Fargo had a corporate history of acquisitions and mergers. According to information on the company's marketing site, "Wells Fargo's goal is to encourage its customers to buy all of their financial products through Wells Fargo—to sell at least eight products to every customer." This sounds like retail sales rather than banking, but as Wells Fargo has posted on the company's website, "We want to satisfy all of our customers' financial needs, help them succeed financially, be the premier provider of financial services in every one of our markets, and be known as one of America's great companies." [https://www.wellsfargo.com/invest_relations/vision_values/6]

Maybe Wells Fargo can pull it off. In 2010 its 280,000 employees in 6,335 retail branches (which they call "stores" in line with their ambitious marketing goals) along with 12,000 automated teller machines servicing more than 48 million customers represent a powerful force to carve a significant niche for Wells Fargo in the banking marketplace.

As of September 2011 Wells Fargo is regarded as one of the Big Four in commercial banking, alongside Bank of America, Citigroup and JPMorgan Chase.

JPMORGAN CHASE & COMPANY
James ("Jamie") Dimon
Chairman and Chief Executive Officer

As a commercial bank on Wall Street, the nation's largest bank holding company, JPMorgan Chase (Chase), stands out—*way* out. It's an immense enterprise that almost defies description. It has over 250,000 employees worldwide, and 2010 income of $17.4 billion. Its total assets in September 2011 were $2.289 trillion.

Its historical path to becoming a leader in investment and commercial banking is strewn with mergers, acquisitions, partnerships, subsidiaries and other business relationships. The merger of J. P. Morgan and Co. and Chase Manhattan Corporation was effectually combining four of the largest and oldest money center banking institutions in New York City (J.P. Morgan, Chase, Chemical and Manufacturers Hanover) into one firm called J.P. Morgan Chase & Co.

The firm comprises the following long, but incomplete, listing of companies now part of Chase:

- Bank of Manhattan Company (from 1799)
- The Chemical Bank of New York (from 1823)
- First Chicago Corporation (from 1863)
- Guaranty Trust Company of New York (from 1866)
- Hanover Bank (from 1873)
- Chase National Bank of the City of New York (from 1877)
- Washington Mutual (from 1889)
- J. P. Morgan & Company (from 1895—House of Morgan)
- City National Bank & Trust Company
- Farmer's Saving & Trust Company
- National Bank of Detroit
- Texas Commerce Bancshares, Inc.
- Louisiana's First Commerce Corporation
- Banc One Corporation
- Providian Financial
- Great Western Bank
- Bank United of Texas
- Bear Stearns

In the midst of the turmoil in the financial markets of 2007-2012, Chase weathered the storm better than most. This was due to the leadership of Mr. James (Jamie) Dimon, CEO. Even before the meltdown began, he was preparing for the worst. He won praise from most of Wall Street for his prescience.

However, on October 28, 2008, the U. S. Treasury transferred $25 billion of TARP money to JPMorgan Chase, the fifth largest transfer of bailout funds during the crisis. In June 2009 $10 billion was returned to the feds. In July 2009 New York Attorney General Andrew Cuomo maintained Chase paid 1,626 employees more than $1 million each in bonuses and paid $3 million each to more than 200 employees.

This raised the question of what was the intent of the federal government by extending the TARP funds. The primary idea of the Troubled Asset Relief Program was to return liquidity to the banking system. Banks were unable to extend credit due to so many loans being classed as non-revenue-producing assets. Lines of credit were frozen, and the wheels of American business were slowing to a halt from a lack of operating funds. It is unclear that TARP funds were used to pay bonuses, since when a dollar is spent from one account, it essentially comes from the same entity—no matter which pocket in the pants the money is drawn from.

It is clearly up to the recipient of TARP money to explain the use of the money and keep the accounting straight between operating capital and TARP relief funds. Bonuses of that magnitude paid to employees are a tough pill for out-of-work American taxpayers to swallow. Mr. Dimon and others in his position had a difficult time explaining their philosophy for doing so.

The Bernard L. Madoff Investment Securities firm used JPMorgan Chase as its primary banker. The trustee overseeing the liquidation of Madoff assets has filed suit against the bank to recover $1 billion in fees and profits and $5.4 billion in damages alleging that the bank knew, or should have known, that Madoff's firm was engaged in fraud. The complaint cites internal e-mails from officers that support these allegations.

Chase's position was further weakened by not disclosing purchases of securities made during a 2009 takeover bid for Dragon Oil, which broke New York Stock Exchange rules.

When you're not big enough to do things by the book, but you're too big to fail, someone must be taking up the slack. Let us hope it is the company's stakeholders and not the American public.

CITIGROUP, INC.
Vikram Pandit, Chief Executive Officer

Nobody can question the fact that Mr. Sanford ("Sandy") Weill created the world's most extensive financial complex. He capped his career by one of the largest mergers in the financial world on April 7, 1998, when he engineered the merger of Citigroup, Inc. and Travelers Group to form Citigroup, Inc. ("Citi"). The organization's 260,000 employees and assets of $1.9 trillion generate operating income of $10.9 billion. Citi has more than two million customers in 140 countries. At the turn of the twenty-first century, Citi was flying as high as you can get. But the bigger you are, the farther you can fall—and fall Citi did.

In a two-year period, Citi's stock market value dropped from $600 billion in 2006 to $6 billion in 2008. Wall Street loves high-flying enterprises but has no mercy when the tide turns. Sandy Weill's personal fortunes took a similar hit, although he retired in 2007. He offered to help during the trials and tribulations of 2008-09, but he received no response. Apparently there is no place in such a large company for a seasoned seventy-six-year-old, no matter what his accomplishments have been.

Two roads took Citi to the top. The first started in 1812 with the opening of business for City Bank of New York. In 1865 the bank's name was changed to The National City Bank of New York. It became the first bank to have a foreign banking department and a foreign office in Buenos Aires in the early 1900s. The purchase of International Banking Corporation pushed the combined assets to over $1 billion and made it the world's largest commercial bank.

In 1976 under CEO Walter Wriston, the bank changed its name to Citibank, N.A., and its holding company became Citicorp. By 1995 Citibank was the largest United States bank and had pioneered Automated Teller Machines (ATMs). It was also the largest issuer of credit cards in the country.

The second road to the top began with an early computer company, Control Data of Minneapolis, whose Commercial Credit division was bought by Sandy Weill. Control Data was taken private in 1986. Two years later, using some cash and Commercial Credit stock, Control Data absorbed Primerica—as well as A. L. Williams and the stock brokerage house Smith Barney. The name of the new conglomerate was Primerica.

In September 1992 Travelers Insurance, whose extensive real estate insurance holdings were badly damaged by Hurricane Andrew, made a "strategic alliance" with Primerica. Within a year, Primerica had acquired Travelers and formed Travelers, Inc. The famous red umbrella trademark of Travelers was part of the deal. Travelers Inc. proceeded to acquire Shearson Lehman and merged it with its Smith Barney division.

In 1995 Travelers Inc. merged with Aetna Property and Casualty and renamed the combination the Travelers Group. In 1997 Travelers Group purchased Salomon Brothers, and on April 6, 1998, Citicorp and Travelers Group announced to the world a merger that would create a $140 billion company with $700 billion in assets.

The two roads to Citi had finally met.

In 2008 Citigroup received a TARP distribution of $25 billion, yet an analysis showed the company was still insolvent in spite of the injection of funds. It was apparent more help would be needed. The government agreed to back $306 billion in loans and securities and to directly invest $20 billion more in the company. The legal walling off of certain assets (or liabilities) inside a corporation is known as ring fencing.

In January 2009 Citigroup stated it was breaking the company into two units: Citicorp for investment and retail banking operations and Citi Holdings for management of assets and brokerage operations. On February 27, 2009, it was disclosed that the government was taking a 36 percent equity position in Citigroup by converting $25 billion of aid money into equity. Shareholders took a hit with the dilution of shares, but this company had taken several hits already.

In 2004 Citigroup was roundly criticized for shaking up the European bond market by quickly selling billions worth of euro bonds, causing the price to drop, and then stepping in and buying more at the lower price.

In 2005 Citigroup Global Markets, Inc., a wholly-owned subsidiary, American Express Financial Advisors and Chase Investment Services were fined a total of $21.25 million for "supervisory violations" regarding mutual funds.

In June 2007 the National Association of Securities Dealers announced fines of $15 million levied against Citigroup Global for poor disclosure of pertinent facts regarding proposed investments by BellSouth employees.

In November 2007 the so-called Terra Securities scandal dragged in Citicorp. Eight municipalities in Norway were sold Terra paper by Citicorp, and the Financial Supervisory Authority of Norway charged that Citicorp provided inadequate information during the sales pitch. Norway withdrew Citigroup's permission to sell such investment paper.

In August 2008 the Attorney General of California caused Citigroup to pay $18 million in refunds and $14 million in restitution to credit card customers whose accounts' positive balances were wrongly transferred to Citigroup's general fund.

A pattern of such activities is deeply troubling and may partially explain why Citigroup finds itself in such a precarious situation.

Citigroup did start to repay TARP funds in December 2009. The government began to market the shares it owned in March 2010. Citi recently repaid the $20 billion balance owed the government, although the Treasury Department still owns more than one-fourth of Citi's common stock.

The stock price has plummeted from $54.38 in early 2007 to a low of $1.03 in early 2009. Current share prices in late 2011 have shown some recovery and have hovered in the $20-$25 range. Citi has been viewed as the riskiest member of the Big Four money-center banks, according to *Barron*'s magazine. It is splitting itself into two businesses, shedding several businesses and shrinking itself by a third. The overhaul marks the end of Citigroup's financial one-stop model, which had been crafted by legendary dealmaker and ex-CEO Sandy Weill.

THE BANK OF NEW YORK MELLON CORPORATION
Gerald L. Hassell
Chief Executive Officer and Chairman

The Bank of New York and the Mellon Financial Corporation joined forces on July 1, 2007, and became The Bank of New York Mellon. It's a powerhouse with 42,900 employees and a net income in 2010 of $2.5 billion on 2010 revenue of $13.9 billion. Its corporate headquarters is in New York City. The history of these two banks makes it the oldest banking corporation in the United States. The founding year of the Bank of New York was 1784; its founder was none other than Alexander Hamilton.

The New York Stock Exchange opened in 1792 with the Bank of New York as the first company to be listed. For 138 years, The Bank of New York prospered without any mergers or acquisitions. In July 1922 it merged with the New York Life Insurance Company, in 1948 with the Fifth Avenue Bank, and in 1966 with Empire Trust Company. Its name, The Bank of New York, survived all these mergers.

T. Mellon & Sons Bank originated in Pittsburgh, Pennsylvania, in 1869. Early firms financed by T. Mellon & Sons were Alcoa, Bethlehem Steel, Gulf Oil and Westinghouse. In 1886 Judge Thomas Mellon stepped down as the bank's head and his son Andrew took over. In 1902 T. Mellon & Sons changed its name to Mellon National Bank.

In 1946 Mellon National merged with the Union Trust Company (founded by son Andrew) with the new name, Mellon National Bank and Trust Company. Over the years this name became Mellon Financial Corporation. On December 4, 2006, The Bank of New York and Mellon Financial merged to become the aforesaid Bank of New York Mellon. The merger was completed on July 2, 2007.

Mr. Tom Renyi, former CEO and Chairman of The Bank of New York, took these two roles for the first year and a half of the merged bank's existence. Then, the former CEO and Chairman of Mellon, Robert P. Kelly, assumed the CEO and Chairman positions of the bank located at One Wall Street.

The financial meltdown of 2008 touched Bank of New York Mellon, and, in October 2008, the bank reluctantly accepted $3 billion of TARP funds. This total amount was paid back to the U.S. Treasury on June 9, 2009, along with $136 million to buy back stock warrants issued to the Fed at the time of receiving the TARP money.

STATE STREET CORPORATION
Joseph (Jay) L. Hooley
Chairman and Chief Executive Officer

For more than 200 years State Street Bank ("State Street") has been a Massachusetts state-chartered financial institution. It was founded in 1792 and has always been headquartered in the financial district of Boston. In October 1999 Citizens Bank purchased the retail and commercial banking services of State Street, so that all remaining resources of the bank could be focused on global investors. The company has operations in twenty-five foreign cities.

State Street Bank and Trust Company is the legal name of the bank, and State Street Corporation is the name of the holding company.

State Street is one of the world's leading providers of financial services to institutional investors, with $17.9 trillion in assets in 2010 and $1.7 trillion under investment management. State Street's website lists the following customer base it now serves:

- Banks and trust companies
- Brokers and financial intermediaries
- Collective investment fund companies, including mutual fund companies and pension plan sponsors
- Corporations, including multinationals
- Government agencies
- High-net-worth individuals and family offices
- Insurance companies
- Investment managers
- Non-profit organizations, endowments and foundations
- Trade and professional organizations

A purchase of Deutsche Bank's securities division in 2003 for $1.5 billion and the acquisition of Investors Bank & Trust for $4.5 billion made State Street the largest security services firm in the United States (surpassing JPMorgan Chase and The Bank of New York Mellon). It is the second-largest custodian of assets in the country. Wall Street knows of State Street, but it's not exactly a household name elsewhere. It is known as a "banker's bank."

State Street was one of nine banks summoned by Treasury Secretary Hank Paulson to announce the establishment of the TARP and to receive their estimates of the amount of aid each would need. It has been reported that some of the nine banks said they neither wanted nor needed the money because of the restrictions that went with it: increased capital ratios, limits on compensations, no annual bonuses, etc. They were given only a few hours to decide if they would participate. But then Washington ruled, and all took some TARP grants. State Street received only $2 billion in TARP funds on October 28, 2008, and repaid it all on June 17, 2009, creating speculation that they were one of the banks "forced" to take the TARP funds out of a desire for unanimity.

It is guesswork to presume that State Street was one of the banks in the Big Nine who took TARP money from the U. S. Treasury "at last rather than at first"—and perhaps even under protest. But a banking company that survived for 211 years without a major merger must have had inner discipline to withstand almost any adversity.

MORGAN STANLEY
James Gorman, Chief Executive Officer
John Mack, Chairman

Morgan Stanley is pretty much unknown to the ordinary person. For most of its history it has been an investment bank financing deals in the billions and trillions of dollars with governments, large national and international firms and institutions.

Formed relatively recently—on September 16, 1935, its founders were Henry S. Morgan (grandson of J. P. Morgan) and Harold Stanley. In the very first year of business they captured 24 percent of the IPOs and private placements. Connections certainly paid off for them. Because of the Banking Act of 1933 (commonly referred to as the Glass-Steagall Act), the founders had to choose between being an investment bank or a commercial bank—and they chose the former.

In 1938 Morgan Stanley was lead underwriter for the distribution of $100 million of debentures for U. S. Steel. By 1952 the bank became a major player to many financial transactions. In 1952 it co-managed the World Bank's $50 million triple-A-rated bond issue, a major feather in its cap. Other notable financing participations were GM's $300 million debt offering, IBM's $231 million stock offering, and AT&T's $250 million debt offering. Its business and investment prowess continued to grow. In the 1960s, '70s and '80s, the bank established itself as a major player in the international scene, with offices in seven countries.

In 1996 Morgan Stanley purchased Van Kamden American Capital. In 1997 it merged with Dean Witter Reynolds and Discover Company. In 1999 AB Asesores of Spain was purchased, and the firm became active in India through a joint venture with JM Financials.

Morgan Stanley occupied the fifty-ninth to the seventy-fourth floors of the South Tower of the World Trade Center. On September 11, 2001, ten employees died in the destruction of the two towers and surrounding structures. While the firm mourned the death of those ten, they marveled that the loss of life was so low among its 3,700 employees officed on twenty-five floors of the building.

Among more recent notable deals, Morgan Stanley managed Google's IPO. It also acquired the Canary Wharf Group. In 2006 Discover Card was spun off.

The sub-prime mortgage crisis arrived in 2007—and the China Investment Corporation poured in $5 billion for equity units to be convertible into as much as 9.9 percent of Morgan Stanley's shares in 2010. This investment infusion offset $9.4 billion of write-downs in mortgage-backed securities while expanding Morgan Stanley's footprint in China.

The bank had prospered, but it hit the same financial rocky road that was producing big bumps and ruts for almost everyone else in the financial game. The Federal Reserve allowed the change from an investment bank to a bank holding company (or commercial bank) so that Morgan Stanley would qualify to receive $10 billion of TARP money from the U.S. Treasury. Eight days later, on September 29, 2008, it was announced that Mitsubishi UFJ Financial Group, Japan's largest bank, would buy a $9 billion equity position in Morgan Stanley. That deal closed in October 2008 with Mitsubishi getting a 21 percent ownership in the firm. On June 17, 2009, Morgan Stanley repaid in full the TARP funds it received in September 2008. Morgan Stanley will likely be more of a household name in the future.

As Morgan Stanley and Goldman Sachs, the last two independent investment banks, become bank holding companies, some analysts have predicted an end to the era of the big investment banks on Wall Street. As *The New York Times* observed on September 21, 2008, "For decades, firms like Morgan Stanley and Goldman Sachs thrived by taking bold bets with their own money, often using enormous amounts of debt to increase their profits, with little outside oversight." In surrendering to more regulation as bank holding companies, the firms will be regulated and be required to take less risk, but they gain access to the lending facilities of the Federal Reserve.

Morgan Stanley was not without some other problems over the years. The bank agreed to pay billions of dollars to settle portions of various legal actions and investigations by Eliot Spitzer, former Attorney General of the state of New York. In addition it cost $54 million to settle a sex discrimination suit brought by the Equal Employment Opportunity Commission. In 2005 the NYSE imposed a $19 million fine for alleged regulatory and supervisory "lapses."

There are other lawsuits outstanding at this date. All of these charges demonstrate the disadvantage of having deep pockets—guilty or not.

MERRILL LYNCH
Merrill Lynch Wealth Management
Brian T. Moynihan, Chairman of the Board
Thomas K. Montag, President and Chief Executive Officer

Brian T. Moynihan was appointed CEO and President of Merrill Lynch Wealth Management ("Merrill") at the same time he was made CEO and President of Bank of America ("BofA") in early 2009 after BofA's parent holding company's purchase of Merrill on September 14, 2008. BofA is apparently operating Merrill as an investment banking and wealth management division. As of September 2011 Tom Montag became CEO of Merrill.

Merrill started business in 1914 as Charles E. Merrill & Company at 7 Wall Street. Shortly thereafter, Edmund C. Lynch joined the company and the name was changed to Merrill, Lynch & Company in 1915. An early 1921 purchase of Pathe Exchange (later to be RKO Pictures) and a controlling interest in Safeway in 1926 were two sound investments.

In 1940 E. A. Pierce & Company and Cassatt & Company agreed to be merged with Merrill. In 1941 the name was changed to Merrill (no comma after Merrill) Lynch, Pierce, Fenner & Beane when Fenner and Beane joined the firm. Because Winthrop H. Smith was instrumental in the firm's growth, the firm's name was changed again in 1958 to Merrill Lynch, Pierce, Fenner & Smith.

In 1971 the company went public and was listed on the NYSE.

Merrill's power on Wall Street and nationwide grew as it built its reputation as an elite "in house" broker network of 15,000 brokers referred to as "The Thundering Herd." Merrill was also known as THE Catholic firm on Wall Street in a financial community dominated by Jewish and White Anglo-Saxon Protestant (WASP) firms. [James B. Stewart, *Den of Thieves*, Touchstone Books, 1992.]

White Weld & Company was acquired in 1978 to enhance Merrill's securities underwriting.

On November 1, 2007, big troubles were disclosed for Merrill. Its CEO, Stanley O'Neal, left the company after being criticized for the way he was mishandling the sub-prime mortgage debacle and for his poor risk management (Merrill lost $2.24 billion in unexpected losses). O'Neal received $161 million in retirement perks, stock options and other benefits. In December 2007 John Thain, then CEO of the New York Stock Exchange, was hired to be the CEO of Merrill. It seems barely possible that things could have gotten any worse—but they did.

In January 2008 Merrill announced a loss of $9.83 billion in the fourth quarter of 2007, and in April 2008 a further loss of $1.97 billion was announced for the first quarter of 2008. The company was hemorrhaging $6.5 million every hour of an eight-hour business day. In addition, Bloomberg News reported in September 2008 that Merrill had lost $51.8 billion in value of mortgage-backed securities as part of the sub-prime mortgage crisis.

In spite of TARP funds, emergency preferred-stock sales, swaps of equity stock for poor assets, outright loans from Japan and China at horrific rates due to the low value of the firm's stock—the situation worsened, and Merrill had to find a buyer.

The Bank of America was caught in a purchase bind when it announced that it had bought Merrill for $38.25 billion in stock. *The Wall Street Journal* reported the deal involved 0.8595 shares of BofA common stock per share of Merrill common stock. BofA paid a 70.1% premium for Merrill stock based on the September 12, 2008, closing price but a 61% discount from Merrill's September 2007 closing share price. The final purchase price was about $50 billion or $29 per share for Merrill's common stock.

But that's not all! Unbeknownst to BofA, Merrill had promised big bonuses to its employees, so *after* September 12, 2008, Merrill paid out cold cash in bonuses totaling $3.6 billion or about a third of the TARP money supplied to Merrill by the government. BofA claims the bank wanted to back out of the purchase deal at this point because of the undisclosed losses and cash bonuses but "the government wouldn't let us." The Treasury Department denies this. Perhaps one day the truth will be known.

The antics of Merrill's CEO John Thain during this period are documented in Chapter 7 of this book, "Greedsters on Wall Street," under the subheading "John Thain." The short version is that Mr. Thain became CEO of Merrill after Mr. O'Neal was deposed in 2007. Mr. Thain's total compensation in 2007 was $83 million (after leaving the job as CEO of the NYSE with a severance bonus of as much as $600 million). Mr. Thain approved the 2008 $3.6 billion in bonuses for Merrill employees, which included an additional $10 million for himself (although he later decided not to take the bonus). As part of the purchase deal, Mr. Thain would move to BofA as its new CEO and Chairman of the Board. He showed up for his new job

December 1, 2008. He resigned on January 22, 2009, after a tense meeting with Mr. Ken Lewis, the CEO he had replaced. Mr. Thain received a total compensation of $93 million for being CEO of BofA for just fifty-three days.

During his two-year tenure at Merrill, Mr. Thain had managed to renovate his office. After his departure from Merrill and BofA, no mention was made of the whereabouts of his much-publicized $35,000 gilded washroom commode and $87,000 office armchairs.

It's very difficult to understand how such huge bonuses could be paid or expected to be paid when so many of the deals were valued in "funny money" and proved to be nothing but toxic assets in the very year the bonuses were paid in full. Few if any clawbacks have occurred to date.

Both Citigroup and BofA (along with its subsidiary Merrill) have hundreds of millions of dollars of toxic assets that sooner or later will have to be written down or sold in a fire sale to get them off the books. The TARP funds paid out in bonuses were intended to offset just these kinds of write-offs and guarantee the banks' return to solvency—not to further enrich those who generated the toxic assets—regardless of salary and bonus contracts.

BAILOUTS AND BAD PAPER

In a two-week period in September 2008, the U. S. Government took over Fannie Mae (a U.S. secondary mortgage lender that works with mortgage banks to provide funds to homebuyers at affordable rates) and Freddie Mac (a U.S. secondary mortgage lender that initiates community development lending projects) and the huge insurer American Insurance Group (AIG). Lehman Brothers, a major global investment bank, filed for bankruptcy. Merrill Lynch was forced into selling to Bank of America. Washington Mutual became the largest commercial bank failure in history.

The Financial Times of London noted on March 13, 2010, "Lehman Brothers was a poorly managed bank that operated an irresponsible business model." When a bank is clearly failing, it has three choices: wind the bank down, sell it, or keep trading in the hope of resurrection. Lehman's board chose the third option and failed.

By early 2009 the financial market collapse wiped out more than $30 TRILLION in market value. "A decade's worth of investment gains" disappeared—and no one knew how to stop the damage to investors. [http://www.efinancialnews.com/story/2010-06-21/fund-management-quarterly-fund-chiefs-need-bright-new-ideas-to-rebuild-assets].

A column by Tyler Cowen in *The New York Times* on March 1, 2009, cited three ways to rescue failing banks:

- The shovel method—shovel money into the banks until they return to profitability;
- The control method—take control of the failing banks, either by nationalizing or by bankruptcy and wait until matters turn the corner;
- The bandage method—patch a bank's problems here and there, now and then, and wait and hope.
  [http://www.nytimes.com/2009/03/01/business/economy/01view.html]

Mr. John C. Bogle, Vanguard Group founder, noted in January 2010, "The investor in America sits at the bottom of the food chain. Many banks are rewarding their employees at shareholder expense. Net losses have not deterred large bonuses and ridiculous perks with money and values right out of the investors' pocket."

On April 2010 at an international meeting of bankers in Washington, D.C., they agreed to "stronger capital standards with new rules to improve both the quantity and the quality and to discourage excessive leverage," according to *The New York Times*. Some of the larger American banks disagreed, stating tighter capital requirements would stifle monetary lending. On May 3, 2010, China raised its banks' reserves against deposits to 17 percent, the third rise in four months. [http://www.nytimes.com/2010/05/26/ business/global/26basel. html].

Those financial institutions receiving bail-out money from the U.S. Government were told to put off evictions of homeowners with distressed mortgages, allow shareholders to vote on executive pay packages, slash dividends, cancel employee training and morale-building exercises and withdraw job offers to foreign citizens. Several recipients receiving bailouts objected to pay and other restrictions and have returned the handouts as soon as was practicable. Some bankers are quoted as calling such restrictions social engineering by the government. [http://www.istockanalyst.com/article/ viewiStockNews/articleid/3108535]

The Wall Street Journal noted on July 20, 2009, that to understand the difficulties of pricing and dealing with certain toxic assets, study the following—an example of "bad paper" purchased by investors of all kinds—who lost billions while trying to sell or break up or repackage the "junk": A $1 billion CDO-2 package of second-tier Collateralized Debt Obligations, like sub-prime mortgages, was created by a large bank in 2005. It had in it 173 investments in tranches (slices) issued by other pools, for example, 130 CDOs (collateralized debt obligations), and 43 CLOs (loan obligations), each composed of hundreds of corporate loans. The bank issued $975 million of four AAA tranches, and three subordinate tranches of $55 million. Banks bought the AAA tranches, and hedge funds bought the subordinated tranches.

Two of the 173 investments held in this CDO-2 were in tranches from another bank earlier in 2005—which was composed mainly of 155 tranches and 40 CDOs. Two of these 155 tranches were from a $1 billion investment pool created in 2004 by a large investment bank and composed of 7,000 mortgage loans (90 percent being sub-prime). That pool had issued $86 million of AAA notes, half of which was purchased by Fannie Mae and Freddie Mac and the rest by a variety of banks, insurance companies, pension funds and money managers. As of July 2009 about 1,800 of the 7,000 mortgages remain in the pool, with a delinquency rate of 20 percent.

How in the world is such a tangled web of paper sorted out by anyone? It is no wonder the job of selling off toxic assets from failed or purchased companies is complicated and successful only at bargain prices and conditions.

FINANCIAL REGULATION AND REFORM

In the summer of 2011, as I put this book together, the Congress of the United States is debating the necessity and the terms of financial regulation legislation that would prevent the kind of economic meltdown in the future that has threatened our financial stability for the last four years.

The Volcker Rule

Congress is still debating whether or not to reestablish the Volcker Rule, which limits the degree of risk banks can take in their lending and investing. New York Senator Charles Schumer stated, "Wall Street is New York's number one economic engine. In spite of that threat to New York, I voted for the Volcker Rule because we need a strong reform." New York City's Mayor Michael Bloomberg feared the financial regulation bill could kill the city's tax base.

However, a New York-area internal poll showed public opinion was overwhelmingly against banks and financial firms and in favor of the Volcker Rule. In support of the reinstatement of the Volcker Rule, Nobel Laureate for Economics Paul Krugman wrote in *The New York Times,* "The lesson from the last few months has been very clear: when banks gamble with other people's money, it's heads they win, tails the rest of us lose."

It will be interesting to see if the banks' lobbyists prevail again over common sense.

SUMMARY

Something has gone very wrong with the expectations on Wall Street as it deals in millions and billions of dollars. Banks and bankers used to be friendly faces down the street, but "Banks Too Big to Fail" has changed all that. It seems billions of dollars have corrupted the very soul of everyday finance. Whom can you trust, whom can you believe?

Of course, there are more good guys than bad guys, but it doesn't take many bad guys to spoil the works. And what is the main cause for this change in attitude from integrity to carelessness and fraud? In our opinion, it is greed. The pursuit of the almighty dollar can become a disease—and it is a compulsive illness where enough is never enough.

Greed reaches up and down at all levels. It is the element of greed that allows these characters to think that their successes are their own, while their failures are the responsibility of the taxpayers. Greed even impacts and affects how one looks at oneself. Their image of themselves must have broken lots of very expensive mirrors.

Let's pay attention to sane beliefs and use common sense. No more annual paychecks 400 times larger than those of the workers who made the paychecks possible. No more retention bonuses to appease those who are willing to jump ship to one with supposedly better sails made of money. No more obscene perks like golden parachutes, golden coffins and golden commodes. Our country can prosper again with fewer greedsters.

Bankers and their banks should lead the way up and out of the moral morass that plagues our country. They are our community leaders, and a healthy community breeds a healthy financial system.

GLOBAL FINANCE WORLD'S 50 SAFEST BANKS 2009

1. KfW—Germany
2. Caisse des Depots et Consignations (CDC)—France
3. Bank Nederlands Gemeenten (BNG)—Netherlands
4. Landwirtschaftliche Rentenban—Germany
5. Zuercher Kantonalbank—Switzerland
6. Rabobank Group—Netherlands
7. Landeskredibank Baden-Wuerttemberg-Foerderbank—Germany
8. NRW.Bank—Germany
9. BNP Paribas—France
10. Royal Bank of Canada—Canada
11. National Australia Bank—Australia
12. Commonwealth Bank of Australia—Australia
13. Banco Santander—Spain
14. Toronto-Dominion Bank—Canada
15. Australia & New Zealand Banking Group—Australia
16. Westpac Banking Corporation—Australia
17. ASB Bank Limited—New Zealand
18. HSBC Holdings pc—United Kingdom
19. Credit Agricole S. A.—France

20. Banco Bilbao Vizcaya Argentaria (BBVA)—Spain
21. Nordea Bank AB (publ)—Sweden
22. Scotiabank–Canada
23. Svenska Handelsbanken—Sweden
24. DBS Bank—Singapore
25. Banco Espanol de Credito S.A. (Banesto)—Spain
26. Caisse centrale Desjardins—Canada
27. Pohjola Bank—inland
28. Deutsche Bank AG–Germany
29. Intesa Sanpaolo—Italy
30. Caja de Ahorros y Pensiones de Barcelona (la Caixa)—Spain
31. Bank of Montreal—Canada
32. The Bank of New York Mellon Corporation—United States
33. DnB NOR Bank—Norway
34. Caixa Geral de Depositos—Portugal
35. United Overseas Bank—Singapore
36. Oversea-Chinese Banking Corp.—Singapore
37. CIBC—Canada
38. National Bank of Kuwait—Kuwait
39. J. P. Morgan Chase & Co.—United States
40. UBS AG—Switzerland
41. Societe Generale (SG)—France
42. Wells Fargo—United States
43. Credit Suisse Group—Switzerland
44. Banque Federative du Credit Mutuel (BFCM)—France
45. Credit Industriel et Commercial (CIC)—France
46. Nationwide Building Society—United Kingdom
47. U. S. Bancorp—United States
48. Shizuoka Bank—Japan
49. Northern Trust Corporation—United States
50. National Bank of Abu Dhabi—UAE

WORLD'S 50 SAFEST BANKS 2009 - *by Dan Keeler*
After two tumultuous years that saw many of the world's most respected banks drop out of the top-50 safest banks list, the dust appears to be settling. Those banks that kept an iron grip on their risk exposure before the financial crisis have consistently topped the table and maintain their standing among the top echelon in this year's ranking. At the same time, the big-name banks that lost their safest bank ranking during the credit crunch are still absent from the list as they struggle to rebuild their credit standing. *Global Finance,* October 2009. [http://www.gfmag.com/archives/ 105-october-2009/2451-features-worlds-safest-banks-by-dan-keeler.html

GREEDSTERS ON WALL STREET

Chapter 7 - Synopsis

"It Has To Change"

The level of integrity of many of Wall Street's high flyers needs to be addressed because they've either lost it or never understood what it implies.

Instead of feeling pride and pleasure in the great, good fortune that propelled their income into the hundreds of millions of dollars in many cases, their insatiable greed pushes them to continue to demand big money contracts, bonuses and perks. They even threaten to leave their employers unless they are awarded large retention bonuses—and those bonuses are frequently not connected to any performance benchmarks at all.

The private financial houses of Wall Street and the stock exchanges were founded to create capital for growing businesses and to permit investment in publicly traded businesses by any individual or institution. Traditionally, our companies produced goods or services, and they grew based on the execution of a sound business plan by a hard-working team of management and labor.

Now, Wall Street greedsters have manipulated and damaged this very effective method for many of us to participate in the nation's commerce, by designing self-serving schemes and financial instruments that game the system and rob investors of their capital. Who knows how much more destruction of assets will be done to the financial system before we find the will to rein in the greedsters on Wall Street.

Chapter 7

GREEDSTERS ON WALL STREET

IT HAS TO CHANGE

On March 19, 2009, Barack Obama, President of the United States, said on television, "There's been systematic and institutionalized greed in this country for the past ten to twelve years. It's a cultural thing; it has to change."

"The Greedsters of Wall Street" occupy the territory of high-flyers of a financial world that has contained some of the greediest executives in the entire history of the United States. ("Greedsters on Main Street" are addressed in Chapter 8 of this book.) They work with millions and billions of dollars every day. Little or none of it is the executives' own money. They are conditioned to believe that their salaries, perks, bonuses and retirement benefits should be aligned with the amount of wealth they are creating in the marketplace.

Who are the people—whether employed by a for-profit or a not-for-profit entity—that work daily and are classed as "workers"? Who are the people employed by the same entities, who draw immense salaries accompanied by lavish bonuses and perks—those that work daily and are classed as "executives"? What quality distinguishes "executives" that they merit so many times the pay of the "workers"?

Workers and executives have at least one thing in common: both receive compensation from the same source. The company hires executive or management staff to lead a healthy, vibrant company; in turn, they depend upon a solid, experienced work force to produce goods or services that create value. Their interdependency must always be balanced. Salaries and wages for each must be fair.

When comparing executive salaries with workers' wages, The Economic Policy Institute found that the ratio in 1970 was 35 to 1. By the year 2000 the ratio had become 100 to 1. Seven years later in 2008 the ratio reached as high as 400 to 1 and by year's end had settled at 365 to 1.

It should be pointed out that by 2008 Department of Labor figures showed the average American worker earned $28.00 per hour. This total wage figure included hourly, overtime, vacations and health benefits for a 52-week/365-day year. The average worker's annual United States wage, by this accounting, is $58,240.00.

Ford Motor Company received concessions from their unions that decreased the average Ford worker's hourly wage from $60 (all inclusive) to $48. On a 52-week/365-day year, the annual wage packet would be $101,640. Apparently Toyota's wage contracts are similar. General Motors has negotiated with its unions, but terms of the agreement have not been released at this writing.

Executive total compensation for the year 2009 reached an all-time high average influenced by the rise in the market value of stock used in bonuses and retirements. A furor was created in 2009 when AIG received $180 billion in federal corporate assistance while paying out $165 million in bonuses. For the year 2010 total average compensation decreased by 10-15 percent as the market value of stock used for compensation purposes decreased. The year 2011 should show total executive average compensation still depressed from the 2009 averages. The march upwards should not commence again until the economy improves. However, even though economic factors have not improved much in 2011, high executive total compensation appears to have resumed.

If the average American worker received $58,280 for 2008 and the average Chief Executive Officer received 365 times that, the CEO's average pay package for that year was $21,257,600. A Wall Street Chief Executive Officer also serving as Chairman of the Board would be included in this average, but his or her salary would be much higher.

If you are shocked by the above statistics, consider the following: In general, any public organization—for profit or not-for-profit—is no better than the team made up of the sum of its parts, in this case, its employees. When an executive is hired to work for an organization, that person becomes a member of the team. As such, the new member assumes the historical value of that team, its experience, its product position in the marketplace, its earning power and the loyalty of current employees. This total intangible sum of values enhances the existing economic machine and adds worth to the company.

This historical expertise and success contributes greatly to the organization and is a component of "goodwill," an accounting term that values the non-tangible assets of a business by quantifying the gap between the cash value of the assets and the market value of a company.

Any executive, especially a CEO, who believes he or she is personally responsible for all or a goodly portion of the wealth created by the company under his or her supervision, is ignoring the intrinsic values inherited from the past business history of the organization. A good executive understands that his or her contribution is layered on to what has already been achieved by previous years of hard work by all staff. He or she esteems the broader experience, well-honed intelligence, maturity, community standing and dedication to the company of long-standing employees. This kind of staff not only enhances the company, but also enriches the community in which it operates.

Greed has become prevalent on Wall Street in the form of bulging profits of the companies and obscene salaries, fringe benefits, pensions, stock options and retirement terms to a few perched on the top rung of the ladder. Total annual compensation for a few exceeds the 365:1 ratio compared to the many who made those profits possible.

The tragedy of outlandishly rich salaries and perks on Wall Street was particularly painful because so much of the compensation was based on *paper* profits. These "profits" were ephemeral. Credit swaps, derivatives, sub-prime mortgages, Ponzi schemes and glib talk led many investors down the road to financial ruin—especially those who were greedy themselves and looking for unusually high profits without doing due diligence or using common sense.

How can a responsible company give a huge bonus to a salesman or account executive that raked in huge fees on deals that are later found to be based on bad paper—especially when that paper turns out to be not only unprofitable, but the cause of losses so enormous that the integrity of the company is threatened! In the case of the recent unraveling of this kind of deal, the financial system of the entire United States and many other countries was threatened.

Prudent oversight, experience and just plain business "smarts" have been so discounted by the egregious returns on criminal greed that it seems no one cares to preserve those attributes on Wall Street. If so, we are headed for another meltdown, and our collective financial affairs may not survive another one.

Some say Wall Street will never be the same. The hugely profitable investment banks like Bear Stearns, Lehman Brothers, Goldman Sachs and Morgan Stanley either failed, have been absorbed by other firms or have become commercial banks by the decision to be bank holding companies. But, never say never. The same inventive minds that create innovation can create swindles. Almost none escaped egg on their faces during this meltdown, and it was due to their own folly and greed. Therefore, this chapter is aptly named "*The Greedsters of Wall Street.*"

Only the future will tell us how much of the risk taken was due to self-deluded misunderstanding of the product—and the ways it could turn into disaster—or how much was due to actual fraud.

If these executives are so smart that they have to be compensated for their superiority, why were so many hoodwinked in the meltdown?

A good CEO is not an autocratic boss but rather a strong leader of the management team, workers and supporting administrative personnel. A CEO should be compensated for his or her attributes and experience, but *no one* is irreplaceable—no matter what he or she may believe. Unreasonable compensation is unsupportable.

Wages and salaries swing like a pendulum, subject to external forces such as state and federal regulations, peer pressures, unions, competition, foreign affairs and wars. Scarcity of materials, new and innovative products and other matters also affect compensation considerations. It is poor business judgment to make long commitments to high salary structures.

Special compensation for a few should be handled wisely and carefully. Boards of directors have been very lax in policing standards for baskets of perks that include hiring bonuses, performance bonuses, bonuses paid on what proved to be worthless paper, retention pay, vacations and access to recreational properties, stock options (and occasional back-dating of same), personal loans, company cars, club fees, deluxe air travel, limousines, tax relief, tax planning, nannies and other child care, *plus* the final egregious benefit known as the "golden coffin." It is hard to justify paying $100 million to the estate of an employee who is deceased. Try placing a consulting phone call to *that* former executive.

A way to curb excessive wages and benefits is to mandate that the board of directors examine and approve salary packages of actively employed senior executives and promptly rescind their benefits if they choose to leave the company prematurely for whatever reason.

The following is a list of some CEOs who, for the most part, serve or served in the dual role of CEO and Chairman of the Board of their respective companies—a combination that is particularly inviting to long-term disasters in compensation and fringe benefits.

JOHN THAIN
Merrill Lynch
Compensation (2007): $83,000,000

John Alexander Thain was born on May 26, 1955, in Antioch, Illinois. His most recent escapades on Wall Street would lead anyone to believe he was born with a stock certificate in his mouth.

Mr. Thain entered into Wall Street history less than a month after he became Merrill Lynch's CEO and Board Chairman when he approved $1,278,000 in renovation funds for his new office, reception room and two conference areas. Heidi Moore writes in her article, "John Thain, Then and Now," *The Wall Street Journal,* January 22, 2009, that some of the items for remodeling included fancy new rugs carrying price tags that totaled $131,000; a $68,000 antique credenza; a pair of guest chairs for $87,000; a parchment waste-paper can for $1,400, and a gilded commode on legs for $35,000. No mention was made of what kind of toilet paper dispenser was installed to match the golden toilet seat.

A lack of education might account for the jaded values of Mr. Thain, but such cannot be the case for him: He received a B.A. in Electrical Engineering from Massachusetts Institute of Technology (M.I.T.) in 1977, followed with an M.B.A. from the Harvard Business School in 1979. His fraternity was Delta Upsilon.

At the age of forty-four he became Co-Chief Operating Officer of Goldman Sachs, a position he held from 1999 to 2003, and received Goldman Sachs stock worth $300 million at the time. This was followed by four years as COO and CEO of the NYSE and NYSE Euronext, Inc. He was discussing the CEO position with Citigroup when contacted by Merrill Lynch. In November 2007 he joined Merrill as CEO and Chairman of the Board succeeding ousted CEO Stan O'Neal, who had received a $250 million golden parachute. Meanwhile, Merrill had lost $8.4 billion in write-downs during the last quarter of Mr. O'Neal's tenure.

At Merrill it seems that Mr. Thain became carried away by greed in his position as a top dog among major Wall Street firms. It was in 2007 that his annual salary, bonuses, perks and stock options for the year totaled a mere $83 million (a compensation package supposedly approved by the board of directors of which he was chairman).

Then Wall Street started to fall apart. Mr. Thain felt it was necessary to find a funding partner to save Merrill from looming bankruptcy. He found Bank of America. BofA purchased Merrill for $50 billion—well above the then current market price of Merrill stock.

After a hasty and incomplete examination of Merrill's books by BofA, it was found that $3.2 billion in 2008 bonuses were to be paid to Merrill employees—including a tidy $10 million to Mr. Thain that he considered appropriate for his role in brokering the Merrill/BofA merger.

Mr. Thain was slated to become the new CEO and board chair of BofA when CEO Ken Lewis retired, but as the purchase deal was consummated in January 2009, Mr. Thain received a call from Mr. Lewis concerning the *multi-billion* dollar loss announced by Merrill for the fourth quarter of 2008. The next day, after a discussion with Mr. Lewis, John Thain was without a job—fired even before he assumed leadership of BofA. Mr. Thain received a total of $93 million for 53 days at BofA.

Unbelievably, BofA went through with its purchase of Merrill despite the 2008 fourth quarter's huge losses and subsequent extensive investigations.

In 2010 Mr. Thain landed as CEO at CIT Group Inc., a commercial lender that has just emerged from bankruptcy and is a fraction of the size of Merrill Lynch. Mr. Thain will now be subject to compensation limits placed on companies that have received TARP funds, and he is expected to work for about $6 million per year. When asked, he stated that he plans to keep his new office exactly the same as it is. He acknowledged his error in judgment in approving the lavish furnishings for his office at Merrill, but defended the decorations as in keeping with the "very nice" office décor of Merrill. He subsequently reimbursed Merrill for the $1.2 million spent on his office renovation. In a recent speech he gave at the Wharton School of Business at the University of Pennsylvania he made the following comments regarding the office renovations: "Now, in hindsight that was a mistake. All right? I admit that was a mistake. I didn't know the world was going to explode, but it did. And that was a mistake and I'm sorry that I did that. If I had that to do over again, I'd furnish it in IKEA."

From $83 million annual salary to $6 million: Greed was a boomerang that became very costly to Mr. Thain.

JAMES "JIMMY" E. CAYNES
Bear Stearns, CEO and Chairman of the Board

It must have been awkward in his social circle for Mr. Caynes: On one hand he was called a championship bridge player, and on the other he was called the worst CEO of all time. The former is certain—he is a championship bridge player. The latter is just one of many opinions held on the "street" regarding his performance as CEO of Bear Stearns Companies. He certainly doesn't lack competitors for the honor of worst CEO of all time.

Mr. Caynes is a hard-driving executive whose enthusiasm for golf and bridge seemed at times to override the business duties for which he was paid handsomely. The collapse of two hedge funds managed at Bear Stearns made it a necessity to sell the parent company to JPMorgan Chase at a near rock-bottom price.

Born on February 14, 1934, he grew up in the tough environment of New York City, where his father was a patent lawyer. Purdue University was his college choice but he didn't finish the four years there. He did his military service in the U.S. Army. Early in his career he sold copiers, scrap iron and municipal bonds—and started to play bridge, a unique combination of vocations and avocations.

A fellow bridge player, Alan Greenberg, steered Mr. Caynes to a brokerage job at the firm of Bear Stearns ("Bear") on Wall Street. He had found his niche. With hard work, and reputedly a perpetual chip on his shoulder, he climbed the ladder to become President of Bear in 1985, CEO in 1993 and Board Chairman in 2001. In 2005 *Forbes* magazine ranked him as 384th on the list of the 400 richest men in the United States, with most of his net worth resting in Bear Stearns stock. In 2006 his take-home pay was $34 million. In 2007 his holding of Bear Stearns stock was estimated to be worth a little bit more than $1 billion.

In March 2008 he sold all of his Bear holdings for "only" $61 million.

What happened? Blame the hedge funds. Bear had two big ones. A hedge fund takes other people's money to play around with, extracts a fee and gets up to a 20 percent cut of the profits (if any). At present they are unregulated. It is estimated that in 2005 there were 8,000 hedge funds with combined total portfolio values of $1 trillion (at the same time, an estimated 8,000 mutual funds had combined portfolios of $8 trillion). Most hedge funds are more tolerant of risk than mutual funds, and therefore the economic downturn that started in 2007 raised havoc with such funds as asset values tumbled. Bear's hedge funds were aggressive: The firm poured hedge fund monies into almost every "new idea" that came along.

Those new ideas included some of the following: credit swaps (swapping one value for another, e.g. currencies); CDOs (bundled collateralized debt obligations or fixed-income securities); derivatives (values derived from hedging risks); options, both "puts" and "calls" (a put is an option to sell shares at a certain price and a call is an option to buy shares at a certain price); and sub-prime paper (e.g., mortgages taken out with inadequate assets to back them; many of these ultimately lost their value and became "toxic assets" as the mortgages defaulted).

The general consensus within Wall Street is that investment houses and brokerage firms have a stable of smart young people who dream up elaborate ways to package and label investment vehicles. These "new products" aren't fully understood by the trade—there is no experience with them. Actually, they are not fully understood by anyone. They make lots of money for the institution that sells them; then they lose lots of money for everyone who buys them. Once the commissions and fees have been booked, someone has made a "killing."

Unfortunately, when the product becomes "toxic," a lot of innocent institutions and investors get "killed."

Mr. Caynes and Bear Stearns rode the market up with these bright new ideas, and they slid down as the market collapsed. In the case of Mr. Caynes, his company stock went from a high of about $170 per share down to $2—plunging over a weekend while he played bridge in a Master's Tournament.

Did he win the bridge tournament? He certainly lost his Bear shirt. Maybe he has learned to pay attention to matters for which he was handsomely paid.

RICHARD "DICK" A. GRASSO
New York Stock Exchange, Inc.
Chief Executive Officer / Chairman of the Board

After having worked for the New York Stock Exchange (NYSE) in New York City since 1968, Mr. Richard Grasso, CEO and Board Chairman, was tossed out on September 17, 2003, by board action for failure to disclose the accumulated compensation of his retirement package. Then, *hyper*-greed kicked in.

Mr. Grasso was paid a severance of $140 million but then filed a suit to recover part of his unpaid pay package, totaling about $44 million. This suit was appealed all the way to the New York Supreme Court. On October 19, 2006, the Supreme Court ruled in favor of the NYSE but that decision was appealed to a higher court.

In July 2008 the New York State Court of Appeals ruled in favor of Mr. Grasso, stating that the NYSE was a public entity at the time of the suit and that the Court had no jurisdiction over the suit. Any further action by Grasso against the NYSE was dismissed.

Mr. Grasso ignored bitter complaints regarding his pay package and walked away with his $184 million. He claimed that the lawsuits cost him $100 million. Not a bad deal even so—$184 million for $100 million, tax deductible.

Mr. Grasso has been quoted as saying, "All of this isn't about money, it's about what's right and what's wrong." However, the amount of money involved has earned him the nickname, "Mr. Graspo."

According to *The New York Times,* the "Grasso case," started by Eliot Spitzer as he examined the historical details regarding Mr. Grasso's compensation, brought into focus the previously hidden and questionable compensation practices that caused large transfers of wealth from shareholders to managers.

Born in New York City in 1946, Mr. Grasso was quite young when his father left the family. He graduated from Newtown High School, and after years at Pace University, he joined the Army. His career started in the NYSE following his military service. From his beginning job as a floor clerk, he advanced through the ranks to become CEO and Board Chairman of the NYSE early in the 1990s. During his tenure at the NYSE, he took public a private company owned by a group of financial specialists. The NYSE began a transformation into high technology electronic and global trading that continues to bring innovation to its universal trading platform.

A thumbnail history of this entity might serve to illuminate the transformations that have occurred.

The New York Stock Exchange at 11 Wall Street in downtown Manhattan is the world's largest stock exchange in terms of the $10.1 trillion average value of listed securities (October 2008). Twenty-four brokers formed the NYSE on May 17, 1792, under the terms of the Buttonwood Agreement, so named because it was signed outdoors under a buttonwood tree. They opened the Exchange on lower Wall Street. The NYSE expanded in listings and volumes over the centuries, but retained its open outcry auction style of matching sellers and buyers of shares until the advent of electronic trading in the early 1990s. Mr. Grasso led the NYSE in the transition to a hybrid exchange that permits the traditional auction style by floor brokers as well as electronic trading by a vast computer communications network.

On March 6, 2006, the board of the NYSE voted to merge with rival Archipelago, an electronic stock exchange company, and named the merged entity the NYSE Group. NYSE Group merged with Euronext N.V. (the European combined stock market), resulting in a milestone for global market finance: the first transatlantic stock exchange. It is named NYSE Euronext.

The electronic trading of securities is still causing unpredictable aberrations in buying and selling shares. Arguably, the advent of the instantaneous automated trade, the ability of individuals to place orders from personal computers and the complex hedging of risk with options and short sales has created a market of speculators as opposed to investors. If this is true, a securities exchange becomes a casino, where designing a game with winners and losers makes money, not evaluating and investing in healthy businesses.

Traditional expectations of investment returns on the profits of well-run companies no longer seem respectable in an environment of excess. In order to justify and pay the outsized salaries and commissions expected today, companies must be merged and acquired, assets leveraged and accounting manipulated. The resulting balance sheet may wow the analysts and pop the stock price for a time, but eventually the unsound financial decisions made will be visible and will weaken even the finest business model. At the end of the cycle the worker has been chiseled to increase the bottom line, the individual investor has been lured and despoiled and the country's economy is deprived of a reliable unit for production of goods and services.

The innovations for which Mr. Grasso was so highly paid played their role in the destruction of asset values for many investors.

MATTHEW C. DEVLIN
Lehman Brothers
"The Golden Goose"

On December 18, 2008, the U. S. Securities and Exchange Commission charged Mr. Matthew C. Devlin with insider trading—a violation of the nation's trading rules and regulations. Several others were charged in the same suit, including some relief defendants (a relief defendant is one who has obtained funds as part of the alleged securities violations by the named defendants "under circumstances in which it is not just, equitable or conscionable for them to retain the illegal profits"). Relief defendants were not active participants in the scheme, but they cannot retain, and must return, tainted profits.

Mr. Devlin, at the time of the violations, was a registered representative of Lehman Brothers, Inc., New York City. The SEC claims that between March 2004 and July 2008 $4.8 million in profits were made from insider trading. Mr. Devlin started sharing insider information on impending corporate transactions that involved takeovers, mergers, acquisitions and other potential actions that would influence the per-share price of a publicly-held stock. In all, there were nine defendants and three relief defendants charged in the suit.

The source of much of the privileged information came from Mr. Devlin's wife, Nina Devlin, a partner in the Brunswick Group, LLC, a financial public relations firm. As you can imagine, pillow talk is often a cause of leaks. The suit maintains Mr. Devlin obtained transaction information on companies such as Rohm & Haas,

Anheuser-Busch, Inc., Ventana Medical Systems, Mercantile Bankshares Corporation, Take-Two Interactive Software, Inc. and Pharmion Corporation.

The SEC documented some of the gifts Mr. Devlin received from "friends" who were recipients of special inside information: Cash (of course), luxury items such as a Cartier watch, a Barney's gift card, a widescreen television, a Ralph Lauren leather jacket and Porsche driving lessons.

As of December 2008 Mr. Devlin has pleaded guilty and according to SEC reports is "cooperating with authorities." This cooperation includes wearing a wire as well as collecting evidence for the feds to aid in sentencing.

The SEC has become much more aggressive in investigating reports of various types of fraud since the disclosure of the Madoff Ponzi scheme. For instance, in April 2008 a Mr. Ted Parmigiani, a former analyst with Lehman Brothers specializing in the semiconductor industry, approached the SEC with more than 4,000 e-mails relating to possible and probable dissemination of information that could be classed as insider information. These e-mails are dated as far back as 2005. Mr. Parmigiani was dismissed from Lehman Brothers by June 2005 due to "performance issues." [http://www.nytimes.com/2009/02/23/business/23hedge.html]

Following the disclosures by Mr. Parmigiani, several individual meetings and phone conversations were held between him and the SEC, including a six-hour grilling on April 30, 2008. On February 19, 2009, Senator Charles E. Grassley (R-Iowa) sent a letter to Mary Schapiro, Chairwoman of the SEC, inquiring about any action taken by the SEC regarding this investigation, and Mr. Grassley received a non-committal answer. John Nester, an SEC spokesman, stated, "We certainly share the Senator's interest in vigorous enforcement against insider trading." No mention was made of any legal enforcement as of February 19, 2009—about ten months after the SEC had made several forays looking into the Parmigiani charges. [http://www.nytimes.com/2009/02/23/business/23hedge.html].

The wheels of justice turn slowly after whistle-blowers sound their alarm, but certainly the government and the SEC are smarting from the lack of attention to the Madoff whistle blowing, and the process of doing "something about it" will be the rule, not necessarily the exception. Fraud is rampant and must be pursued; it is a time-consuming and laborious process to do so.

EARNEST STANLEY O'NEAL
Merrill Lynch
Former Chief Executive Officer (2006)

Earnest Stanley O'Neal was born on October 7, 1951, in Roanoke, Alabama. (His family lived in Wedowee, Alabama, but the nearest hospital willing to admit African-Americans was in Roanoke.) His father was a farmer, and his mother was a cleaning lady. As a youngster, O'Neal lived in a house with no indoor plumbing. The family had no automobile. Mr. O'Neal worked on his grandfather's farm in the corn and cotton fields. He sold and delivered newspapers to help out the family.

At the age of twelve his family moved into a federal housing project in Atlanta, and his father took a job in a General Motors assembly plant nearby. Mr. O'Neal was one of the first African-Americans to attend the newly integrated West Fulton High School.

On the advice of his father, O'Neal entered college at the General Motors Institute (later renamed Kettering University), where he studied engineering and industrial administration. In 1974 he graduated in the top 20 percent of his class with a Bachelor of Arts in Industrial Administration. A scholarship allowed him to attend Harvard Business School, where he graduated in 1978 with honors and an MBA in Finance.

His first job after graduation was in GM's treasurer's office in New York City. By 1982 he worked in a similar position in Madrid, Spain. He returned to New York in 1984 and was responsible for the

New York office's acquisitions and mergers. After eight years with GM he obtained his first Wall Street job in the high-yield Finance Group of Merrill Lynch, and he was continually promoted from that time on. He was successful in the junk-bond area of financing and by 1996 was head of Merrill's capital markets group where he gained a broad understanding of working with clients around the world.

In 1997 Mr. O'Neal was named an executive vice president and became a member of the executive management committee. His star was rising quickly—he was becoming experienced in all phases of the business. In 1998 he gained the title of Chief Financial Officer and direct management of several important divisions. In 2000 he became president of the prime retail brokerage business with responsibility for 16,000 brokers and financial advisors, six million benefit plans, 800 branch offices and $1.3 trillion in client assets. He was a very, very big deal in the highest circles of Wall Street finance.

Riding high in July 2001, Mr. O'Neal was appointed Chief Operating Officer and President of Merrill. Many negative factors came together in 2001, but chief among them was the tragic loss of Merrill's main offices across the street from the World Trade Center on September 11. A $1.3 billion loss was recorded for the fourth quarter of 2001. Reacting to falling revenues and profits by April 2002, O'Neal fired 15,000 employees, reorganized top management and closed branches in South Africa, Canada and Australia and most of the offices in Japan.

In May 2002, Merrill paid $100 million to settle charges of misleading investors. In the September 2002 issue of *Fortune* magazine, David Rynecki wrote of O'Neal, "He's ripping apart the securities firm, piece by piece. He's making enemies, he's not apologizing—it might just work." He became CEO on December 2, 2002.

Business magazine stated in 2007 that O'Neal received an annual compensation in 2006 of $46.4 million, including a bonus of $18.5 million and stock options worth $26.8 million.

As CEO, Mr. O'Neal must have known the seeds of destruction were being sown and that the ground was being prepared for the fatal collapse of the company and its eventual sale to Bank of America in 2008-2009.

Such is the rising and faltering of one of Wall Street's brightest stars. As CEO and board chairman, he crafted a handsome retirement package for himself that came in handy when the board ousted him in late 2007. His golden parachute was valued at $161.5 million at the time of his retirement. Just another day on greedy Wall Street.

IVAN FREDERICK BOESKY
Arbitrageur Extraordinaire
The Take-Over King Fined $100 Million

Mr. Ivan Boesky made his reputation—and his fortune—by becoming one of the first risk arbitrageurs of the 1980s. Arbitrage is simply the notion of trading similar goods by buying low and selling high. Arbitrageurs like Boesky, Carl Icahn and others ferreted out corporations that were likely take-over candidates; bought or threatened to buy large blocks of the target company's stock; pressured the majority ownership with a large nuisance position; demanded director representation on the board; threatened to re-organize and sell off portions of the company; and, in general, made it clear that as an unfriendly shareholder they could potentially orchestrate a hostile takeover of the corporation.

The likely result of such actions was for the company to offer above-market prices to remove the investor—making it possible for him to reap millions just by being a prickly thorn under the saddle. The process was very successful for such "raiders" as T. Boone Pickens and Irving Jacobs. In some cases the threatened takeover would shake things up and cure ills in a company, force the company to clean house and become more efficient and streamline its production. The company's financials would improve, the stock price would rise and the raider would back off, sell the position at a profit and walk away with a tidy gain.

Born in Detroit, Michigan, in 1937 Mr. Boesky attended Mumford High School and matriculated at Wayne State University, Eastern Michigan University and University of Michigan. After several years with the Central Intelligence Agency, he enrolled in the Detroit College of Law (without an undergraduate degree) and completed his J. D. in 1965.

In 1966 Mr. Boesky became a stock analyst on Wall Street. In 1975 the family fortune of his wife, Seema Silberstein, bankrolled the formation of his own arbitrage company. He was an astute trader and by the mid-1980s his net worth was estimated to be $200 million.

The first half of the 1980s was a golden age for mergers and acquisitions. Mr. Boesky excelled at company takeovers by sniffing out information in advance of public announcements of mergers, sales and acquisitions. But he grew careless or lazy and began to seek *insider* information—not public information.

About 3,000 corporate mergers and acquisitions valued at $300 billion were consummated in the marketplace of 1986. Mr. Boesky bought a large block of Gulf+Western stock, the share price rose and he sold it prior to the takeover that he knew in advance would happen. When the Maxxam Group tendered an $800 million offer to buy Pacific Lumber, Mr. Boesky had bought 10,000 shares three days prior to the offer. He also traded illegally on inside information from Mr. Dennis Levine of Drexel Burnham Lambert and paid Levine part of the profits he made from the trading.

On November 14, 1986, the SEC charged Mr. Boesky with illegal stock manipulation based on insider information. He was sentenced to prison, barred from dealing in securities and made to pay $100 million in penalties.

In order to bargain for a more lenient sentence, Mr. Boesky agreed to "rat out" his takeover-artist and junk-bond dealer associates, and he wore a wire to secretly tape conversations for the feds to use against them. Mr. Boesky also was allowed by the SEC to sell off stocks and securities to reduce liabilities outstanding. This action was later widely criticized.

On May 18, 1986, just before being charged with fraud, he gave a commencement address to the University of California's Business School in which he flatly stated, "I think being greedy is healthy—you can be greedy and still feel good about yourself."

One wonders how he felt six months later when he was tossed into prison. His greedy nature was active doing business and was still active in the plea-bargaining process, no matter the cost.

Prison inmates usually don't have mercy for a rat.

RALPH CIOFFI
High Flyer and Risk Taker

Mr. Ralph Cioffi was a picture of dejection, grasping the arm of his wife as they left a Brooklyn courthouse on June 29, 2008, after being indicted and making bail for mail and securities fraud. What a comedown for a star athlete who was universally proclaimed to be an all-around nice guy.

That's what greed can do to a fellow.

Born on January 5, 1956, in South Burlington, Vermont, he grew up in that same town on the shores of Lake Champlain. His *alma maters,* Rice Memorial High School and St. Michael's College, were both within a few miles of his hometown. He was a successful fullback, running back and guard in college sports, an A student in economics and math and graduated from St. Michael's with honors in Business Administration in 1978.

A biographical article on Bloomberg's site, published by Yalman Onaran and Jody Shenne in 2007, portrays Mr. Cioffi as "a happy and upbeat fellow who didn't hang out with the party crowd," and someone who "got along with everybody." He seemed to be a man who exuded decency, integrity and a commitment to his family and community.

Mr. Cioffi joined Bear, Stearns & Company on Wall Street and soon had made many close relationships with the large institutional investors that ran the big pension funds. His specialty became structured products, which included mortgage-backed bonds. Thomas Pearce, a fellow worker for eleven years at Bear, said Mr. Cioffi was not "some Wall Street hedge fund guy who is full of himself, but rather a family man with lots of integrity. You can't find people inside or outside of business who disliked him." [Bloomberg.com, July 3, 2007. [http://www.bloomberg.com/ apps/news?pid=newsarchive &sid =azWrpTVCph08&refer=home].

Structured finance became a rapidly growing business for Bear, and the Onaran and Shenne article on Bloomberg notes that Mr. Cioffi was responsible for the first offerings of "complex financial products widely used today." His sales offerings were products backed by "non-risky assets" or principal-protected notes that guaranteed the investors would get their investment back in case of failure.

The first such fund he started earned for investors a 46.8 percent return between October 2003 and March 2007. His second fund, High Grade Structural Credit Strategies Enhanced Leverage Fund starting in August 2006, returned 7 percent in its first six months. In February 2007 the two funds started to lose money, and by June the second fund was down by 20 percent and the first fund by 10 percent.

The two funds were highly leveraged (using their assets to borrow money to invest in the funds). The asset-backed bonds in the portfolios decreased in value, investors started to demand their monies back, borrowed money couldn't be sold off and cash became short. The media played up his problems and Bear finally replaced him with more seasoned managers.

Mr. Cioffi and his closest associate, Matthew Tannin, struggled mightily to save the two funds but they both collapsed with heavy losses to investors. Early in 2007 Mr. Cioffi withdrew over $2 million of his own money from the funds without telling his investors—and in the meantime continued to extol the safety of the assets backing his funds and assuring investors that all would be well.

On June 19, 2008, the FBI charged Mr. Cioffi, Mr. Tannin and three other Bear managers with fraud and insider trading, stating that since March 2007 the bad situation in the funds they managed was getting worse, but investors were not properly informed. The funds collapsed in the summer of 2007. The investors lost at least $1.4 billion in unrecoverable toxic assets.

The FBI posted the following statement: "Mortgage fraud and related securities pose a significant threat to our economy, to the stability of the Nation's housing and to the peace of mind to millions of American homeowners."

"Operation Malicious Mortgage" is the FBI's program against mortgage fraud. It is a concerted, joint law enforcement and prosecutorial effort "aimed at disrupting individuals and groups engaged in mortgage fraud," according to the FBI's official press release. "This effort is an example of our unified commitment to address this significant crime problem." [http://www.justice.gov/opa/pr/2008/June/08-odag-551.html].

It's also a prime example of the Wall Street saying, "Your reputation is only as good as your last trade." Probably no one needs to remind Mr. Cioffi of that fact.

MICHAEL ROBERT MILKEN
Dethroned "Junk Bond King"
Again Worth $2.1 Billion in 2007

Mr. Milken was charged with ninety-eight counts of racketeering and securities fraud in 1989, but was convicted of only six securities charges. He has been called the Junk Bond King, and some detractors call him the epitome of greed on Wall Street.

After paying a $200 million fine, he still has enough money to be listed as the 458th richest person in the world, with $2.1 billion, according to *Forbes* magazine. It would seem proper that if someone had gained their wealth through fraudulent schemes, he should be financially wiped out of the ill-gotten gains. But the illegal profits could be channeled into good works for the public—and that is what Michael Milken has chosen to do.

He has been philanthropic with large sums of his money. In fact, *Fortune* magazine has called him "The Man Who Changed Medicine" in its cover article in the November 2004 issue. He has concentrated his charitable efforts towards research and education with emphasis on prostate cancer. In January 1993 he was diagnosed with advanced prostate cancer that had spread to his lymph nodes. This is usually a clear signal that death will occur within two years, but he has survived that dire prediction.

He was born on July 4, 1946, in Encino, California, into an upper-middle-class Jewish family. He attended Birmingham High School. In 1968 he graduated Phi Beta Kappa from the University of California at Berkeley and went on to graduate school at the Wharton School of Business at the University of Pennsylvania. Among the host of data he learned there was the concept proposed by Mr. W. Braddock Hickman, a President of the Federal Reserve Bank of Cleveland: "A portfolio of non-investment grade bonds offered 'risk adjusted' returns greater than that of an investment grade portfolio." That statement became the cornerstone of a remarkable—if illegal—profession for Mr. Milken.

Mr. Milken landed a summer job with Drexel Harriman Ripley that led to a position with Drexel Firestone as head of their low-grade bond research division. In 1973 Drexel merged with Burnham and Company. He retained his position with the firm and by 1976 his compensation was $5 million annually.

High-yield bonds produce greater interest payments than "normal" bonds because the underlying asset is a greater risk than the assets of better-rated bonds.

Mr. Milken tapped into a huge source of trading by gathering together bundles of high-yield bonds and using the old saying, "there is safety in numbers." He convinced investors to place their money in the new type of bundled securities to gain more interest income at reduced risk. The growing economy made these bundles possible until the market contracted. Then the diminished asset valuations behind too many "junk bonds" weakened the ability of the bonds to keep delivering higher interest rates, and bond values fell. The phrase coined for these assets was "toxic," and the term "toxic assets" and "sub-prime mortgages and loan papers" became buzzwords again used for the financial crises of the 2007-2012 debacle.

The market and "good times" were good for Mr. Milken—during the 1980s at least. He made a fortune several times over. It is common for undue success to turn the head of reason and for greed to take over. Mr. Milken worked hard and long and his reputation grew by leaps and bounds. Ultimately, his tactics were questioned. In 1989 a grand jury indicted him on ninety-eight counts of racketeering and fraud. Ivan Boesky gave evidence that implicated him in illegal practices and insider transactions. At his sentencing, Judge Kimba Wood told Mr. Milken, "You were willing to commit only crimes that were unlikely to be detected."

He eventually agreed to plead guilty to a total of eight securities and tax violations. He was sentenced to prison and served a little less than two years. He paid several hundred million dollars in fines—by some accounts he paid out over a billion dollars—and was barred from working in the securities business for the rest of his life.

By May 2009 Michael Milken was involved in several successful businesses worth in excess of a billion dollars. He is a highly talented individual who was turned wrong by greed. He appears to be trying to make up for his past, and we wish him well.

RICHARD SEVERIN FULD
"The Gorilla"
Six-Year Average Annual Compensation: $63.9 million

According to *The Wall Street Journal*, Dick Fuld had prospered while being CEO and board chairman of the Lehman Brothers bond house on Wall Street. *Barron's* magazine listed Mr. Fuld as "one of the world's best CEOs" and called him "Mr. Wall Street." That was in March 2008.

On September 15, 2008, Lehman filed for bankruptcy, and exposure to details of the businesses of Lehman has given cause for some experts to declare Mr. Fuld one of the worst CEOs in the financial business. Stars can fall much faster than they rise.

While facing an irate Senate committee investigating the bankruptcy, Mr. Fuld felt the rage of Senator Henry Waxman, who asked, "Your company is now bankrupt, our economy is in crisis, but you get to keep $480 million. I have a very basic question for you, is that fair?"

No. It is not fair.

Richard Severin "Dick" Fuld was born on April 26, 1946, in New York City. After high school he attended the University of Colorado at Boulder, and graduated in 1969 with a BA degree. He then attended New York University's Stern School of Business and graduated with an MBA in 1973.

While in Boulder, he joined the Naval Reserve Office Training Corps, but his dreams of being an Air Force pilot ended abruptly when he engaged his commanding officer in a fistfight. Mr. Fuld claimed he was defending a cadet from verbal abuse by the same officer.

He joined Lehman on Wall Street in 1969 and stayed with the firm his entire career on Wall Street. He prospered while Lehman merged with Kuhn, Loeb & Co. and again when Shearson/American Express acquired that merged entity in 1984. A merger with E. F. Hutton was followed in 1994 by a decision by American Express to spin off Lehman (plus assimilated entities) into just Lehman Brothers again. Mr. Fuld was named CEO and board chairman, having survived the mergers and spinoff. He held those posts until the firm's demise due to bankruptcy.

Mr. Fuld earned the nickname "Gorilla" for his aggressiveness and hard-as-nails dealing. He was an ace squash player, but as Bloomberg's website ultimately noted, "the one-time international squash player accustomed to working the angles, finally found one he couldn't master." [http://www.bloomberg.com/apps/news?pid=newsarchive&sid=aVZKah.at5fY].

Astute financial deals under Mr. Fuld assured record earnings, and in October 2003 Lehman acquired the successful firm of Neuberger Berman for $2.6 billion. In January 2004 *Institutional Investor* listed Dick Fuld first in its annual Best CEOs in the Brokers and Asset Managers category.

Success has its own costs. Mr. Fuld was regarded as an "unbearably intense man." [http://business.timesonline.co.uk/ tol/business/industry_sectors/ banking_ and_finance/article5336179.ece].

When other executives were exercising in a training room along with Fuld, the bankruptcy of the firm was broadcast over the public address system. Vicki Ward, a U. S. journalist, said, "two very senior sources - one incredibly senior source" had confirmed to her: "He went to the gym after ... Lehman was announced as going under," she told CNBC. "He was on a treadmill with a heart monitor on. Someone was in the corner pumping iron, and he walked over and he knocked him out cold." [http://www.telegraph.co.uk/finance/financetopics/financialcrisis/3150319/Richard-Fuld-punched-in-face-in-Lehman-Brothers-gym.html].

No love was lost for Mr. Fuld—if there ever was any—when the chips were down, and values were gone. All of the dreams and the hard work were for naught. The making of many enemies and but few friends is not much reward for a lifetime lived at the fastest pace possible on Wall Street.

However, as Mr. Waxman said in the Senate hearing on the bankruptcy, "You get to keep $480 million?" Even if he does keep it, it can't be worth the money to lose the respect of one's peers on Wall Street.

The "Gorilla" couldn't muscle his way through the disaster he'd created.

SANFORD I. WEILL
Founder of Citigroup, Inc.
Compensation: $785 million over Five Years

Sanford "Sandy" Weill was and is one of Wall Street's outstanding successes—success by anyone's standards.

Born in Brooklyn, New York, on March 16, 1933, Mr. Weill grew up in a dynamic Jewish neighborhood. He chose Cornell University in Ithaca, New York, for his college studies, joined the Air Force ROTC while there to become an Air Force pilot but later dropped it due to a curtailment in defense spending at the national level.

His business career started with a job as a runner for the Wall Street house of Bear Stearns but soon moved into the main office, and with legendary drive and meritorious work, became a stockbroker for the "Bear." His penchant for Wall Street and its myriad deals—and money—led him into one of the most successful careers in the world of investments.

At the age of twenty-seven Mr. Weill and three partners formed a small brokerage house. Over the next twenty years they made fifteen acquisitions that culminated in the financial firm of Shearson Hayden Stone (Shearson). American Express bought Shearson in 1981 for $930 million. Sandy Weill followed the sale by becoming president of American Express.

The New York Times detailed Mr. Weill's continued rise in the financial world. He went to Minneapolis in 1986 and convinced the Control Data Corporation to spin off its Commercial Credit Division into a separate entity, went public with it and sold 82 percent of the spin-off for $850 million. He became president of Commercial Credit and invested $7 million of his own money in the 18 percent ownership balance. Part of the deal was for Sandy Weill to inherit Gulf Insurance, an offshoot of Commercial Credit. [Norris, Floyd. "Citigroup's Climb to Riches, One Merger at a Time with Sanford I. Weill," *New York Times*, July 17, 2003.]

Within two years, Mr. Weill and his friends had made Commercial Credit very valuable and parlayed that value into buying Primerica for $1.5 billion. In this deal Sandy harvested the Wall Street brokerage house Smith Barney and the A. I. Williams Insurance Company. This new package of companies was labeled Primerica Financial Service, and all values were continued under the brand of Primerica Corporation.

In 1992 Primerica Corporation bought 27 percent of Travelers Insurance for $772.5 million after selling off some "non-strategic" assets. In 1993 again under the banner of Primerica, Sandy Weill bought Shearson back from American Express for $1.2 billion—adding 8,400 financial brokers to its sales force. Primerica then bought the balance of 73 percent of The Travelers Companies, Inc. (Travelers) with Primerica stock worth $4 billion, and The Travelers Group was formed.

In 1996 Travelers bought the property and casualty operations of Aetna Insurance for a mere $4 billion. In 1997 Travelers bought Saloman, Inc., the parent company of Salomon Brothers, a major Wall Street house, for $9.1 billion. Saloman was then merged with Smith Barney to create the second largest securities firm in the world at that time.

In 1998 the grandest move of all occurred when Travelers merged with Citicorp, the parent company of Citibank, to form Citigroup, Inc. Sandy Weill's group now supplied the most credit cards in the world, had the second-largest bank in the United States and had 100 million customers in 100 countries using its financial services. On the day this grand merger was announced, Citigroup was valued at $70.6 billion. By the end of that day the value was $83.6 billion, a neat jump of $13 billion within just a few hours.

In a report by *Forbes* magazine dated April 26, 2001, Mr. Weill was paid a total compensation over a five-year period of $785 million. At the time he owned one half of one percent of Citigroup, and was "a hired hand and fabulously overpaid one by our measure," said *Forbes*.

Citigroup had a five-year growth rate of 21.3 percent. In the same time period, Morgan Stanley Dean Witter grew 26.5 percent; Fleet Boston grew 23.4 percent; Wells Fargo grew 24.2 percent; and Charles Schwab grew 33 percent. In the same five-year period combined total compensation for the CEOs of these four companies was $458.8 million, about 58 percent of what was paid to Mr. Weill. Add the five-year compensation of the CEOs of Washington Mutual, Bear Stearns, Freddie Mac, Lehman Brothers and AIG to the $458.8 million and the grand total *still* didn't reach Mr. Weill's five-year period total, according to the *Forbes* article.

In 2000 Mr. Weill became both CEO and Chairman of the Board. Citigroup's earnings for 2001 were $13 billion. In 2003 he relinquished his role as CEO, and in 2006 he stepped down as Chairman of the Board.

Was that the point when enough was enough for Sanford Weill? Operations of Citigroup were turned over to a succession of executives; each was paid exorbitant salaries, bonuses and perks—much of it in shares of stock.

This climbing towards the top of the financial game came to a screeching halt in the meltdown of 2008. It was said that Mr. Weill lost half a billion dollars in value—in just one day.

Of course in 1998 he made billions of dollars in just one day. He has been very generous with his money in supporting dozens of worthy causes—in particular his *alma mater*, Cornell University.

Maybe he is now relaxing and enjoying the fruits of a most active, successful yet hectic career. But knowing Sandy Weill, his head is whirling with new plans. He can be counted on to be back in the fray.

On October 25, 2009, *The Wall Street Journal* published an extensive article, "Six Steps to Revitalize the Financial System," by Sanford I. Weill and Judah Kraushaar (the latter is managing partner of Roaring Brook Capital). Their prelude to explaining the Six Steps included the statement: "Our policy leaders should focus directly on how to create and enhance market discipline. Our country needs to strive for transparency in financial-company balance sheets and establish new rules of the road."

A very condensed version of the six steps follows:

<u>Six Steps to Revitalize the Financial System</u>
By Weill and Kraushaar

Make the Federal Reserve the super-regulator responsible for overseeing systemic risk.

- As much as possible test complex instruments regularly for market valuation and clear them through a central clearing house.
- Reform and revitalize the securitization market.
- Engage the rating agencies by regulator scrutiny.
- Overhaul capital requirements and reserve policies.
- Align executive compensation with long-term returns. [http://online.wsj.com/article/SB1000142405274870433590457449513061229 1304.html].

SUMMARY

It has not been an enjoyable task to write about greed on Wall Street. Most of the "players" in Chapter 7 of this book and throughout the narrative are not friends or acquaintances of the author. But a few are. No apologies are given for what has been written, as all facts portrayed are true as far as the author is concerned. Greed is a disease that affects us all—there's no substitute for the truth in that matter.

Life on Wall Street can be cruel. Expectations are not always fulfilled—even to the size of a bonus, for instance. Many believe the millions of dollars they do receive in any one year—salary, bonus, perks and other compensation—are fully justified based upon the long hours worked and the creativity put into such work.

In my experience a few million dollars a year should compensate for the needs of most anyone. Who really needs multiple numbers of fancy cars, more than two mansions to occupy for short periods, acres of walls to hang art work for occasional private viewing, expensive clothes, jewelry and lady friends who are terribly expensive and almost certainly destabilizing to personal lives. But, who am I to dictate such moral decisions.

Each of us should ascertain that we indeed have a conscience—and then follow it.

GREEDSTERS ON MAIN STREET

Chapter 8 – Synopsis

"No Geographic Limits"

How do you identify a greedster on Main Street? Big fat salaries (in the mega-millions); huge bonuses; long lists of perquisites like nannies, toiletries and box seats for sporting events; forced-retirement packages called Golden Parachutes, and death benefits called Golden Coffins that pay the greedsters' estates long after the executives are deceased.

Wall Street and Main Street meet where the money is. This game is rigged to benefit the greedsters. Shareholders have the voting power to elect independent boards, but they must exercise it. The evidence is that lax boards of directors have too many "cozy" ties to management and are rubber-stamping powerful CEOs. The result is companies taking too much risk in order to pump up stock prices artificially and reward executive management with excessive compensation.

Companies across the United States find themselves under pressure to create paper profits that do not represent real revenue and value from real assets. Instead executives manipulate and magnify assets through mergers and acquisitions, shift operating losses to phony subsidiaries and use creative accounting methods to inflate the bottom line.

Stories like those in this chapter have eroded investors' confidence in owning equities. When shareholders cannot trust the audited financial statements, cannot trust management to perform their jobs with integrity and cannot trust that the board of directors is monitoring a company's business behavior, they grow unwilling to own equities.

Sound management of good companies will always be reflected in reasonable compensation plans and straightforward public disclosures. Finding such companies in which to invest has become a real challenge, but it is a necessary responsibility of each stakeholder.

Chapter 8

GREEDSTERS ON MAIN STREET

With severe criticism of Wall Street's financial houses and commercial and investment banks, it is only natural to believe it's only Wall Street that is consumed by greed. Not so. Pools of money are everywhere, and CEOs of many companies are as greedy as the principals on Wall Street.

In this chapter, thirteen executives have been profiled who exemplify greed on Main Street.

It's no coincidence that in every case listed in previous chapters their company was at the mercy of one person, serving as both CEO *and* Chairman of the Board of Directors. That should never happen. When it is permitted to occur, shareholders should revolt and vote that person out. It's a great risk not to do that.

RICHARD M. SCRUSHY
Cooked the Books at HealthSouth

Richard M. Scrushy was born in August 1952 in Selma, Alabama. He went from being a middle-class citizen of Selma to becoming the third-highest-paid executive in the United States in 1997. He directed illegal bookkeeping of the business affairs of HealthSouth to inflate earnings and thereby increase the per-share price of the stock so Mr. Scrushy could sell his own shares of company stock at higher prices. He's now behind bars.

His upbringing didn't necessarily prepare him for the world of high finance. His father repaired cash registers; his mother worked as a nurse and respiratory therapist. Mr. Scrushy learned how to play the piano and guitar by the age of twelve, and he earned his own spending money doing odd jobs around town using his middle name, Marin.

He dropped out of Parrish High School in his senior year to marry his girlfriend who was pregnant and needed his support. They lived in a Selma trailer park and existed on pick-up jobs. He finished high school with a graduate equivalency diploma, and acting upon his mother's advice, enrolled in Wallace State Community College. A year later he transferred to Jefferson State Community College and then transferred to the respiratory therapy program at the University of Alabama at Birmingham ("UAB").

Upon graduation from UAB he was offered a teaching position there and was promoted, at the age of twenty-four, to Program Director after two-and-a-half years. By that time he and his wife had two children. He divorced her and accepted a teaching position at Wallace State College in Dotham, Alabama. There he married his second wife, in the mid-1970s, and they had four children. He divorced her and married a third time in 1997, producing three more offspring. Three wives and nine children in twenty-seven years.

Mr. Scrushy found his business future in health care. In the late 1970s he was offered a job with the Lifemark Corporation, a Houston healthcare company. He left teaching and within a few years "he was helping run a $100 million operation that included pharmacy, physical rehabilitation and a hospital acquisition division." [Burke, Monte (2001-01-21). "Back To Life". *Forbes*. Retrieved 2009-05-19.] While with Lifemark, he moved to St. Louis, Missouri, where he worked as regional director of the respiratory therapy division.

In 1980 Congress passed the Omnibus Budget Reconciliation Act, which recognized Comprehensive Outpatient Rehabilitation Facilities (CORF) and made such services eligible for Medicare coverage.

Mr. Scrushy returned to Houston to become the company's chief operating officer. There he devised a plan for an outpatient diagnostics and rehabilitation clinic chain. Lifemark turned the plan down; Mr. Scrushy left Lifemark in 1983.

On January 23, 1984, Mr. Scrushy founded Amcare (ambulatory care) in Birmingham, Alabama. In September 1984, Amcare opened its first outpatient rehabilitation service in Little Rock, Arkansas. Amcare changed its name to HealthSouth in late 1984.

In 1986 HealthSouth's revenues increased by 256 percent and added locations in Jackson, Mississippi, and Miami, Florida, to expand its services. Medicare was supplying a fountain of money to the chain. In September 1986 HealthSouth's stock began trading on the NASDAQ exchange.

In 1987 HealthSouth increased its reach by adding worker's compensation and sports medicine to its array of outpatient services. Business leaped forward. The company began a new program called "WorkStart" aimed at returning injured workers to their jobs more quickly. Neurorehabilitation Systems of America was acquired, which added a Detroit-based conglomerate of rehabilitation programs for patients recovering from brain surgery.

By the end of 1987 HealthSouth was growing fat and happy with its revenues soaring, $100 million in assets, 1,200 employees and eighteen chain clinics in twelve states. Life was very rich indeed.

In September 1988 HealthSouth was listed on the "big board," the New York Stock Exchange, with the symbol HLSH. It was the thirteenth healthcare services company to be listed. Do you suppose Mr. Scrushy is superstitious? It seems he should have been.

In 1989 an internal auditor at HealthSouth was fired for allegedly drawing attention to mounting financial problems within the company and for claiming that he was pressured to meet certain earnings targets.

In 1991 Medicare accused HealthSouth of illegally adding costs to reports for outpatient therapy and input rehabilitation for the corporation's Bakersfield Rehabilitation Hospital.

In 1998 Medicare changed its funding arrangements in an attempt to reduce fraud and exploitation of loopholes and thereby reduced payments by $100 billion. Mr. Scrushy maintained it would make no difference to HealthSouth's procedures, but by the end of the year, profits had dropped by 93 percent. Something certainly had made a difference.

At about the same time Blue Cross Blue Shield of Alabama investigated and determined that HealthSouth had "improperly billed Medicare for therapy by students, interns, athletic trainers and other unlicensed aides." Additional lawsuits followed regarding Medicare fraud by "billing for services never provided, delivering poor care, treating patients without a formal plan of care and using unlicensed therapists."

In March 2003 the SEC filed a civil action against Mr. Scrushy and HealthSouth, alleging they had falsified at least $2.7 *billion* worth of profit between 1996 and 2002. On December 30, 2004, HealthSouth agreed to pay the government $325 million to "settle allegations that the company defrauded Medicare and other health care programs."

On February 6, 2003, the FBI announced that it would begin a criminal investigation into the "trading of shares of the HealthSouth Corporation" and possible securities law violations. The FBI filed a criminal complaint against HealthSouth's CFO Weston Smith and Mr. Scrushy. The SEC brought civil charges against them under the Sarbanes-Oxley Act. On November 4, 2003, Mr. Scrushy was the first CEO to be indicted under the act by the U. S. Department of Justice in the trial "United States of America vs. Richard M. Scrushy." The final indictment was thirty-six counts of conspiracy, money laundering, securities fraud and mail fraud. Mr. Scrushy was also accused of using intimidation, threats and cash payments to coerce top executives into committing fraud. These executives called themselves "The Family" and referred to practices of "creative accounting" and "filling the gap." Mr. Scrushy denied his involvement.

He did his best to block a possible guilty verdict. He knew that 70 percent of Birmingham, Alabama's population and eleven of the eighteen jurors were African-American. Mike Wallace interviewed him on "60 Minutes" in a segment titled "Cooking the Books." Mr. Scrushy began a morning talk show with his wife, called "Viewpoint"; backed a city-wide forty-day prayer movement referred to as "City, thou art loosed"; and joined the predominantly African-American Guiding Light Church.

On June 28, 2005, a jury of his peers acquitted Mr. Scrushy of all charges.

Within a few years HealthSouth had become a major player in the healthcare field. Using their early experience in sports medicine, the company gained international attention as they signed up sports stars such as Michael Jordan, Roger Clemens, Bo Jackson and others to popularize their programs.

In 2001 HealthSouth was the largest operator of inpatient and outpatient rehabilitation facilities, freestanding outpatient surgery centers and freestanding diagnostic centers in the country. It had gross revenues of $4.3 billion, more than 2,000 facilities in all fifty states of the United States, as well as facilities in Australia, Puerto Rico, Saudi Arabia and the United Kingdom. The facilities were treating more than 100,000 patients a day and employed over 60,000 people.

Mr. Scrushy had a tiger by the tail. Despite the acquittal of all charges on June 28, 2005, a federal grand jury in Montgomery, Alabama, on October 26, 2005, indicted Mr. Scrushy for twenty counts of money laundering, extortion, obstruction of justice, racketeering, and bribery of Alabama's Governor Don Siegelman. The prosecutor alleged that Mr. Scrushy had agreed to cover over $500,000 of Mr. Siegelman's debts in return for the governor giving Mr. Scrushy a seat on the Certificates of Need Board—which reviews hospitals and approves construction of facilities for Alabama.

This trial lasted six weeks and both Mr. Scrushy and the Governor were each found guilty of several of the charges.

On June 28, 2007, some two years after his indictment, Mr. Scrushy was sentenced to six years and ten months in a federal prison and ordered to pay $267,000 to United Way of Alabama in restitution. Governor Siegelman received similar sentences. Immediately after sentencing, both were carted off to a federal prison in Atlanta, Georgia. They briefly shared the same cell.

After losing lower court appeals, his final legal step may be an appeal to the U. S. Supreme Court. Who knows when that may occur? He was transferred to a low-security prison in Beaumont, Texas, to await further appeals.

On May 7, 2009, a new civil trial on behalf of HealthSouth investors brought Mr. Scrushy back in court in Birmingham. Closing arguments were made on May 27, 2009. On June 18, 2009, Judge Horn ordered Mr. Scrushy to pay $2.87 *billion* in damages. The Judge said, "Scrushy knew of and actively participated in the fraud." Mr. Scrushy has the right to appeal.

RAMALINGA RAJU
Satyam Computer Scandal—India's ENRON

Ramalinga Raju formed Satyam Computer Services, Ltd. of Hyderabad, India, in 1987 as an information and technology (IT) company. It was a huge success. By 2008 Satyam had listed its stock on the NYSE and Euronext, had a network that covered sixty countries, employed 40,000 people and served more than 654 global clients including 185 companies listed in the Fortune 500.

Mr. Raju was CEO and Chairman of the Board of Satyam from its inception in 1987 to January 7, 2009, when he made the startling announcement that the company had been practicing a massive corporate fraud that would total more than $1.5 billion. He promptly resigned from the board of directors with the comment, "It was like riding a tiger, not knowing how to get off without being eaten."

Apparently Mr. Raju had a strong social conscience, and his company had played major roles in supporting programs for the underprivileged. Upon disclosing the fraud, he stated, "neither myself or any of our spouses sold any company shares in the last eight years—excepting a small proportion declared and sold for philanthropic purposes."

What is hard to understand is how a huge gap of over a billion dollars in cash could be "overlooked" by Satyam's accounting firm, Price Waterhouse, over the ten-year period they served as auditors. Current accounting examinations show the gap, and the question has been raised as to where the missing money has gone. It must be assumed that Mr. Raju and his family were the recipients of most, if not all, of it.

In early 2008 Satyam attempted to purchase two infrastructure companies for billions of dollars—Maytas Infrastructure and Maytas Properties. The acquisitions fell through and precipitated a crisis for Satyam. The Raju family owned both of the proposed acquisitions and actual cash for the deals was not available. It now appears that these two deals were further attempts by the Raju family to cover up cash manipulations in effect since 2001.

Mr. Ramalinga Raju and his brother, B. Rama Raju, were immediately arrested and charged with criminal breach of trust, criminal conspiracy, falsification of records and forgery. India's criminal system acts promptly. It also was disclosed that Mr. Raju had violated insider-trading rules with multiple *benami* (dummy) accounts through relatives and friends. He used the accounts to trade Satyam shares, thereby inflating the volume and share prices. It is suspected that this procedure was used to siphon off vast amounts of money from Satyam through 6,603 phony invoices and forged certificates of deposit—to cover deposits that never existed.

According to Indian law, Mr. Raju and members of his family may be sentenced to prison for life.

Such is an instance of fraud beyond the United States. Beware: There is no safe haven from fraud and greed today.

SANJAY KUMAR
Computer Associates, International
"There's No Excuse for My Conduct"

Mr. Kumar was born in Colombo, Sri Lanka, in 1961. He immigrated to the United States in 1976 and settled with his family in South Carolina. He attended Furman University from 1980 to 1983, but never received a degree.

Mr. Kumar joined UCCEL Corporation, and within a few months was director of software development. In 1987 Computer Associates acquired UCCEL in an $800 million buyout, and Mr. Kumar became an employee of Computer Associates ("CA").

In 1988, Charles Wang, founder and CEO of CA, made Mr. Kumar Director of Planning. In 1989 he was named Senior Vice President of Planning and in 1993 became Executive Vice President of Operations. In 1994 at the age of thirty-one, Mr. Kumar was promoted to President and Chief Operating Officer (COO) of Computer Associates, capping a remarkable rise within CA.

In 2000 Mr. Kumar replaced Mr. Charles Wang as CEO and in 2002 became Chairman of the Board. The company became his overall responsibility two years later when the roof fell in.

In April 2004 Mr. Kumar resigned from both positions—CEO and chairmanship of CA's board—when an investigation of securities fraud and obstruction of justice formally commenced. He left the firm on June 4, 2004.

On September 22, 2004, a federal grand jury in Brooklyn, New York, indicted Mr. Kumar on $2.2 billion fraud charges. On April 24, 2006, the forty-four-year-old Mr. Kumar pleaded guilty before Judge Glasser to securities fraud and obstruction of justice, and on November 2, 2006, he was sentenced to twelve years in prison and fined $8 million for his role in the massive accounting frauds at CA. Following those twelve years, he will be on supervised release for three more years.

Six months later Judge Glasser set a fine of $798.6 million, of which at least $52 million must be paid by December 31, 2008. Also, after his twelve years of prison, Mr. Kumar may pay the government 20 percent of his "future gross annual pay for restitution."

Huge penalties to be sure, but the massive frauds included pervasive lying, falsifying documents, backdating contracts and misleading shareholders and regulators.

Let this be a lesson to all—play it straight or don't play at all. Greed shows others no favors, so don't expect it to show you one when payback time comes.

ANGELO R. MOZILO
Countrywide Financial
"Mozilo the Worst American CEO of All Time"—CNBC

For thirty-nine years Mr. Angelo Mozilo was CEO and Board Chairman of Countrywide Financial. In 2008 the company and Mr. Mozilo were questioned regarding deceptive lending procedures that made Countrywide one of the leading originators of home mortgages. You would think that after thirty-nine years at the helm of such an important company Mr. Mozilo would value a clean record of operations.

Between 1982 and 2003 the price of a share of Countrywide rose 23,000 percent and the asset portfolio of the company became over-weighted with sub-prime mortgage paper. By 2003 the total of sub-prime loans had mushroomed to $600 *billion*. From 2005 to 2007 Mr. Mozilo sold a majority of his shares of Countrywide stock for a profit of $291.5 million.

In 1969 Mr. Angelo Mozilo and Mr. David Loeb founded Countrywide Financial. When Mr. Loeb died in 2003 Mr. Mozilo became "Mr. Countrywide." Their company stock was initially listed as a penny stock on the Over the Counter (OTC) market, and in 1985 the stock was listed on the NYSE with the symbol CFC. Sub-prime mortgage loans became the new fad in financial products, low-interest rates and prosperity added fire to the sub-prime market and Countrywide became a leading lender of poor risk mortgages. That was their undoing.

Mr. Mozilo has been criticized as a headstrong protagonist who became blinded by ambition and pride (and may we add greed), which helped create the national housing fiasco. Competitors both admired and feared him. When the housing market tanked, the jobless rate increased in the mid-2000s; the rate of mortgage delinquencies soared; home foreclosures became an ugly reality; and book values of sub-prime paper cratered. Countrywide was caught in the worst of situations, facing severe cash shortages and looming bankruptcy.

One option for Mr. Mozilo was to sell a lot of his stock holdings in Countrywide, knowing ahead of time that the stock value must deteriorate. He sold in the twelve months ending in August 2007 while "publicly touting the stock and using shareholder funds to buy back stock to support the share price." From February 2007 to March 2008 the shareholders lost an equity value of about $23 *billion* when the stock price per share fell from $45 to a shade above $5.

In 2006 Mr. Mozilo received total compensation of about $48.1 million, and he cashed out formerly issued stock options worth additional millions. In June 2008 it was announced in the press that Countrywide had a "Friends of Angelo" group that received below-market-rate mortgages from Countrywide—and Senator

Chris Dodd was one of the recipients. As Chairman of the Senate's Budget Committee, Senator Dodd proposed the government buy up to $400 billion in defaulted mortgages. Both Franklin Raines and James Johnson, former CEOs of Fannie Mae, also were "Friends of Angelo." Mr. Raines received more than $3 million in loans from Countrywide while he was CEO of Fannie Mae.

In December 2007 Mr. Mozilo made a phone call to Mr. Kenneth Lewis, CEO of Bank of America. On January 11, 2008, BofA announced an agreement to purchase Countrywide with BofA's stock. BofA dispatched sixty analysts from its headquarters in Charlotte, North Carolina, to Countrywide's headquarters in Calabasas, California, to check the books of Countrywide for its legal and financial status. BofA offered a purchase price of $4 billion in BofA stock (a fraction of the $24 billion asset value of a mere year prior to the sale). Countrywide shareholders approved the sale on June 25, 2008, and closed the deal on June 26, 2008. BofA announced that more than 7,500 Countrywide jobs would be lost over the following two years.

In June 2008 the Attorney General's office of Illinois filed a civil lawsuit against Countrywide claiming "unfair and deceptive" practices to get homeowners to apply for risky mortgages beyond their means. California filed a similar suit the same day. In August 2008 Connecticut's Attorney General filed suit for deceptive lending practices. In October 2008 BofA settled all such suits and modified terms of troubled loans worth $8.4 billion. States involved in the settlement of suits were Arizona, California, Connecticut, Florida, Iowa, Michigan, North Carolina, Ohio, Texas and Washington. Other states may follow.

Mr. Mozilo is "taking it easy" these days, presumably counting his millions. He still does not believe he caused or contributed to the mortgage crisis.

An important element of greed is the inability to acknowledge wrongdoing or accept responsibility for failure. How can the criminally greedy fail to learn such a simple concept as right from wrong?

DANNY PANG
Dead at the Age of Forty-two—A Consummate Liar

Mr. Danny Pang, a Taiwanese immigrant, was born in Taiwan on December 15, 1966, and died suddenly in Newport Beach, California, on September 12, 2009. He lived up to his name of "pang" by apparently having a sudden, sharp pain—physically or emotionally—at the moment he died. An autopsy report one day after death ruled out foul play, but on September 18, 2009, an autopsy leak stated his body contained barbiturates and THC, the active ingredient of marijuana.

As a high-flyer in the financial and social worlds of southern California, he was well known, hobnobbing with the likes of media mogul Sumner Redstone, former defense secretary Frank Carlucci and Lockheed Martin CEO, Norman Augustine. Elsewhere, he was not well known except in his native country of Taiwan.

Mr. Pang was CEO of a $4 billion investment fund. At the time of his death, he was free on $1 million bail while under indictment by the SEC for lying about his credentials, forging insurance documents and running a Ponzi scheme on his investors. Mr. Michael On, president of Beyond Asset Management Company in Taipei, was quoted as saying, "Pang's death is a surprise, but it won't make any difference; investors won't get their money back. People have to realize there's no windfall from these investments."

There are apparently no windfalls from all sorts of things that Mr. Pang claimed. The University of California Irvine records show that Mr. Pang never received an MBA degree or any other degree from the University as he had claimed. When confronted with this fact, Mr. Pang countered by saying he used a Chinese name while earning the degrees at U of C Irvine. He also has stated he worked at Morgan Stanley on Wall Street as a senior vice president and a senior high-tech advisor, but the firm has no record of ever employing him. The CEO of another investment firm says Pang was fired after it was revealed he had stolen $3 million from an escrow account at the firm. Mr. Pang explained away this act by saying, "I just needed the money."

A few weeks prior to being fired, Mr. Pang's wife opened their home's front door to a "well-dressed man" who shot her dead. The murder has never been solved.

Mr. Pang and a local entrepreneur, Mr. Heip Trinh, founded Private Equity Management Group (PEM). Investors were told their money would be used to purchase life insurance policies of older people, and upon their deaths the PEM Group would receive full proceeds as the beneficiary. It seems fake insurance policies were used to mislead investors and new money was continually raised to keep some investors happy. Pang admitted it was a Ponzi scheme. When investors complained they weren't receiving returns on their investments as promised, Mr. Pang said, "Everybody is living longer."

Most investors were in Taiwan and Mr. Pang made several trips there, staying in the presidential suite at the swank Grand Formosa Regent Taipei Hotel. On June 12, 2007, Mr. Pang hired a jet and took several women from PEM's California office to a party in Las Vegas. After winning big in a casino, Mr. Pang threw "stacks of $10,000" around to the women during the return flight.

Upon his untimely death, one former associate commented, "He was a consummate liar. He could lie about anything with a straight face." He stole millions of dollars, lived high and wide on investors' money and apparently died without grace.

What a legacy to leave behind.

JOHN J. RIGAS
Convicted of Fifteen Counts of Securities Fraud
Sentenced to Fifteen Years in Prison

John Rigas ruled the roost at Adelphia Communications for more than fifty years, but fraudulent management and personal greed took him down, out and into federal prison for fifteen years. His son Timothy, as CFO, followed him to prison—but for twenty years.

"Adelphia" is the Greek word for "brothers." As operated by the Rigas clan, Adelphia should be identified as "family-hood."

Adelphia Communications Corporation listed John Rigas as one of its founders in 1952, and most of his fifty years of corporate service was in officer roles. His brother, Gus, helped to found the company, and sons Timothy and Michael held major positions in Adelphia as well. Timothy served as CFO in later years. The Rigas family comprised a majority of the directors of the company; John Rigas's desires and will were always approved by his board.

This Coudersport, Pennsylvania, company grew up with the nascent cable television industry, borrowed heavily to finance acquisitions of suburban cable television networks and became the fifth-largest cable supplier in the United States. They serviced 5.6 million customers over an area of thirty states.

The company also launched high-speed Internet and long-distance telephone service. Fraud and the illegal misdirection of large sums of money from the company resulted in its bankruptcy and sale to Time Warner Cable and Comcast in 2006. Adelphia Communications no longer exists.

Mr. Rigas and his family were sports enthusiasts. In 1990 they launched Empire Sports Network, added a sports talk station and in 1997 bought the NHL's Buffalo Sabres hockey team. In 1999 Adelphia purchased naming rights to the professional football stadium in Nashville, Tennessee, promptly naming it Adelphia Stadium and just as promptly having the name removed in 2002 when the company missed a payment on the purchase contract prior to filing for bankruptcy.

In May 2002 John Rigas was indicted on bank, wire and securities fraud, along with his two sons Timothy and Michael (Director of Operations, later cleared of any wrong doing). The company collapsed after prosecutors proved the Rigases used "complicated cash-management systems" to spread money around to various family-owned entities and as a cover for stealing $100 million for themselves.

The company collapsed into bankruptcy in 2002 when it revealed $2.3 *billion* of unrecorded loans to the Rigas family. Why such a huge debt was not disclosed on financial statements was never publicly stated.

John and Timothy Rigas were indicted on May 2002 and convicted in June 2004. On June 27, 2005, they were sentenced to a federal prison for fifteen years in John's case (due to his advanced age and sickness) and twenty years for Timothy. Appeals for lower court re-trials were all dismissed as was an appeal denied at the U. S. Supreme Court level. After a mistrial, son Michael did a plea bargain and was given a sentence of ten months of home confinement and two years' probation.

The maxim "crime does not pay" holds true for this family.

DR. KENNETH LEE "KEN" LAY
CEO and Board Chairman of Enron
Dead but Not Forgotten

In the May 25, 2009, issue of *The New Yorker*, a quote credited to artist Alice Neel stated: "All experience is great, providing you live through it. If it kills you, you've gone too far."

Dr. Kenneth Lay died on July 5, 2006, at the age of sixty-four in Snowmass, Colorado, while on a vacation prior to entering prison for "corporate abuse and accounting fraud." He was facing the rest of his life in prison. Was it poetic justice or cowardice? Maybe he just continued to go too far.

The term "Enron" is now synonymous with the greed displayed by its executives—with Dr. Lay leading the pack as CEO and Board Chairman for eight years. His resignation from Enron on January 23, 2006, was the result of a scandal that shook the United States and presaged the downfall of America's (and the world's) financial markets.

Dr. Lay was born in Tyrone, Missouri, on April 25, 1942, to a lay Baptist preacher and part-time tractor salesman. He was eleven years old before he lived in a house with indoor plumbing. Moving to Columbia, Missouri, Dr. Lay attended Hickman High School, and then went on to the University of Missouri where he received bachelor's and master's degrees in economics while working part-time as a painter and patching together scholarships, loans and earned income to pay for his education. He was well liked and was president of the local chapter of Beta Theta Pi fraternity. He continued his studies in economics at the University of Houston.

In 1968 he served two years in the Navy. A mentor, Professor Pinkney Walker, used his connections to get Kenneth Lay posted at the Pentagon as a Navy procurement officer, and during this period he married and had two children. He received his doctor of philosophy degree in economics from the University of Houston in 1970.

Upon graduation his first job was with the Exxon Mobil Corporation. In 1970 Pinkney Walker, his former economics professor, was appointed to the Federal Power Commission, and he took Dr. Lay along as his chief assistant. Good work led to an appointment as Deputy Under-Secretary for Energy in October 1972, where he answered directly to Rogers Morton, Secretary of the Interior. Being a friend of Texan George Bush, future President of the United States, didn't hurt. Even adopted Texans stick together.

His service in government during this period of energy crises gave Dr. Lay the opportunity to identify future business opportunities, and the following years saw his rapid rise to executive corporate positions.

After two years in Washington D. C., he returned to the private sector via an executive position with Florida Gas. Later he joined Houston Natural Gas, a large regional pipeline operator. Houston Natural Gas and Dr. Lay were involved in the acquisition of Lay's former employer, Florida Gas. Dr. Lay became CEO of the combined companies in 1985. He then turned his attention to Internorth.

Internorth, the largest natural gas pipeline company in America, was based in Omaha, Nebraska. It was a fair merger target, as company officials were fearful of a takeover by venture capitalist Irwin Jacobs of Minneapolis, who had bought a third of Internorth's shares. The merged company, HNG/Internorth, bought out Jacobs's stock position for $357 million, but incurred huge debt in doing so. It was later disclosed that $230 million of the stock purchase funds came from the company's employee retirement funds. In a masterful coup, HNG took control of the merged HNG/Internorth's board of directors. Internorth's CEO was fired, and in 1986 Dr. Kenneth Lay became CEO of HNG/Internorth. After much debate, the board adopted a new name: Enron.

In 1987 a bank notified Enron of missing money in a crude-oil account, and Dr. Lay dismissed the thought of fraud. In October of that year, Enron lost $150 million when that scam was exposed.

In 1989 Dr. Lay used his creative mind to form a "gas bank." Natural gas was deregulated by that time, and a gas bank that assured gas supplies in time of scarcity or stabilized natural gas prices in times of plenty was a boon to large users of natural gas.

The Enron Board of Directors gave Dr. Lay a special "bonus" in 1990 as compensation for good work, along with several million shares of Enron stock. Don't forget, Dr. Lay was both CEO and board chairman at the time. Jeffrey K. Skilling was hired during this period.

In 1991 President George H. W. Bush offered Dr. Lay the Cabinet post of Secretary of Commerce, but the offer was declined on the advice of his old professor, Pinkney Walker, who later said, "The position was not important enough for a person of Lay's stature."

Enron's CFO, Andrew Fastow, came up with a new use of the gas bank. He created "Cactus," a dummy corporation followed by 3,500 other dummies created by Enron. The idea was for Enron to charge these in-house corporations with accumulated debts and thereby keep the liabilities off of Enron's books—enlarging Enron's stated profit. In 1993 Enron's profits were $387 million; in 1994,

$453 million; in 1995, $520 million. In 1995 an Enron executive warned Dr. Lay of accounting irregularities, but he was ignored.

In 1997 Ken Lay and Jeff Skilling decided Enron should be an energy company. This led to major lobbying to get electricity deregulated. That happened first in California. On November 5, 1997, Enron's board approved a new off-the-books dummy corporation called Chewco. This dummy company hid $2.6 *billion* in debt while inflating profits by $405 million. With the frauds being committed systematically by Enron's executives, investors never had a chance.

By 1998 Enron had private jets, and Lay owned 20 houses and estates in Colorado and Texas. His female protégé, Rebecca Mark, set up another dummy business front called Azurix to deal with water as a commercial commodity. The financial press lauded Enron's prescience in identifying this new commodity. The enterprise was a failure.

In December 1999 Dr. Lay was considered by President-elect George W. Bush to be Secretary of the Treasury of the United States of America. He was not the final choice. During 1999 Dr. Lay received compensation from Enron in excess of $6.2 million. Mr. Fastow was allowed to form an inside company called Raptor, which was set up to buy and sell Enron stock and inflate the share price. As CFO, Mr. Fastow could manipulate Raptor, and he personally gained in the process. Raptor cost Enron $700 million that year.

In 2000 a year-end report stated, "Government investigators discovered that Enron's dummy corporations had traded natural gas and electricity *among themselves* with each trade increasingly leveraging the price until the commodities were sold to California for several times their actual market value." This practice bankrupted businesses and households, made people homeless and devastated lives. Enron claimed earnings of *$101 billion* that year.

In February 2001 Dr. Lay stepped down as CEO and Jeff Skilling took his place, with Lay remaining board chairman. In May Vice Chairman of the Board J. Clifford Baxter warned of finding "accounting irregularities." The warning was ignored. In August Skilling resigned "for personal reasons" and Dr. Lay was once again named CEO. In October Dr. Lay admitted that Enron was "missing" $1.2 billion.

In 2001 an investigative committee of the board of directors delivered "a scathing report on Enron's disastrous financial schemes." Enron declared bankruptcy on December 2, 2001. The company was $30 billion in debt, couldn't pay its bills, had defrauded its investors of $67 billion and fleeced its 21,000 employees of their retirement savings and their jobs.

On January 23, 2002, Dr. Lay resigned as CEO and Chairman of the Board. On the *TODAY* show on January 28, wife Linda Lay declared she and her husband were broke and were selling off their properties. Late in January, Vice Chairman of the Board Baxter was found dead in a locked car with a gunshot wound to the head. Enron's stock dropped from a high of $80 per share to $0.26 per share.

In July 7, 2004, Dr. Lay was indicted on eleven counts of wire fraud, securities fraud and making false statements to banks. On May 26, 2006, Dr. Lay was found guilty of ten of the eleven counts and could have been sentenced to up to twenty-five years in prison.

He died on July 5, 2006 of an apparent heart attack, escaping that prison time. His conviction was vacated because of his death, so his life's record carried no fraud convictions. His estate escaped paying the heavy fines that could have been adjudicated because he had no opportunity to appeal the guilty verdict at the trial court level.

So ended the Enron saga and Dr. Kenneth Lee Lay. You could say death was the only winner over greed. Finally, Dr. Lay learned when "enough is enough."

BERNARD JOHN EBBERS
Chief Executive Officer—Worldcom, Inc.
"The Telecom Cowboy"

Bernie Ebbers, nicknamed "the Telecom Cowboy," rode World-Com, Inc. into the ditch via the largest accounting fraud in U. S.

corporate history. That's hard to do—and he claims he doesn't know any accounting. You better believe that.

He was born in Edmonton, Canada, on August 27, 1941, 103 days before the bombing of Pearl Harbor. His father was a traveling salesman, and before Mr. Ebbers settled down back in Edmonton, the family had also lived in California and New Mexico. After his high school education, he attended the University of Alberta and Calvin College in Canada before enrolling in Mississippi College on a basketball scholarship.

His basketball scholarship ended when an injury forced him off the team in his senior year. In between school terms, he had jobs as a bouncer and a milkman, about as far apart as two occupations can be. His business career started with the operation of a chain of motels in Mississippi until, in 1983, he and other investors put money into a startup company called Long Distance Discount Services (LDDS).

Two years later he was named CEO of the new company. Over the next ten years, LDDS acquired more than sixty start-up telecommunications companies as they were formed, prospered and then sold to LDDS.

In 1995 LDDS changed its name to WorldCom. In 1996 WorldCom acquired MFS Communications, a company that had recently acquired UUNet, a company with an Internet-based network. This acquisition was worth $12 billion. At that time it was one of the largest corporate acquisitions in U. S. business history.

On October 1, 1997, WorldCom announced it was tendering an unsolicited bid for $40 billion to purchase MCI, and the deal closed in September 1998. Mr. Ebbers was really stepping out and up in the business world. In 1999 Mr. Ebbers proclaimed that they would buy Sprint Communications for the paltry sum of $115 billion. The deal collapsed due to regulatory complications.

This binge of acquisitions used primarily WorldCom stock as collateral for loans—stock whose price per share had continued to escalate. Why worry about using your company stock when you're sure the company is worth mega-billions? It hit a high of $80 per share, but shortly thereafter a downturn in the telecom market and weakness in the overall market caused the WorldCom share value to slide. Banks began to call the loans procured on margin using stock as collateral, and something had to be done quickly to find the necessary cash. To protect Mr. Ebbers from selling shares he had pledged against the loans, the board lent him corporate funds to pay his obligations.

On April 30, 2002, Mr. Ebbers resigned, and part of his separation package was a combined promissory note to the company for the money his board of directors had advanced him. This personal note was for $408.2 million.

At the height of his fortunes in early 1999, Mr. Ebbers's net worth was an estimated $1.4 billion, and he was 174th on the *Fortune* list of the 400 richest individuals. Besides his considerable holdings of WorldCom stock, he owned a 500,000-acre ranch in British Columbia; co-owned with his brother a 28,000-acre farm in Monterey, Louisiana; a majority interest in 540,000 acres of timberland in four states; a large livestock and crop farm; majority ownership of Columbus Lumber; a yacht and repair company in Georgia; nine hotels in Mississippi and Tennessee; trucking firm KLLM purchased with a partner for $30 million; and he was half-owner of a minor league hockey team.

In July 2001 he was proposed as the Chair for the President's National Security Telecommunications Advisory Committee. On June 25, 2002, WorldCom admitted to $3.85 billion in accounting misstatements, an amount that later grew to $11 billion.

On May 25, 2004, a federal indictment listed nine felonies, including false statements with security regulators and fraud. On July 13, 2005, Mr. Ebbers was sentenced to twenty-five years in federal prison.

His earliest possible release date is July 2028. He will be eighty-five years old. Some WorldCom investors sued Mr. Ebbers and others at WorldCom. Those suits settled in 2005. Over 830,000 individuals divided up $6.13 billion plus interest. It is estimated Mr. Ebbers, now in prison, had assets left totaling $50,000.

ALBERT J. DUNLAP
Chainsaw Al—Rambo in Pinstripes
"Ruthless at Sunbeam"

The Sunbeam-Oster Corporation needed new blood—whether products or marketing or executive leadership. In desperation, the board turned to Albert J. Dunlap for leadership in turning around flagging profits, upgrading its line of products and changing the way the corporation did business. Mr. Dunlap was to take the company to new heights; instead, he ran it into the ground.

The combined branding of Sunbeam and Oster in 1989 was considered a sure winner by blending the two old-line companies with their established line of small appliances. Both companies had been separate within the complex of Allegheny International and joined together after the bankruptcy of Allegheny in 1988.

All of us probably grew up with Sunbeam's Mixmaster mixers, Coffeemasters, CG waffle irons, Rain King sprinklers and T20 toasters. Oster Manufacturing of Racine, Wisconsin became famous early in the 1900s for its electric clippers, other beauty products, small electric motors for military planes during World War II and the famous Osterizer blender after the war. With established product lines like that, the combination of the two companies seemed certain to insure business success.

New products added to the old lines produced robust sales into the early 1990s—then the troubles began. Sales slowed, the board of directors was unhappy with existing lead executives and a search began for a new chief. A new CEO at Sunbeam-Oster arrived in 1996 in the person of Albert J. Dunlap, who had turned around the troubled companies of Lily Tulip Cup, Scott Paper and Crown Zellerbach. Mr. Dunlap's reputation as a stern, merciless CEO led to his nicknames "Chainsaw Al" and "Rambo in Pinstripes." He lived up to his reputation immediately upon arriving on the scene at Sunbeam.

He slashed payrolls and discarded projects and product lines as "old fashioned" and denounced his staff with angry tirades no matter who they were or what they did. Debt rose, but revenue fell. Sunbeam's stock price fell as well.

After two years Sunbeam's General Counsel, David Fannin, addressed a meeting of the board of directors in June 1998. He said, "The day-to-day atmosphere at the company has really deteriorated. Al is no longer in touch with the business and what's going on at the company. Al isn't talking to people—he has cut himself off." [http://www.businessweek.com/1999/99_42/b3651099.html].

The board (mostly hand-picked by Dunlap) was aghast at Fannin's statements, and after stormy discussions (without Dunlap present), it voted to fire Dunlap at once. It was further disclosed that the projected $80.9 million deficit in the second quarter of the fiscal year was actually $200 million. Dunlap *had* driven the company into the ground.

Losses at Sunbeam continued after Mr. Dunlap left the company, but Dunlap continued to profit from his past reputation. He traveled to Australia after he was fired as a participant in leadership lectures with Norman Schwartzkopf and Mikhail Gorbachev. A series of five lectures netted Mr. Dunlap $500,000. In his lectures, he commonly used one-liners. His favorite was, "If you want a friend, buy a dog. I've got two." That means two dogs—not two human friends.

In 2002 the SEC sued Mr. Dunlap for fraudulent accounting practices during 1998. He paid $500,000 to settle the suit, but also accepted the ruling that he could never again be an officer or director of a public company. Later in 2002 Sunbeam executives, including Dunlap, settled a Sunbeam shareholder's suit for $15 million for fraudulently raising stock prices.

During the SEC suit it came to light that a quarter of a century ago Mr. Dunlap had been fired by Nitec Paper Corporation for manipulating the reporting of amazingly high profits to justify high payouts to himself.

Leopards never change their spots. Rambo doesn't have many friends either.

DR. WILLIAM W. McGUIRE
Backdated Stock Options

The saga of Dr. William W. McGuire and the United Health Group of Minneapolis seemed to unravel and come to an end when the SEC and the IRS agreed to a settlement with Dr. McGuire on the charge of backdating stock options granted to him as part of his compensation as CEO and Chairman of the Board of United Health.

The settlement was a trivial matter—the value of the 29.6 million stock options in question was set at $2.1 billion—not exactly hay in anybody's loft. His 2005 total compensation was between $60 million and $124.8 million in stock options.

At issue in the settlement was the granting of more millions in stock options to Dr. McGuire as part of a 1996 compensation package that included salary and perks. Part of the option grants specified that Dr. McGuire could himself choose when the options were granted (also known as backdating the options) so that he could pick pricing dates for the most favorable spread when he exercised those options.

Exercising the options when the stock price was higher than the grant date allowed Dr. McGuire to insure the greatest profit on the sale of those shares.

JOHN ("JACK") FRANCIS WELCH
CEO/Chairman—General Electric
"Neutron Jack"

Born in November 1935 in Salem, Massachusetts, Mr. Welch is a graduate of the University of Massachusetts with a chemical engineering major and MS and PhD degrees from the University of Illinois. He joined General Electric ("GE") in 1960, was made a Vice President in 1972, a Vice Chairman in 1977 and Chairman and Chief Executive Officer in 1981. *Fortune* magazine named him "Manager of the Century" in 1999. He obviously had blazed a bright trail of successes while at the helm of GE. On his retirement day in 2001 the market capitalization of GE was more than $400 billion.

Today Mr. Welch is married to his third wife and is a "special partner" to her. When Mr. Welch retired from GE, the company released few details of his retirement compensation except to state he was retained at an annual $86,000 "consultant" retainer, and as long as he was an employee, GE would cover his living costs for the rest of his life. *The New York Times* quoted a 2001 GE proxy statement that retirement benefits given Mr. Welch were "unconditional and irrevocable." He was receiving an annual salary at retirement of $16.9 million per year.

In 2002 court filings associated with divorce proceedings by his second wife made public the further perks Mr. Welch received on retirement from GE, in addition to the annual $86,000 "consultant" fee:

- Use of an $80,000 per month Manhattan apartment owned by GE
- Use of GE's Boeing 737 jet plane, valued at $291,890 per month
- Use of GE's helicopter
- A cook
- A housekeeping staff
- Restaurant costs
- Country club fees
- Security service costs
- Costs of financial planning
- Toiletries
- Laundry
- Limousines
- Postage
- Newspapers
- Dry Cleaning

- Flowers
- Wine
- Use of seats at Wimbledon tennis tournament in England
- Use of courtside seats for New York Knicks basketball games
- Use of courtside seats for the U. S. Open Tennis Tournament
- Use of box seats for Boston Red Sox baseball games
- Use of box seats for New York Yankees baseball games

Mr. Welch gave up most of his perks at the time of his divorce from his second wife (who listed monthly expenses of $126,820). He is now married to his third wife. Mr. Welch claims his divorce cost him $100 million. However the above list contains only "small change" compared to the rumored GE stock "bonus" tendered to Mr. Welch upon his retirement, which may have totaled as much as $800,000,000. Yes, that is *$800 million.*

In our opinion, this kind of excessive retirement package of perks, bonuses and salaries is the direct result of Mr. Welch being both Chairman of the Board and Chief Executive Officer—at the same time. Excessive compensation delivered by a board action to an employee—with the board's chairman being that employee—is an example of poor corporate governance, to say nothing of pure greed on the part of that chairman.

The post-divorce, post-retirement Jack Welch still resides in style. He has a condo in Boston that cost him $5.5 million in 2004, a residence in Boston's Beacon Hill neighborhood and a custom-designed summer residence in Nantucket, Massachusetts.

A dynamic, active life and three wives take their toll. In 1995 he underwent a triple heart bypass surgery. Still, don't waste time pitying Jack Welch—he is getting around quite well.

JOSEPH NACCHIO
Qwest Communications International, Inc.
Historic Telecom Scandal

Mr. Joseph Nacchio was both CEO and Chairman of the Board of Qwest Communications from 1997 to 2002. He and Qwest have had a pile of legal problems due to the conviction of Mr. Nacchio on nineteen counts of insider trading and $3 billion in accounting irregularities within the company.

According to law, any conviction can be appealed to a higher court. Mr. Nacchio has done so, and two higher courts have ruled against him. He is now in the process of appealing to the United States Supreme Court. In the meantime the company has agreed to an SEC fine of $250 million for "misconduct."

Mr. Phillip Anschutz founded Qwest Communications International, Inc. in 1996. Using existing right-of-ways of Southern Pacific railroad, which he already owned, he had digital and fiber optic infrastructures laid in place. With several key mergers and acquisitions, Qwest became a major provider of local communications, extensive long-distance and broadband data services in fourteen states in the western United States.

Financial information for 2007 reveals annual revenue for Qwest of $13,778,000,000, net income of $2,917,000,000, total assets of $22,532,000,000 and 36,519 employees. A big footprint, indeed.

Mr. Joseph Nacchio was born in Brooklyn, New York, on June 22, 1949. His father was a bartender and longshoreman in New York City. Mr. Nacchio received a fine education, gathering a BS in electrical engineering, an MBA from New York University and a master's degree in management as a Sloan Fellow from MIT—hardly the caliber of education of most convicted felons.

Shortly after Qwest was formed, Mr. Nacchio was hired and served as CEO and Board Chairman from 1997 until his resignation from the company in 2002. In October 2004 the SEC sued Qwest "in a settled injunctive action" in which the company agreed to pay a $250 million penalty for the misconduct of Mr. Nacchio and eight other Qwest employees, stating that it was the result of misleading the investing public about the company's revenue and growth by "fraudulently recognizing over $3 billion in revenues and excluding $71.3 millions in expenses." [http://www.ethicalcorp.com/ content.asp?ContentID=2738]

On March 15, 2005, the SEC formally charged Mr. Nacchio and eight other employees for making "false and misleading statements to the investing public in annual, quarterly and current reports, in registration statements that incorporated Qwest's financial statements, and in other public statements, including earnings releases and investor calls." [http://www.sec.gov/News/press/ 2005-36.html].

On July 27, 2007, Mr. Nacchio was sentenced to six years in federal prison and given a federal registry number. Judge Edward Nottingham also ordered Mr. Nacchio to pay a $19 million fine and forfeit $52 million gained in fraudulent stock sales. On April 14, 2009, while his third court appeal to set aside such terms of sentencing was underway at the United States Supreme Court, he had the door slammed on him at the Federal Prison in Schuylkill County, Pennsylvania.

When Mr. Nacchio was indicted on December 20, 2005, on forty-two counts of insider trading, he was required to surrender his passport for fear he would flee the country. That was a far cry from the late 1990s when he served on two federal advisory panels—the Network Reliability and Interoperability Council and the National Security Telecommunications Advisory Committee—and was given top-secret clearance.

How does that square with the Federal Prison Registry #33973-013?

CHARLES HUMPHREY KEATING
Lincoln Savings and Loan Association
A $3.4 Billion Loss for Our Government

In his teens and early college years Charles Keating excelled as a breaststroke swimmer, set many records and earned a second place in the 1946 National AAU Championships. In his later years, as an aggressive businessman, he came in second again—when swimming in debt, he lost to the federal government on fraud charges.

Born on December 4, 1923, in Cincinnati, Ohio, his schooling included St. Xavier High School, where he obtained good grades and was on the swim team for four years as well as a participant in track and football. He helped St. Xavier win three Greater Catholic League swimming championships. He graduated from there in 1941.

After one semester at the University of Cincinnati, he left school and enlisted in the United States Navy as the country entered World War II. He was assigned to the Naval Air Force and was trained to fly carrier-based F6F Hellcats. He saw no combat, but one night he did screw up a Hellcat when he forgot to lower his landing gear and belly-landed. He was uninjured, but the plane was wrecked.

Leaving the Navy in 1945, he returned to the University of Cincinnati and worked out a plan with them to receive credit for his military service, complete six months of liberal arts courses and then enroll in law school. An All-American athlete, he continued his swimming achievements: In 1946 he won a major swim meet by defeating favorites Cornell and Yale by one foot before a packed house at Yale.

Mr. Keating continued a lifelong commitment to competitive swimming, and his son and grandson have been serious competitors at the Olympic level. He has sponsored and contributed to swimming and aquatic centers in Cincinnati and in Arizona.

He graduated from law school in 1948 and in 1949 married "an athletically-minded Catholic from an established Cincinnati family."

[Binstein, Michael; Bowden, Charles (1993). *Trust Me: Charles Keating and the Missing Billions*. Random House. ISBN 0-679-41699-4. p. 77.]

Mr. Keating joined a law firm and pursued various other commercial activities on the side. In 1952 with his brother and a law school friend, he founded the law firm of Keating, Muething & Keating. Their main client was Carl Lindner, Jr. who was aggressively accumulating ice cream stores, supermarkets, real estate and savings and loans. He ultimately became the firm's sole client. [Binstein and Bowden, *Trust Me*, pp. 88, 92.] In 1958, Mr. Keating was admitted to the U. S. Supreme Court bar.

In 1960 Lindner and Keating formed American Financial Corporation (in later years Mr. Keating was occasionally referred to as a founder), and AFC created several subsidiaries and financial products—all linked and all financed with generous lines of credit. Mr. Keating became a board member of AFC in 1963. Transactions between AFC and its subsidiaries became large and complex. One stock analyst in 1977 said, "I've never come across a company that has so much strange paper on its books." [Loomis, Carol J. (January 1977). "Carl Lindner's Singular Financial Empire." *Fortune*.]

In 1972 Mr. Keating left his law firm and joined AFC as Executive Vice President. By this time AFC had become a $1 billion company and was publicly traded. Mr. Keating gained a reputation for ruthlessly firing redundant employees after the company's numerous acquisitions. Carol Loomis asserts in the *Fortune* article that he was thought to be both aggressive and arrogant. In 1975 and 1976 several lawsuits by disgruntled shareholders were filed against AFC, and Mr. Keating was on the receiving end of complaints involving unsecured loans and stock warrants. The SEC charged both Mr. Lindner and Mr. Keating with having defrauded investors for their own benefit and for filing false reports to the SEC.

In 1976 Mr. Keating moved to Phoenix, Arizona, to operate American Continental Homes, an ailing AFC subsidiary spun off to Mr. Keating as part of his severance from AFC. In 1979 the SEC settled with AFC, and Mr. Keating signed a consent agreement. In such an agreement, generally the accused neither admits nor denies guilt but agrees to certain sanctions imposed by the agency. In this agreement, Keating vowed never to violate federal fraud and securities statutes again.

Moving to Phoenix gave Mr. Keating a much-needed new beginning. The home-building firm was losing money, but Mr. Keating began acquiring subsidiaries to form a group of linked companies in the same fashion as AFC had done. By the 1980s the company was a huge builder of single-family homes and had assets exceeding $6 billion and over 2,000 employees. Mr. Keating was a charismatic figure to his employees, who were well paid and hardworking, but Ms. Loomis noted in her 1977 article in *Fortune,* "It seems almost impossible to find anyone who actually likes Charles Keating."

The Phoenix City Council must have been an exception. They were given healthy campaign contributions in return for approving real estate developments and water features for Keating's projects.

There were other groups who either liked him or needed him: part of the complexity of Mr. Keating's aggressive character was a fierce religious faith, a passion to defeat pornography and support of Republican conservative, pro-business candidates. He was campaign manager for a few months of John Connally's failed presidential campaign in 1979. He once lent his helicopter to Mother Teresa so that she could travel to remote American Indian reservations during a trip she made to Arizona.

In 1984 his company bought Lincoln Savings and Loan Association, a slow-growth, conservatively operated thrift institution. In the early years of the Reagan administration, savings and loans had become deregulated—permitting deposits to be invested in riskier ventures. Mr. Keating promptly fired existing management, and within four years he had increased Lincoln's assets from $1.1 billion to $5.5 billion, investing in high-yield junk bonds, risky real estate schemes and questionable land investments.

In 1985 the Federal Home Loan Bank Board (FHLBB) became fearful of misuses of depositors' money since deregulation, and targeted Lincoln for examination in early 1986. Only 10 percent of the assets of a savings and loan were permitted to be in direct investments, and all hell broke loose in late 1986 when FHLBB found Lincoln had $135 million in unreported losses and had surpassed the allowed regulated investment limits by $600 million. Lincoln was in grave danger of insolvency.

Enter the Keating Five.

Mr. Keating enlisted help from five senators to urge the FHLBB to ease up on its regulations and to obtain some preferential help. These five senators were Alan Cranston (D-CA), Dennis DeConcini (D-AZ), John Glenn (D-OH), John McCain (R-AZ) and Donald Riegle (D-OH). Mr. Keating had made or would be making contributions to their political campaigns to the tune of $1.3 million. Senator McCain was a personal friend, who "had made several trips at Mr. Keating's expense, sometimes aboard American Continental's jet, for vacations at Mr. Keating's opulent Bahamas retreat at Cat Cay." [Nowicki, Dan and Muller, Bill (2007-03-01). "John McCain Report: The Keating Five". *The Arizona Republic*. Retrieved 2007-11-23.]

After being asked to lean on the FHLBB to give Lincoln a lenient audit, Mr. McCain refused to meet with Mr. Keating (who called McCain a "wimp" behind his back). [Alexander, Paul (2002). *Man of the People: The Life of John McCain*. Hoboken, New Jersey: John Wiley & Sons. ISBN 0-471-22829-X. pp. 108–111.] The group of Senators did meet twice with FHLBB in April 1987, and the result was that FHLBB took no action against Lincoln. This gave Keating time to do some restructuring of the problem investments. Later on in 1991 the Senate Ethics Committee rebuked the five senators.

Lincoln stayed in business from mid-1987 to April 1989, and its assets grew from $3.91 billion to $5.46 billion. Mr. Keating "was triumphant, having defeated the regulators." [Binstein and Bowden, *Trust Me*, p. 42.] In October 1988 Lincoln opened "The Phoenician," an extravagant resort at the base of Camelback Mountain, at a cost of over $300 million. At the same time Lincoln was planning a

20,000-acre real estate development called Estrella that was to be a model city for the twenty-first century with mixed-use commercial and residential properties. A real estate downturn in Phoenix destroyed those grandiose plans.

American Continental (Lincoln's parent) went bankrupt in April 1989 and was seized by the FHLBB. Its bonds became worthless. The total loss to the government for covering Lincoln's losses to depositors was $3.4 billion.

Mr. Keating blamed the business failures and losses on the government and its restrictive regulations. In September 1990 Mr. Keating and his associates were indicted in the State of California on forty-two counts of duping Lincoln's depositors. He was convicted in December 1991 on seventeen counts of fraud, racketeering and conspiracy. In April 1992 California Superior Court Judge Lance gave him the maximum ten year sentence, and Mr. Keating went to Federal prison in Tucson. In January 1993 a Federal conviction resulted in a twelve and a half year prison sentence based on seventy-three counts of fraud, racketeering and conspiracy. Mr. Keating was also ordered to pay restitution of $122 million to the government, but Mr. Keating said he was $10 million in debt and had no assets to sell. In another lawsuit, Mr. Keating claimed to be bankrupt, so the judge made him agree that any hidden assets that came to light would be used to pay penalties.

But that's not the end of the story. Mr. Keating had been spending as much as $1 million a month on legal counsel, and after court appeals and legal discussions, in April 1996 a California Appeals Court overturned Judge Ito's California State sentence. In December 1996 the same Appeals Court ruled error in the federal conviction based upon the State conviction appeal and threw out the federal conviction. Mr. Keating was a free man after only four-and-a-half years in prison.

In April 1999 at a retrial of the federal case, Mr. Keating pleaded guilty on four counts of wire and bankruptcy fraud. The prosecutors dropped all other charges, the Court sentenced Mr. Keating to four years in prison and then gave him credit for the four-and-a-half years he had already served—so he was a free-free man. In October 2000 the U. S. Supreme Court refused to hear a federal appeal of the State conviction. All conviction records have been erased. Mr. Keating is now maintaining a low profile in real estate in Phoenix, Arizona.

So Charles Humphrey Keating has served his time and had his record expunged? So it seems. A lot of lobbying, a lot of lawyers, a lot of money and a lot of time can make a lot of difference in outcome.

GREEDSTER SALARIES

A last word needs to be said concerning greedy salaries. When we read about celebrity salaries whether it is Hollywood figures, sports figures, media moguls, financial tycoons, titans of corporate America or the most highly regarded members of the professions of medicine, law, and education—we think that we should all aspire to earn these lofty salaries.

The truth is that we can't all earn this kind of salary. For the average American, the lottery is their only hope of achieving mega-riches. By allowing the rich and powerful to garner the resources of our country in order to live grandiose lives of luxury and excess, we deprive the average Joe of a decent, livable salary. These greedy salaries do *harm*.

The macroeconomists can better explain the distribution of income through a society, the seeds of inflationary cycles, the costs of lengthy recessions when the "bubble" bursts—but the bottom line is that prosperity in our country for the most people is painfully contracted by boom/bust economic cycles. By the time recovery occurs, the next expansion is already contracting. The middle class is the first to feel the pain, and the last to feel the gain.

With 2009 being a year of toxic assets and horrible losses, you'd think salaries, bonuses and compensation overall would suffer not only on Wall Street, but on Main Street as well. Not so:

1. Randall Stephenson, AT&T CEO, received a total pay in 2009 of $29.2 million—1,123 times the AT&T annual worker's wage of $10.00 per hour.
2. Jamie Dimon, CEO of JPMorgan Chase, was an exception. He dragged down only $1.3 million in 2009—compared to $35 million in 2008.
3. Thomas M. Ryan, CEO of CVS Pharmacy, picked up $30.4 million in 2009—1,461 times the annual average CVS worker at $8.00 per hour.
4. Robert Iger, CEO of the Walt Disney Company, put $29 million into his pocket in 2009—1,123 times the annual average worker's wage at his company of $10.00 per hour.
5. James Skinner, CEO of McDonald's, squeezed out $17.6 million in 2009, 933 times the annual wage of his average worker of $7.25 per hour.
6. Gregg Steinhafel, CEO of Target Corporation, hit the bulls-eye of $16.1 million in 2009, 728 times the annual wages of $7.25 per hour for his workers.
7. Howard Schultz, CEO of Starbucks, reaped $9.9 million in 2009, 423 times the annual wage of a $9.00 per hour barista.
8. Mark Parker, CEO of Nike, took in $7.3 million, which is 311 times the wage of his workers at $9.00 per hour.
9. James Senegal, CEO of Costco, drew only $2.3 million in 2009—115 times that of the annual wage of his $11.00 per hour workers.

The media has had a field day reporting contractual salaries for certain lead figures in the sports world. Consider the five-year salary of $19.2 million annually to be paid to basketball player LeBron James, now of the Miami Heat. Owners of several other clubs flocked to Cleveland to woo the self-named "King" to no avail. On top of his annual salary, Mr. James is assured of endorsements paying him as follows:

1. Nike—$12 million
2. Coca Cola—$5 million
3. McDonalds—$5 million
4. State Fair—$5 million
5. Upper Deck—$2 to 3 million
6. MSN—$2 to 3 million
7. Cub Cadet—$1 million
8. Wiiplay—$1 million

[Data: Burns Entertainment/Sports Marketing]

After the infamous telecast of James' choice of Miami over Cleveland and others, the positive rating of James by his public dropped from 92% to 79% in one day. His salary with Miami plus endorsements will total $54 million per year—that is $660,000 per game for a season of eighty-two games. The public will pay and pay—and pay.

Phil Jackson, the former NBA Lakers' coach, earned nearly $12 million in 2010 before becoming a free agent in 2011. He is weighing his options as to where he will be coach in the future. You can bet his annual salary would be in the multi-millions of dollars per year. That's the way the basketball bounces these days.

Yankees third baseman and star hitter, Alex Rodriguez (or "A-Rod" as he is known), has the richest contract in baseball history, and that will earn him $27.5 million per year through 2017. Yes, he's a game-winning player and all that goes with it, but playing baseball used to be a fun game. The fans are the ones that now pay through their noses to be entertained by watching Mr. Rodriguez.

Philadelphia's first baseman, Ryan Howard, has signed a new five-year contract worth $125 MILLION. For the baseball seasons of 2012 through 2016, he will average $25 million per year!

In July 2010 it was announced that the New Jersey Devils hockey team signed a contract with Ilya Kovalchuk for seventeen years totaling $102 million. Ilya gets $95 million over the first ten years and $7 million over the last seven years. By the end of the contract, Ilya will be forty-four years old.

In 2009 the highest paid executives of companies listed in the S & P 500 were:

Carol Bartz	Yahoo!	$47.2 million
Marc Casper	Thermo Fisher Scientific	$34.1 million
J. Raymond Elliot	Boston Scientific	$33.3 million
Ray Irani	Occidental Petroleum	$31.4 million

The Wall Street Journal listed the salaries of college presidents for the college year 2007-2008.

Rensselaer Polytechnic Institute, New York	$1.5 million
Suffolk University – Oklahoma	$ 1.49 million
Webster University – Missouri	$ 1.43 million
American University – Washington, D. C.	$ 1.42 million
Columbia University – New York	$ 1.38 million
DePauw University – Indiana	$ 1.3 million
Vanderbilt University – Tennessee	$ 1.28 million

Twenty-three private colleges averaged in excess of $1 million
The median for all colleges and universities– $358,746

The legal profession extracts fancy fees. Top lawyers bill clients $750 to $1,000 per hour, and charge $400 per hour for "associates." One bankruptcy firm working on the AIG case has collected millions of dollars in fees, including a charge of $2.54 for chewing gum.

Executives of media companies aren't exactly shy about taking fat salaries for the year 2009.

Leslie Moonves, CBS	$43 million
Philippe Dauman, Viacom	$34 million
Sumner Redstone, Viacom & CBS	$33 million
Brian Roberts, Comcast	$25 million
Stephen Burke, Comcast	$31 million

The fine arts are no exception when it comes to annual salaries. For the year 2009:

Zarin Menfa, New York Philharmonic	$ 2.67 million
Peter Gelb, Metropolitan Opera	$ 1.35 million
Glen Lowry, Museum of Modern Art	$ 1.32 million
Reynold Levy, Lincoln Center for Performing Arts	$ 1.18 million
Earl Potter, III, National Gallery of Art	$ 1.06 million
Clive Gillinson, Carnegie Hall	Less than $1 million
Joan Rosenbaum, Jewish Museum	$ 249,000

In a time when we don't fully understand what kind of changes are occurring to our planet; when we don't know what the lives of our children and our grandchildren may be; when we don't know what innovations will be necessary to cope with the crises of depletion of resources—wouldn't it make sense to figure out what we really need to live? We could re-build the infrastructure and economy of our country to provide good lives for all, and not just for the lucky few born with the talent to make money or the greedy appetite to take it from others.

THE LAX STANDARDS OF THE BOARDS OF DIRECTORS

Chapter 9 – Synopsis

"Ultimate Responsibilities"

Several reasons have been cited by the professionals as to the causes of the financial turmoil of the 2007 to 2012 period and beyond. Boards of directors of our companies are at least partially at fault. The failure to demand full transparency, the laxity of measuring the degree of risks taken by the corporate body and the failure to maintain a reasonable check on levels of executive compensations are all board responsibilities—and they were not properly executed in too many cases.

The "cozy" relationships between most CEOs and their boards resulted in flawed performances by boards when executing their duty to the shareholders whom they represent.

The CEO and the board chairman should never be one and the same person, although this combination has become a common practice.

A suggested corporate organizational chart is included in this book for the makeup of any public stock corporation with an independent full-time outside auditor, an internal SEC compliance officer and a strong but independent relationship between the company's board of directors and its CEO. The board of directors should and must do more than merely give a rubber stamp of approval to CEO requests.

Chapter 9

THE LAX STANDARDS OF BOARDS OF DIRECTORS

UNDERSTANDING SHAREHOLDER RESPONSIBILITY

There is no shortage of culprits to bear the blame for the financial crisis of 2007-2012. But, in my opinion, the fundamental responsibility for the excesses of compensation and laxity of control over the Chief Executive Officer of a corporation should and must rest on the shoulders of the independent boards of directors of publicly traded companies. Many boards of directors failed to exercise their obligations to the shareholders they served during this crisis.

In the period of 2007-2012 ten of the twenty largest bankruptcies in United States business history occurred. The giant corporations that declared bankruptcy were not only from the financial and real estate industries but also included General Motors and Lyondell Chemical Company.

Corporate employees, including the CEO, the President (if that office is separately occupied), the CFO and other senior officers, bypassed or inadequately informed their boards of corporate matters of the highest significance to the corporations' solvency.

Corporate bylaws place the final responsibility for major acts and decisions of a company on its directors under the leadership of the Chairman of the Board. Many boards have been and continue to be weak—not due to the members' unsuitability to serve *per se,* but rather due to a hasty and careless selection process that does not create a truly independent board.

Strong boards of directors must again assume their defined roles of control and oversight of corporate decisions.

Any corporation that markets its ownership by selling shares of stock to the public is actually owned by its investors, the shareholders. In the company's annual report and at the annual meeting of shareholders, the shareholders are advised of the qualifications of a slate of nominees to be elected to the board of directors for a term stated in the corporate bylaws. The shareholders elect the board based on one vote per share of stock owned. Frequently, smaller shareholders submit a proxy by mail to vote their shares. The controlling majority of the outstanding shares tend to be in the hands of principals in the company and institutional shareholders. But it is the responsibility of all shareholders to examine carefully the reports submitted to them. Diligent shareholders can and do attend the annual meeting and do question management about the slate of directors to be elected, corporate activities, debt obligations, executive compensation and other issues.

The board of directors is designed to oversee, monitor and control the decisions and actions of employees who are performing in the workplace on behalf of the company. These actions must conform to the law and be compliant with the requirements of the SEC and other federal and state regulations. The board must also conduct the business of the company within the dictates of its own corporate bylaws.

One of the primary functions of a board is to recruit and approve senior management for the company. The board hires, and can fire, the CEO. The board can terminate any senior officer of the corporation who fails to perform duties or behaves in an irresponsible manner.

Compensation for the senior officers is also decided and approved by the board of directors. Overall corporate salaries can, and should, be determined and monitored by the board.

Awarding excessive annual salaries, obscene "retention bonuses," outrageous "performance bonuses," expensive fringe benefits ("perks"), "golden parachutes," "golden coffins" and other innovative compensation packages must be approved by the board of directors—and the ultimate responsibility for how these decisions impact the financial health of the company rests with them.

The board must also approve all decisions with major consequences to a company. Contracts, mergers and acquisitions, debt obligations, risk management and employee stock option plans are all matters that should come before the board.

Choosing an independent auditor to review and prepare financial statements for the corporation is one of the single most important functions of the board. The board's relationship with the auditors must be completely ethical and without conflicts of interest. Reputable auditors certify to a board of directors that the financial management of a company is sound and in accordance with generally accepted accounting principles, that the company is in compliance with applicable rules and regulations and that corporate taxes are being paid in a timely fashion. They can also consult on industry-wide benchmarks for salaries and bonuses and the percentage of the budget that can responsibly be distributed in compensation to employees.

The general counsel and in-house legal staff generally retain an outside law firm(s) to review corporate documents, contracts, assess legal liabilities and risks and conduct specialized legal matters such as stock issues, debt offerings, litigation and other issues beyond the scope of inside counsel. The choice of outside legal counsel is also subject to the approval by the board of directors.

In summary, *a public stock company is owned by its SHAREHOLDERS who elect an INDEPENDENT BOARD OF DIRECTORS to represent them and supervise the activities of the company IN THEIR BEHALF.*

THE BOARD MEETING
More Political than Politics

Being a director on a public company's board is a serious job. Being responsible for decisions that may have lasting and unpredictable effects is not the only risk undertaken—there is also exposure to liability by serving on the board. Shareholders, customers, creditors and competitors can and do include directors and officers of a company as defendants in lawsuits. Liability insurance policies that protect boards of directors are available, but such protection carries an expensive premium. Imagine being sued as a director of Merrill Lynch or Enron or AIG's board! Few today would join a board of such a company without directors' and officers' liability insurance coverage—and yet it must be stated that not being indemnified would increase the due diligence of directors in executing their responsibilities.

Muriel Humphrey, wife of former Vice-President Hubert Humphrey, was a board member for each of the thirty-five mutual funds of the Investors Group, Inc. She and two other women served as directors, and they represented 2,000,000 women shareholders. On board meeting days, a luncheon at the Minneapolis Club was served. After a particularly stormy board meeting one noonday, Mrs. Humphrey paused on the street curb to say, "You know, these board meetings are more political than politics."

She was right, and being a good board member has many ramifications. Among the major issues faced by directors are dealing with audits, contracts, performances and frivolous lawsuits. Directors' opinions and voting alliances will shift issue to issue based on their background and information. The board is a team, but one in which each member must think and act on decisions independently.

CEO AND CHAIRMAN OF THE BOARD
They Must Not Be the Same Person

One of the most important issues facing a director is keeping the company's CEO on a short leash. A good CEO runs a tight ship, but knows when he or she is about to cross the line that will require board action. Most issues require multiple decisions on a continuum from major to minor—discerning when a decision must be taken to the board can be quite difficult. The chairman of the board must constantly remain apprised of current business conditions that may have an impact on the company.

The board chairman MUST be an independent director. Too frequently the CEO is also the chairman of the board. It is bad practice to allow the CEO to decide the agenda of the board. The evidence for chief executive officers' inability to resist their own greed is clear and compelling. The CEO as chairman of the board can direct his or her own compensation and that of the company's executive officers. The officers will then be in collusion with the CEO to manipulate excessive salaries, bonuses and perquisites for all concerned.

A classic case of a greedy CEO and board chairman is John Rigas, founder of Adelphia Communications ("Adelphia") detailed in an earlier chapter. An early leader in cable operations, Rigas had a successful company collapse around him due to an unwarranted binge of cash withdrawals by him and his family. Adelphia's board rubber stamped actions by Rigas because four members of his family (including three of his sons) were on the nine-person board. The result was a raid on this successful company's assets and cash that totaled a staggering $2.3 billion. The money was spread among several family-owned companies and a long list of personal luxuries totaling over $100 million. The expenditures included a golf course, a hockey team and real property on which Adelphia paid $2 million just in building and property maintenance fees. Adriana Huffington alleges in *Pigs at the Trough* that the senior Rigas bought a piece of property for $465,000 and promptly sold the timber rights to Adelphia for a measly $26 million! [Huffington, Arianna, *Pigs at the Trough: How Corporate Greed and Political Corruption Are Undermining America,* (New York: Three Rivers Press, 2004).]

After John Rigas and son Timothy were convicted of bank and securities fraud, the common stock of Adelphia dropped 99 percent and shareholder equity took a $6 *billion* hit. The federal prosecutor, Jacob S. Frenkel, was quoted as follows in the *Pittsburgh Post-Gazette*, "The Adelphia Corporation is the ultimate in corporate board rooms out of control. This is big time looting of a public company." [http://www.post-gazette.com/pg/04191/343793-28.stm].

Another example of a public stock corporation with a compromised board of directors is Global Crossing, Ltd. This corporation was a Tier One global communications provider and developer of fiber optic cable networks. It operated in more than sixty countries with headquarters in Hamilton, Bermuda. In 1997 founder Gary Winnick created Global Crossing by absorbing a venture capital company owned by him and three associates. Winnick was named CEO and Chairman of the Board for at least a year, and a procession of CEO's followed him almost annually. Through acquisitions with cash and stock, the company appeared to prosper. But in some of these transactions nothing of value was exchanged—fraudulent accounting made it appear that the transactions were profitable on the financial statements. Within four-years-time after Winnick cashed in on almost $420 million of Global Crossing shares in 1997, other executives also reaped nearly $900 million. By 2002 the cash draw and stock sales proved too heavy a load for this company, and Global Crossing filed for bankruptcy—but not before Winnick made an additional $734 million selling his shares before the company's stock price tumbled. At the time it was the third-largest bankruptcy in U.S. history (the Global Crossing bankruptcy is now ranked fifteenth largest in our business history according to http://www.bankruptcydata.com).

A point of interest: In 1998 former president George H. W. Bush was given $50,000 of Global Crossing stock for making a speech in Japan on behalf of the corporation. He sold his stock over the next two years and realized a profit of more than $4.5 million as Global Crossing shares experienced a major increase in per share value due to acquisitions and revenue. It is clearly very lucrative to be connected to a company with a friendly board of directors. [http://archive.newsmax.com/archives/articles/2002/2/15/154416.shtml].

Merrill Lynch is another example of the flagrant misuse of power by a CEO who is also serving as Chairman of the Board. In October 2007 the Board of Directors ousted Mr. Stanley O'Neal as CEO and installed John Thain as both CEO and board chairman. On his watch the "net" *profits* in 2008 for Merrill Lynch were *negative* $7,777,000,000—a loss in the billions of dollars—and this 100-year-old company had to be put on the auction block. Bank of America quickly offered $50 billion for Merrill Lynch but wanted to back out of the purchase when it was disclosed that the 2008 loss would be much greater than stated earlier.

As the deal was about to close in late 2008, Thain pushed through a bonus package of $700 million for Merrill employees—including a $10 million bonus for himself. He had lost more than ten times his bonus amount in 2008 as CEO of Merrill Lynch. The resultant outrage echoed from end to end of Wall Street. Thain responded by waiving the $10 million bonus but did accept a senior executive position with Bank of America. His tenure at BofA lasted two weeks before he was forced to resign. The government ultimately guaranteed about $97 million in losses of BofA's assets—most of it coming from Merrill. In late 2009, with the bank under investigation for the irregularities in the acquisition of Merrill, BofA's beleaguered CEO Ken Lewis, age sixty-two, also announced his retirement.

The following are major examples of the relationships of corporate CEO's, their recent compensations and their affiliations with other corporate boards:

Kenneth D. Lewis, *Bank of America*, (formerly with Goldman Sachs)
    CEO and Chairman of the Board since 2001
    2007 Total compensation: $20,404,000
    2008 Total compensation: $9,003,467
    Total wealth (2008): $202,061,123

James M. Crachiolo, *Ameriprise Financial*
    CEO and Chairman of the Board since 2005
    2007 Total compensation: $23,053,075
    2008 Total compensation: $ 11, 970,932
    Total wealth: $60,895,407
    Former board member: Tech Data

Kenneth I. Chenault, *American Express*
    CEO and Chairman of the Board since 2000
    2007 Total compensation: $7,807,209
    2008 Total compensation: N/A
    Total wealth: $163,053,178
    Board member: Procter & Gamble; IBM

Frederic M. Poses, *Trane Co.*
    CEO and Chairman of the Board since 2000
    2007 Total compensation: $7,807,209
    2008 Total compensation: N/A
    Chairman of the Board: Tyco Electronics
    Board member: Centex; Raytheon

Warren E. Buffett, *Berkshire-Hathaway*
   CEO and Chairman of the Board since 1970
   2007 Total compensation: $175,000
   2008 Total compensation: $175,000
   Total wealth: $61,704,795,280
   Former board member: Washington Post
   Former board member: Gillette
   Former board member: Coca Cola

Lloyd Blankfein, *Goldman Sachs*
   CEO and Chairman of the Board since 2006
   2007 Total compensation: $53,965,418
   2008 Total compensation: $-n/a-
   Total wealth: $593,507,665

John T. Chambers, *Cisco*
   CEO since 1995 and Chairman of the Board since 2006
   2007 Total compensation: $12,801,773
   2008 Total compensation: $18,767,149
   Total wealth: $272,414,200
   Former board member: Wal-Mart

James D. Sinegal, *Costco*
   President/CEO/Board Member
   2007 Total compensation: $3,120,888
   2008 Total compensation: $3,767,149
   Total wealth: $180,946,187

Douglas R. Conant, *The Campbell Soup Company*
   President/CEO/Board member
   2007 Total compensation: $9,518,299
   2008 Total compensation; $9,508,001
   Total wealth: $93,147,405

Seven of the nine CEOs of the above corporations are both CEO and Chairman of the Board of their respective companies. Their total compensations for 2007 and 2008 were large, with 2008 on average less than 2007, indicating that the better part of compensation packages were in stock or stock options, the value of which had taken a hit in 2008. However, the size of compensation indicates an obvious tie between the CEO and board-approved compensation.

A strong movement is afoot to sever that tie between CEOs and their board chairmanships. In March 2009 more than fifty leaders of industry, investment and government met to endorse board oversight of company managers by splitting the two functions. The group announced such a splitting would enhance overall performance—and not just limited to increased shareholder returns. They were considering proposing to the New York Stock Exchange and NASDAQ "to adopt listing rules requiring separation of CEO and Chairmanship of the Board."

More than 37 percent of U.S. companies now require such separation. About 79 percent of British companies require separation, and all German and Dutch companies have "two-tier" CEO-Chairmanship separation. Why is the United States so far behind?

According to The Corporate Library, a corporate research firm in Portland, Maine, "businesses with single CEO/Chairman tend to have less shareholder-friendly governance practices, long-tenured leaders, infrequent board meetings and 'classified' boards that serve staggered terms rather than annual terms—all of which make it "more difficult to retain independent board control." [http://online.wsj.com/article/ SB123816562313557465.html]. A board that continues to allow the CEO to also serve as chairman of the board is a manifestation of a board that is reluctant to challenge a strong CEO, and it is all the more reason to separate the two functions.

After its April 2008 annual meeting directors of the Seattle thrift, Washington Mutual, voted its CEO, Kerry Killinger, out of the position of Chairman of the Board (which he had cornered for seventeen years), and in September they ousted him as CEO, just before the corporation was seized by the federal government. The dual role of Mr. Killinger as CEO-Chairman of the Board was death to that once-thriving thrift corporation.

Mr. Dennis Carey, a senior partner in the "head hunter" firm of Korn/Ferry has a contrary opinion, "Most CEOs prefer to chair their boards because one boss at the helm [of the company] is better than two." [http://online.wsj.com/ article/SB123816562313557465.html]. The negative issues of unclear chain of command and conflicts between the two executives *can* distract management and staff from the corporate goals.

That is not the sentiment expressed by Mr. Harry Pearce, Chairman of the Board of MDU, a natural resources company in Bismarck, North Dakota and a retired former Vice Chairman of General Motors. After the experience of being a lead director for five years, he insists upon debates by the full board about issues such as risk management. "A board with an outside chairman is better equipped to assure that appropriate risks are being assessed." [http://online.wsj.com/article/SB123816562313557465.html].

A recent social study pointed out that 37 percent of the independent directors on bank boards had important ties to the CEO such as club memberships, college affiliations or congenial volunteer relationships with the same charitable or community organizations. A UCLA Anderson School of Management study of 20,000 board members of 2,080 firms from 1999 to 2007 found that personal connections between CEOs and independent directors correlated with earnings restatements and merger decisions that hurt companies' earnings performance.

Recipients of TARP bailout money had a higher than industry average of connections between CEOs and independent directors who were "cozy" colleagues. [http://www.usatoday.com/money/industries/banking/2009-04-02-gm-aig-citigroup-tarp_N.html]. However, the Anderson School of Management study found *no* relationships between AIG's CEO Martin Sullivan and his board while the insurance industry as a whole had 20 percent of independent directors with personal ties to the CEO. When Sullivan took over from Maurice R. ("Hank") Greenburg as CEO of AIG in 2005, more than 60 percent of AIG's independent directors had ties with Greenburg who had been named CEO by company founder Cornelius Vander Starr in 1968 and served as CEO for thirty-seven years.

As CEO Sanford ("Sandy") Weill was adding acquisitions to Citigroup, as many as eight of his directors had close ties with him, and this was "far above the norm" according to the Anderson School report. [http://www.usatoday.com/money/industries/banking/2009-04-02-gm-aig-citigroup-tarp_N.html].

* * *

What can investors learn from this?

Lesson #1: *The CEO and the board chairman should never be the same person.*
Lesson #2: *A company that has a majority of its Board of Directors related to the CEO does not have an independent board.*
Lesson #3: *The Board of Directors must be strictly independent from the CEO despite social relationships that may exist among them.*

NUMBER OF MEMBERS ON A BOARD OF DIRECTORS

The number of members on a board of directors is a further critical issue. First of all, the number should always be an odd one to avoid a tie vote on important and controversial issues. Too few board members make it easy for a small group to control an important issue. Conversely, too large a number can become unmanageable (General Motors which declared bankruptcy in June 2009 had twenty-nine directors on its board prior to reorganization).

In my experience, companies found nine to thirteen directors to be ideal. This board complement is large enough for diversity in gender, race, location, expertise, and general business acumen. It is possible to achieve a quorum despite absences due to weather or illness.

Enlisting a strong and diversified board can be difficult. Directors are now subject to lawsuits, public exposure and unwanted media attention. Serving on the board of a developing company is hard work. In spite of these negative aspects of board participation, if offered the opportunity, we urge every qualified person to serve as a director of a for-profit or not-for-profit organization. The well being of our financial system depends on integrity and commitment to sound business practice.

BOARD MEMBER COMPENSATION

Compensation for board members encompasses a wide range of appropriate remuneration. Remember, the board member must keep abreast of company affairs. This may entail a good deal of effort beyond attendance at monthly, bi-monthly or quarterly meetings. Generally an annual fee is paid for basic attendance with reimbursement for other expenses such as travel. A valid reason for non-attendance at a meeting counts as being present as long as voting on certain issues can be accomplished by conference telephone calls or video.

A recent compensation survey reported an average board of directors, *in total*, costs a company about $500,000 annually—with a high figure of $2,500,000 and $50,000 at the low end. It is customary for a director of a not-for-profit organization to serve without a fee. Some privately held corporations, depending upon conditions, pay very nominal fees to their directors. The majority of publicly held corporations pay additional fees for committee work, per diem expenses and travel costs.

A board of directors generally has the following committees: executive, audit, compensation, governance, personnel and real estate. An independent director can serve on more than one committee at a time, and, depending on the issues at hand and the company involved, can easily "earn" more than $100,000 annually. A typical, fair annual director's fee in 2010 for a moderately sized company should be $50,000 with the chairman paid $60,000. An additional $2,500 for service on a board committee (plus out-of-pocket expenses) is adequate compensation.

MULTIPLE BOARD CONFLICTS

A director of one board may serve on other unrelated boards, but it is extremely poor practice to serve on conflicting boards. There are "professional" directors who can earn annual incomes in excess of $1 million just serving on corporate boards. If a corporation is involved in a merger, lawsuit or in severe financial trouble, a director may attend extensive meetings and earn several million dollars in fees. In this way, a corporate director can make board service financially worthwhile, but the director may also be subject to judgments for damages from corporate liabilities or lawsuits.

LIABILITIES OF DIRECTORS

With each passing year, liabilities associated with serving on corporate boards increase. Attracting a panel of qualified, independent directors has become an arduous task. Today not many things in life are free—being a respectable independent director on a corporate board of consequence is a risk that must be carefully and fully examined.

The acceleration of fees paid to independent directors may help to offset the liability risk. But in many states declaring bankruptcy insulates the corporation from shareholder suits for poor performance. The door is left open, however, for shareholders to sue independent directors for malfeasance of duty. If a corporation has a recent record of losing billions of dollars, and the value per share has dropped dramatically, shareholders may sue directors for poor performance. Many very large corporations have declared bankruptcy in recent years. Shareholder lawsuits pose a serious threat to an individual director, and, if successful, damages can be assessed that run to millions of dollars.

Indemnification of directors by the corporation may mean that the company will reimburse directors for expenses incurred defending lawsuits brought against them while serving on the board of directors. Officers and directors' liability insurance is increasingly difficult to find, and adequate coverage can be prohibitively expensive.

Recognizing that liability issues would inhibit independent directors from joining boards, many states have created statutes allowing indemnification and insurance for officers and directors by corporations. But before joining a board, the pertinent business law for the state governing the corporation's business activities must be carefully examined by the potential director or his counsel.

Harvey Golub, formerly a senior partner of McKinsey and Co., CEO and Chairman of the Board of American Express and a director of Dow Jones & Co., Inc., is now Chairman of the Board of Campbell Soup Company (2011). He was formerly board chair for AIG, but resigned due to severe conflicts with the CEO. According to Equilar, an executive compensation data base, his chairman's fee at Campbell Soup is approximately $775,000 annually plus perquisites and retirement agreements that extend his total director's compensation to well over a million dollars.

In our opinion, his personal liability exposure is increased by the number of other corporations and organizations that he serves: trustee of American Enterprise Institute, board chair of Clientlogic Corporation, treasurer of Lincoln Center for the Performing Arts, trustee of New York-Presbyterian Hospital, board chair of Reader's Digest Association, Inc. and board chair of Ripplewood Holdings

LLC. As a "professional" director, he is exposed to a great deal of risk.

The March 24, 2008 issue of *Industry Week* cited a study by The Corporate Library that found the total board compensation for over 3,000 corporations averaged over $1 million. However 32 percent of those surveyed paid their boards less than $500,000 total. At the extreme end of those surveyed, Valero Energy paid about $30,000,000 annually to its Board "with most of that sum going to a single director."

Liability threats aside, if the average *individual* board member of a major company receives $500,000 annually as compensation for six regular meetings consuming one day each plus two days travel and as many days of preparation and study of board materials provided prior to the meeting, their thirty-six days of service would equate to remuneration of nearly $14,000 per day.

Even with extra days spent monitoring company affairs, a board chair receiving $1 million per year in compensation could receive as much as $30,000 per day or $3,500 per hour or more for an eight-hour day. Not bad—but never forget the risks involved. A $5 million dollar judgment in a shareholder suit would quickly wipe out this income. The hope that the chair's fees will hedge the possible liabilities is a gamble the chairman of the board must be willing to assume.

WEAKNESSES OF DIRECTORS

At the time of publication of this book, financial developments dominate media coverage. A case in point is General Motors. Long regarded as the soundest and most continually profitable U.S. corporation, GM filed for bankruptcy on June 1, 2009, after a cry for help by GM to the government because they were "too big to fail." Even the $19.4 billion infused by the government couldn't save what was once the world's largest company.

Among the thousands of reasons that GM failed, two serious issues surfaced: **The Board of Directors was lax in its oversight** *and weak in its leadership. The CEO was also the Chairman of the Board of Directors.*

The *Wall Street Journal* of March 31, 2009, ran an article about GM's board. It was composed of eleven independent directors (nine men, two women), and the CEO/Chairman was the only GM executive on the board. This board of March 2009 was defined as "a collection of failed CEOs." On March 30 President Obama agreed to further help GM with additional billions if they cleaned up their act, fired CEO Rick Wagoner, and appointed an independent director as chairman of the board. [It should be noted that while he was immediately removed as CEO, Mr. Wagoner's "instant" retirement payout amounted to more than $20,000,000 even though during his tenure as CEO he had lost billions of dollars for GM and its shareholders.]

The old GM board of eleven independent directors and its one insider, CEO Rick Wagoner, were regarded as lax (meaning "weak") because most of the directors had been on the board for years, were retired CEOs of other companies and were years removed from carrying the sole responsibility for current managerial practices. Ralph Ward, editor of *Boardroom Insider,* had remarked, "Replacing such an entrenched board will be a nightmare situation to attract good people."

A new Corporate Governance Guidelines for GM was passed in July, amended in September 2009 and posted on the company's website. Criteria for the selection of directors is clearly set forth. It's a very tough assignment to locate and recruit such a board. Who would want to serve under these circumstances? But, interestingly, while the corporate governance guidelines clearly intended that the CEO and the chairman of the board be different individuals, the same person holding both positions was not prohibited. Former AT&T CEO, Edward E. Whitacre, Jr., did indeed assume both as interim positions. On January 28, 2010, Whitacre dropped the "interim" title and accepted the board's invitation to become Chairman of the Board and CEO of General Motors.

Detailed history of a corporation like GM is available on the Internet, and it is prudent for shareholders to inform themselves about such management overhauls. Information regarding new directors to be elected at an annual meeting of a public corporation will be in the proxy material mailed to every shareholder with proper notice before the meeting. If you are a shareholder, be sure to read it carefully. Usually, a new director will have biographical information provided such as experience, directorships of other companies, and stock ownership if it is a material position. Watch for conflicts of interest—be wary of service on multiple boards of similar companies or competitors.

Interlocking boards are also of concern—"You serve on my board, and I'll serve on yours." These reciprocal arrangements can be hard to determine, but through strategic questions and inquiries they can be smoked out. "Old-boy" networks are common in financial circles.

AGE LIMITS FOR DIRECTORS

Many boards have age limits for members. The ranks of retired CEOs are a common source for recruiting board members. Those executives who retire early are prime candidates as their experiences are valuable and timely. They frequently miss the challenges of "big business." A retirement age for a director is usually seventy-five years. One group of mutual funds had former president Gerald Ford as a director. When he reached the age of seventy-five, an amendment to the corporate bylaws was passed as follows: "it is not mandatory for an ex-President of the United States to leave the Board at age seventy-five."

LENGTH OF SERVICE ON THE BOARD OF DIRECTORS

Age aside, the term length of a director's service is often determined by "class" with each "class" serving an initial three years with two successive terms totaling a maximum of nine years of service. When first elected to a board, the new director becomes a member of the "Class of 2010" and, if re-elected twice, would serve until 2019. If the class term was two years, a total of six years could be served. Having class terms makes it possible for the standing board members to provide continuity for the corporation. Staggered terms are sometimes used to "pack" a board, arranging new board members to come and go on irregular years to maintain friendly board control.

"INSIDERS" SHOULD BE IN THE MINORITY

Another issue is how many directors are allowed to sit on the board from within the company in question. It's common to have at least one company "liaison" director from the executive branch of the company to provide information and answer questions from the board. The CEO of the company usually fulfills that role, but may or may not have a vote. Certainly, the CEO should not have a vote on his or her personal compensation, employment or retirement terms and conditions.

It is most important for the board to be strictly independent of the company on whose board they serve. One way to assure that is to have a majority of the voting board be independent directors—or even better, have a super-majority to avoid company partiality when the chips are down on an important issue. Know your votes.

Voting control is always a thorny issue, especially if an issue splits the independent directors. When independent directors split, inside directors can join with the side necessary to get a favored vote. When push comes to shove, fewer company-oriented directors on the board are better.

This is why, as Muriel Humphrey has said, "Serving on boards is more political than politics." The company and the board personnel are human beings with personal views. A board member should serve with the best interest of the company in mind. However there can be times when loyalties are tested or one or more factors are in dispute. A nominal number of seven, nine or eleven (always an odd number) of independent directors can usually resolve these kinds of conflicts, but a super-majority is convenient for one side. There is nothing worse than dissension at the board level, but a board's purpose is to discuss or debate the issues and vote each to his or her own mind as to what is best for the company—friendship or family relationships aside.

BOARD OVERSIGHT OF EXECUTIVE COMPENSATION

The disclosure of excessive CEO salaries for 2008-2011 has put extreme pressure on the compensation committee of boards of directors. To quote Dean Thomas Cooley of Stern School of Business of New York University, "Executive salary excesses are the fault of the Compensation Committee of the respective Board of Directors." Proper and reasonable oversight is a prime duty of the each board's compensation committee.

FINANCIAL OVERSIGHT BY BOARDS

The Sarbanes-Oxley Act of 2002 is commonly referred to as "SOX" but is officially called Bill 166 Statute 745, enacted on July 31, 2002 as the "Public Accounting Reform and Investor Protection Act of 2002." This bill has raised the responsibility of boards and more particularly their audit committees regarding the financial affairs of the corporation they represent. Internal control of accounting and auditing of the company is a *direct* responsibility of the board of directors on behalf of the shareholders. Lack of detailed oversight by boards is just one of the causes of the 2007-2011 meltdown. Consequently most public companies have hired or will hire an independent internal auditor, on duty at all times, to report to the senior officers of the company, the board chairman and the board's audit committee.

An internal employee or SEC regulator should assess compliance with appropriate federal regulations.

The board's audit committee must have a majority of its members who are of independent status, and at least one member must be an expert in accounting practices, if not a certified public accountant.

These added responsibilities imposed upon the boards of directors, and more specifically audit committee members, have had a profound effect on those who serve as expert advisers. Liability insurance premiums go up and up linked with the exposure to greater potential damages. This situation has resulted in a two-fold impact on the total cost of a corporate board: insurance premiums for coverage to indemnify directors escalates as threats of liability rise, and fees paid to directors rise as fewer qualified executives are available to serve as board members in these circumstances.

THE GOVERNMENT AS A SHAREHOLDER

Government infusion of capital as bailout money, massive loans of billions of dollars to ailing companies and the resultant equity position in many of these companies by the federal government have made it a shareholder and major creditor of private businesses. Government has tremendous leverage on management when it attains an ownership portion of a company, and the government is flexing its ownership muscles by demanding resignations of CEOs in charge when companies began to founder. Board chairs are being replaced by other board members or are forcefully removed from the boards entirely.

Instances of the government being a powerful stockholder are very clear with General Motors, AIG, Merrill Lynch, Bank of America and a myriad of others who have accepted TARP money. Many are assiduously repaying their TARP bailouts to get rid of the U. S. government as a shareholder. Until the government is reimbursed its TARP money and other advances *with interest*, goateed Uncle Sam in his red, white and blue hat has bought into the corporate family with wads of shares in his hind pocket. He will be involved in resolving issues of executive employment contracts, compensation, adequate independent board oversight, and the concomitant costs of the troubled companies.

As already cited, in March 2009 General Motors received billions of dollars in loans from the federal government—and that's us. Details of the loan stipulated that a majority of its twelve-person Board of Directors had to be replaced "over a period of several months." CEO Rick Wagoner (not Chairman of the Board) was the only GM employee on the board and had to retire on orders from this new and powerful shareholder and creditor—a highly unusual demand. A current board member, Kent Kresa, was named interim board chairman and Frederick ("Fritz") Henderson took over as CEO of the corporation.

The GM corporate "nightmare" has been resolved—at least partly. By August 3, 2009, the new board of thirteen directors met for the first time at GM headquarters in Detroit. Seven of the thirteen directors were new to the board and attended their first two-day board meeting with Edward E. Whitacre, Jr., the newly named interim board chairman. Mr. Whitacre took the job of chairman after being assured by the government that its Automotive Task Force would be phased out at some later date. (Mr. Whitacre's concern was that he didn't wish to serve two masters: the Board of Directors of GM *and* the federal government's task force. As CEO, he has the daunting challenge of re-structuring GM in order to find and deliver $50 billion (plus interest) to pay back the government bailout loan.)

ANNUAL DAYS SERVED BY A DIRECTOR

Increased emphasis on the duties and responsibilities of boards of directors has resulted in directors who, on average, worked 223 days on combined board service in 2008 compared to 190 days in 2005 [National Association of Corporate Directors, Washington, D.C.]. A computation of reasonable board service days came up with 270 days of service based upon the following factors for a board of nine directors:

Number of meetings per year: 6
Actual meeting days per year: 6
Travel days per year: 12
Home study per year: 6
Total: 30 days per year x 9 members = 270 total work days for the board
Total per director: About 13% of the year

ESTABLISHING A NEW BOARD OF DIRECTORS

Enlarging the structure of a board, changing board rules and responsibilities and/or setting up a new board should be done with a modern configuration and make-up. The following is a guide to accomplish a good, up-to-date working board of directors.

- Choose seven to thirteen directors or more, but always have an uneven number.
- A majority of directors must be truly independent from any employee of the company.
- One independent director should be a certified public accountant.
- The chair (preferably someone having a CPA designation) must be appointed by the board to serve as liaison

between the board and the independent auditor of the company.
- The independent members of the board are responsible for the major actions of the company. Detailed and firm oversight of the company is an essential responsibility of each director.
- A broad and ample directors' and officers' liability insurance coverage should be provided because oversight responsibility is essential.
- The board must be informed that the buck stops with them. They are responsible for all actions of the company and the consequences of those actions.

QUALIFICATIONS OF THE CANDIDATES FOR A NEW BOARD SLATE

A company is essentially no better than its board of directors, and the board of directors is no better than the *sum* of its directors. New directors should be chosen carefully and wisely. The following list is a footprint of what makes the ideal director. Any candidate for the board should have positive marks in the majority of the following categories:

1. <u>Personal independence is a most vital requirement</u>. Defining the state of a director's independence means there can be *no* close ties with any senior officer of the company, no blood relationship, no club membership, no school, college or fraternal association. The "Good Buddy" or "Old Boy" network should play no part in relationships between one director and another director or between the director and the company's CEO, CFO, president or other senior executive officer.

2. <u>Oversight of general business activities is an essential qualification</u>. A director should not be chosen for strength in one specialized area. Well-rounded advisors with many interests are desirable. Oversight requires understanding of the many facets of the company, its products or services and its employees.
3. <u>Age is a factor</u>. Business maturity is required to make quick decisions. It takes years to appreciate and act on the angles of a company's business. A minimum age of forty years is a reasonable guideline. It is always possible that a situation will arise that requires stamina, long hours and grueling discussions. The ability to withstand such pressures becomes difficult with age, and an arbitrary age limit of seventy-five seems to be the norm. Special circumstances can arise and be met by altering the bylaws of the corporation.
4. <u>Gender, race and religion are non-issues.</u> These should not be determining factors in the process of choosing any candidate. The overall strength of the board is the priority.
5. <u>Personality</u>. Eye-to-eye, person-to-person contact occurs on many levels in business. A good director interacts well with others, is socially adept and displays qualities of leadership in any setting.
6. <u>Unimpeachable moral integrity</u>. A director represents the business standards of the company. Serious legal or moral complications in the director's past or present must be carefully examined during deliberations to nominate a potential director.
7. <u>Balanced demographic representation strengthens a board</u>. The United States is a big country, and one region does not necessarily think like another. A United States senator in Washington, D.C. once said, "The Senate's views on national matters often stop at the

Potomac River." A balanced view on corporate matters often requires sensitivity to local issues. Geographical balance is an asset during board deliberations.

8. <u>General experience, intellect, confidence and ability to verbalize articulately.</u> These are great assets for a potential director. Difficult decisions will be faced as a director, and these attributes are valuable resources in board discussions.

9. <u>Availability</u>. Steady and regular attendance at scheduled meetings is not only necessary, but in special circumstances such as mergers, sale of assets or of the company, fraud and other legal challenges, immediate attention may be required. Occasionally prolonged days of meetings are necessary. Computer or phone "attendance" is not the same as sitting at the table with other board members. Reasonable willingness to be available for special meetings is a must.

10. <u>Length of service</u>. It takes time in terms of months, if not years, to get the "feel" of a company and its market—especially if it is in a highly competitive environment. The knowledge to solve problems intelligently comes with length of service. Serving as a director for only a year or so often accomplishes little. Likewise knowledge accumulated with too lengthy service can become a liability with loss of flexibility or entrenched attitudes. Unlimited length of service is usually controlled by term limits and retirement age rules in the company's bylaws.

11. <u>Compensation</u>. Balancing the increased need for directors who are reasonably schooled in economics and accounting and who have general business experience is the increased cost of attracting such candidates to the board. No longer is serving as a director just an addition to an individual's *curriculum vitae*—it entails

greater involvement and greatly increased personal liability.

12. <u>Acceptance of responsibility</u>. Don't forget: *the buck stops with the board of directors*. If a company performs poorly or is subject to misdemeanors or serious massive fraud, it is the board that must answer to the shareholders. The board can fire the CEO or other officers and can sue them for illegal acts, but the board is the legal entity that takes the action and assumes the ultimate responsibility. It behooves the corporation to properly inform and protect its directors from an ever-increasing threat of litigation and the massive costs attached thereto. However, Berkshire Hathaway and other companies have concluded that directors who are indemnified may not be as diligent and cautious in making decisions as those who are not.

There are many good companies that concentrate on supplying assistance in identifying director candidates. Korn/Ferry International in Washington, D. C. is one well-known firm; another is Spencer Stuart in New York City. Both are seasoned "head hunters" and deal with a high volume of placements. An August 2009 news items in *The Wall Street Journal* listed Spencer Stuart as having 329 recruiters. It has been estimated that Stuart conducts at least half of all *Fortune* 500 companies' board searches and at least 400 worldwide. Likewise, our experiences with Korn/Ferry International have been positive ones.

EXECUTIVE COMMITTEE

An essential ingredient to an efficient and meaningful board of directors is a lean, but powerful, executive committee made up of from three to five members of the existing board (including the chairman of the board). The executive committee is a standing committee, available on reasonable notice, to act or advise on behalf of the full board between regular meetings depending upon the issue or issues at hand.

The executive committee meets on demand, but, at the least, schedules a meeting before each board meeting to prepare a report to the board on the period since the last meeting. The major issues, including mergers, acquisitions, salaries and other compensation matters are previewed for the board, and a summary presented to the board for final action. Board meeting agendas can be set by this committee.

The chair of the executive committee can be the chairman of the board or any designated executive committee member. The company's CEO usually is NOT in attendance and sensitive corporate matters such as bonuses and compensation can be discussed freely.

The company's internal auditor, the CFO and even the independent outside auditor are available to the executive committee on demand. If the company has a SEC compliance officer, that person would also be available for consultations. The CEO may or may not be called for information. At any time, the executive committee chair will have the CEO or his counterpart available.

Members of the executive committee will receive double the usual committee fees. Travel and other expenses will be paid for members must be on call.

The company is required to keep the executive committee and its board informed on major details of operations past, present and future.

DIVERSIFICATION

America is a diverse country with different cultures, languages, religions, experiences and beliefs. There are regional concerns that are of paramount importance to certain areas that are unknown to other parts of the country. The mix makes our country great. An independent board of directors must keep geographical representation, race, gender, and age diversity in mind, but overall, the experience and qualifications of the candidate are the central issue. A board should represent, as far as possible, a cross-section of those people who are its shareholders.

SUGGESTED ORGANIZATIONAL CHART FOR A PUBLIC STOCK CORPORATION AND THE INDEPENDENT BOARD OF DIRECTORS

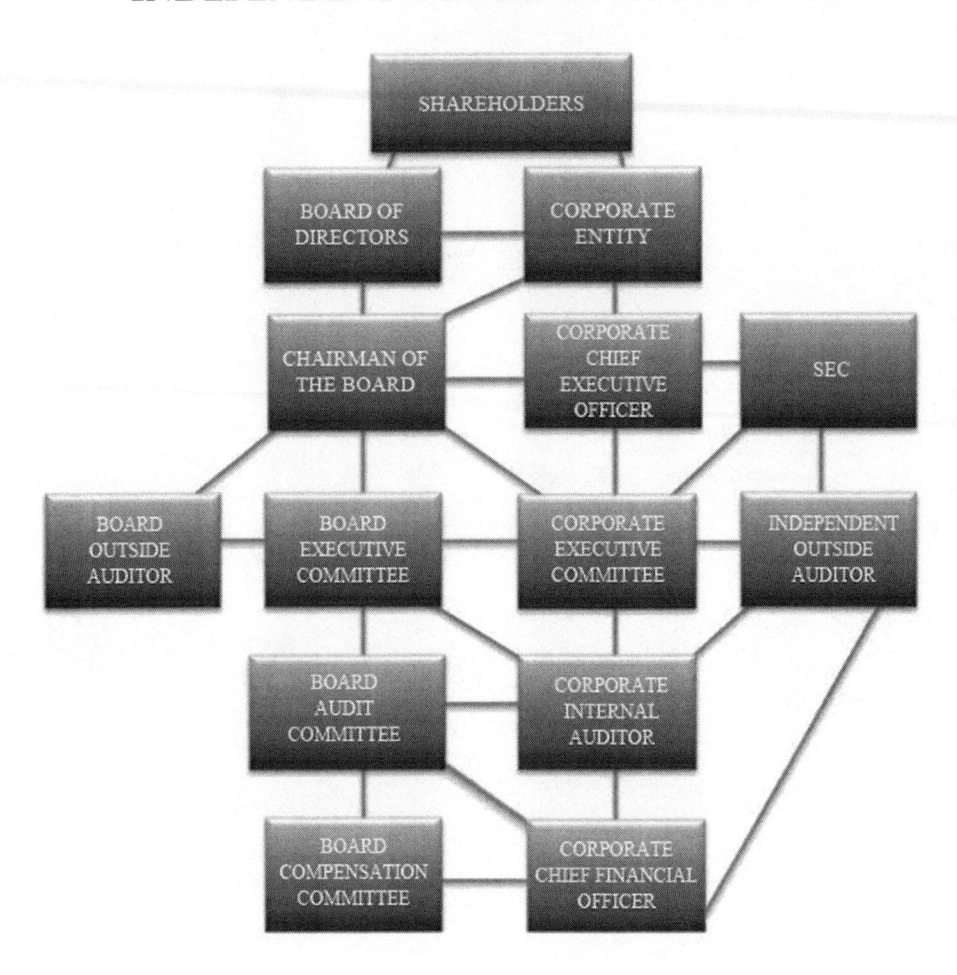

THE FEDERAL RESERVE SYSTEM

Synopsis – Chapter 10

"Bad Decisions"

The Federal Reserve System is not controlled by anyone or any branch of the federal government. The current system was created in 1913, although the origin of a central bank goes back to 1791 when the First Bank of the United States was formed.

Off and on for 122 years, the central bank that services the monetary needs of the United States of America has led a volatile life. It was shut down in 1811, was reborn as the Second Bank of the United States in 1816, and closed again due to corruption in 1836. There was no national bank until 1863 when a series of national banks were created. The Panic of 1907 made it clear that a more stable banking system was needed.

In 1913 the Federal Reserve System was formed via the Federal Reserve Act, and its bank became today's Third National Bank of the United States.

The "Fed" is our nation's central bank, and serves our government much the way your local bank serves you–but in an enormous and complicated form.

Chapter 10

THE FEDERAL RESERVE SYSTEM

The Federal Reserve System as the nation's central bank is needed, but few understand just what "The Fed" is. How is it constituted and how does it affect our monetary supply?

The Federal Reserve Act of 1913 established a central banking system for the United States and is a relatively new addition to the potpourri of historic bureaus and alphabetic commissions, committees, and other bodies governing, regulating or liquidating new and old national financial entities.

"The Fed," "Federal Reserve System" or just "Federal Reserve" is not a political animal under the control of any of the three branches of the United States government. Instead, *it is a freestanding and independent entity.* Even though it operates within the government, the seven-member Board of Governors and its Chairman and Vice Chairman are all appointed by the President and confirmed by the U. S. Senate.

The Fed is our nation's bank. Just like your own bank, it takes in deposits, makes loans and pays bills—all on behalf of the United States government, but really on your behalf, as the citizens are the government.

In spite of its complexities, the Fed is a body composed of five parts:

- The United States is divided into twelve federal banking districts each with its own Federal Reserve Bank with a nine-member board of directors, who act as fiscal agents for the United States Treasury.
- Each district is represented by its local governor who serves for fourteen years on the Fed's Board of Governors in Washington.
- The President of the United States appoints each *independent* Fed district's governor.
- There are a large number of member banks that subscribe to non-transferable stock in their regional Federal Reserve Bank.
- The Federal Open Market Committee of the Federal Reserve determines the key monetary policies for the country. It has a board of governors consisting of seven independent Fed board members and five presidents rotating from the twelve independent Fed Districts.

There is no central banking system in the world that has an independent outside entity that creates its own currency. The United States has its Department of the Treasury, Bureau of the Mint and Bureau of Engraving and Printing, both of which produce the nation's cash supply. The cash supply is sold to the Federal Reserve banks at a manufacturing cost of about four cents per bill, which the Fed in turn distributes to other financial institutions. The cost of coinage is unlisted.

The Federal Reserve System was formed by trial and error over a period of 122 years, from 1791 to 1913, until it finally settled in its present form for the last ninety-eight years. In 1781 the Articles of Confederation & Perpetual Union gave the government power to "emit bills of credit" and later to subscribe privately a national bank similar to the Bank of England. Its charter was revoked in 1785. In 1791 the First Bank of the United States was formed but shut down in 1811 by President Madison. For five years there was no central bank until the Second National Bank of the United States started up in 1816—only to be shut down in 1836 by President Jackson "because of considerable corruption."

From 1837 to 1862 there was a "Free Bank Era"; an "Independent Treasury System" from 1846 to 1921; a period of "National Banks" from 1863 to 1913, and then came the formation of the third central banking system, triggered by the Panic of 1907 that made it clear a new banking system was needed to provide "more elastic currency" and to "insert more liquidity" into the system. [Report of the National Monetary Commission. January 9, 1912, letter from the Secretary of the Commission and a draft bill to incorporate the National Reserve Association of the United States, and for other purposes. Sen. Doc. No. 243. 62d Congress. U.S. Government Printing Office. 1912.]

In 1913 the "Federal Reserve Act" passed through Congress with little support from Republicans but near-unanimous support from the Democrats. The Senate vote was 43 to 25 according to a December 24, 1913, newspaper clipping. The Third National Bank was formed in 1913 and is going strong after ninety-eight years. Our country has gone through times of great financial stress since 1913: World War I through 1918; the United States and United Kingdom crises of 1920; the German crisis of 1922; the French franc crisis of 1924; the stock market crash of Black Tuesday, October 29, 1929; the Austrian Crisis of May 11, 1931; the United States Banking Crisis of 1933; the near panic of the U. S. after the French Capitulation in 1940 during World War II; the 1949 United States recession; the 1980 Farmland crisis and the Silver Thursday Mania of March 28, 1980; the 1985 United States Dollar crisis; the 1987 Black Monday crash on October 19; the 1989 Japanese yen bubble deflation; the 1990 United States junk bond collapse and the failure of Drexel, Burnham Lambert in the following February; and then a whole series of crises from 2002 through 2011 with major mergers, acquisitions, and bankruptcies of very large corporations and institutions where billions of dollars were lost or made. The Federal Reserve System has steered us through these troubled times, but not without instability, economic recessions and the Great Depression, and the very recent near catastrophe for the nation's banking system.

The Federal Reserve System is a "self-funding" enterprise. To track the complexity of the system, a "Consolidated Statement of Condition of All Federal Reserve Banks" is issued weekly by the system, showing the status of each of the twelve Federal Reserve Banks, as well as consolidated figures for all of the banks. A copy of this statement is shown at the end of this chapter.

In times of crisis, the Fed has been unable to prevent speculators and "bottom feeders" from scouring the garbage pits of finance for cheap deals at the expense of the unfortunate. Why are speculators allowed to practice their trade much like looters who welcome earthquakes, typhoons, tornadoes and mass fires to pick over what remains at the expense of those who have lost almost everything?

It seems to us that if the Federal Reserve System is in business to protect the "little" investor from the "big" and to help manage the flow of money, then it must be absolutely tough with those who flout the movement of assets and money and fancy balance sheet maneuvers. Those financial miscreants should be barred for life from serving as CEO or president or CFO or chairman of the board of directors or any other responsible executive position within our nation's financial network. Those executives who have demanded special terms of employment and severance have all too frequently been proven inept at best, or scoundrels perpetrating frauds at worst. They have no apologies for their actions and too few have been remanded to prison for extended periods. Many have millions of dollars stashed away overseas. Those financially crippled for life are doomed to live out the consequences of greedsters' fraud, greed, and reckless gambling with other peoples' money.

Should the federal government take the position, "You knew the rules of acceptable financial behavior, now it is the turn of the society you wronged to take away what you gained?" Why not? Bailouts should be temporary and values should be returned to those defrauded.

The Federal Reserve System is not without its detractors. Many of the critics have tried to make changes—or at least make points—that date back to the very origin of the central banking concept in 1791. Sincere attempts for change are regularly raised in Congress, the latest being by the current ranking member of the Monetary Policy Subcommittee, Ron Paul, who ran an unsuccessful Libertarian Party campaign for President in 2008 and is a Republican candidate for President in 2012.

Criticisms range far and wide, but a few (in condensed form) are as follows:

1. The Federal Reserve Banking System is under the influence of New York City and Wall Street, and their counterparts overseas, both East and West.
2. The Fed is running a monetary policy that is too tight, not allowing rapid enough increases or decreases in interest rates to follow master economic change—appeasing Wall Street instead of Main Street.
3. Assets and liabilities data of the Fed are not regularly published publicly. Transparency should be absolute.
4. It has been claimed by detractors that data compiled by the Fed "are misleading, exaggerated or falsified" to fulfill some type of political manipulation.

5. The Fed is unaccountable, or otherwise not independent, if following orders from the president of the United States or Wall Street interests.

There's a saying, "The only way to throw criticisms at someone above you in the pecking order of business is to kick them in the pants." It is hard to see who is in the position to take that action.

Monthly changes in the CPI (Consumer Price Index) reflect the ups and downs in the inflation or deflation rates. The Bureau of Labor Statistics determines the CPI by "measuring the average price level of a fixed basket of goods and services." The Bureau of Labor Statistics tracks a number of types of indices, but the CPI index is most commonly used. Track the CPI and unemployment or employment figures and you have two of the major data that the Fed might use to change interest rates. But the Federal Open Market Committee seems to make this decisive economic decision without any known formula.

This is just one of the decisions made by the Federal Reserve that makes a material impact on the financial climate of the United States.

The Fed's website posts financial information on a monthly, quarterly and annual basis at www.federalreserve.gov.

"The Board of Governors of the Federal Reserve's financial statements are audited annually by an independent audit firm retained by the Board's Office of Inspector General. The audit firm also provides a report on compliance and on internal control over financial reporting in accordance with government auditing standards. The Office of Inspector General conducts audits, reviews, and investigations relating to the Board's programs and operations as well as of Board functions delegated to the Reserve Banks." [http://www.federalreserve.gov/monetarypolicy/bst_fedfinancials.htm]

An example of a balance sheet posted on the Fed's website follows:

Table 1. Assets, Liabilities, and Capital of the Federal Reserve System
Billions of dollars

Item	Current June 30, 2010	Change from May 26, 2010	Change from July 1, 2009
Total assets	**2,334**	**−4**	**+326**
Selected assets			
Securities held outright	2,060	+3	+836
U.S. Treasury securities[1]	777	+*	+114
Federal agency debt securities[1]	165	−2	+67
Mortgage-backed securities[2]	1,118	+5	+656
Memo: Overnight securities lending[3]	14	+11	+7
Memo: Net commitments to purchase mortgage-backed securities[4]	16	−20	−124
Lending to depository institutions[5]	1	−4	−35
Central bank liquidity swaps[6]	1	+*	−114
Lending through other credit facilities	43	−2	−98
Net portfolio holdings of Commercial Paper Funding Facility LLC[7]	*	−*	−115
Term Asset-Backed Securities Loan Facility[8]	43	−2	+17
Net portfolio holdings of TALF LLC[9]	1	+1	+1
Support for specific institutions	118	−1	+12
Credit extended to American International Group, Inc., net[10]	25	−1	−18
Net portfolio holdings of Maiden Lane LLC[11]	28	+*	+2
Net portfolio holdings of Maiden Lane II LLC[11]	16	−*	−*
Net portfolio holdings of Maiden Lane III LLC[11]	23	−*	+3
Preferred interests in AIA Aurora LLC and ALICO Holdings LLC[8]	26	+1	+26
Total liabilities	**2,278**	**−4**	**+319**
Selected liabilities			
Federal Reserve notes in circulation	904	+4	+33
Term deposits held by depository institutions	1	+1	+1
Other deposits held by depository institutions	972	−116	+246
U.S. Treasury, general account	88	+71	+10
U.S. Treasury, supplementary financing account	200	+*	+*
Other deposits	28	+28	+28
Total capital	**56**	**+1**	**+7**

Unaudited. Components may not sum to totals because of rounding.
* Less than $500 million.
1. Face value.
2. Guaranteed by Fannie Mae, Freddie Mac, and Ginnie Mae. Current face value, which is the remaining principal balance of the underlying mortgages. Does not include unsettled transactions.
3. Securities loans under the overnight facility are off-balance-sheet transactions. These loans are shown here as a memo item to indicate the portion of securities held outright that have been lent through this program.
4. Current face value. Includes commitments associated with outright purchases, dollar rolls, and coupon swaps.
5. Total of primary, secondary, and seasonal credit.
6. Dollar value of the foreign currency held under these agreements valued at the exchange rate to be used when the foreign currency is returned to the foreign central bank.
7. Includes about $1 million in other investments as of June 30, 2010.
8. Book value.
9. As of June 30, 2010, TALF LLC had purchased no assets from the FRBNY.
10. Excludes credit extended to Maiden Lane II and III LLCs.
11. Fair value, reflecting values as of March 31, 2010. Fair value reflects an estimate of the price that would be received upon selling an asset if the transaction were to be conducted in an orderly market on the measurement date. Fair values are updated quarterly.

The Federal Reserve's current financial statements can be found at http://www.federalreserve.gov.

Chapter 11

FINAL THOUGHTS

During the forty-eight months of researching, compiling, writing, editing and finalizing data for *The Greedsters*, many relevant incidents of misdeeds and neglect of duty by corporations, their boards of directors, their executives, and employees were uncovered. Innumerable legal and illegal schemes to defraud others have been documented. Malfeasance and incompetence on the part of public officials was exposed.

Most of the factors that have contributed to our country's financial woes were examined, dissected and then chosen for emphasis in this book. Many legal schemes are as fraught with danger to the investor as are the illegal ones. Play it safe and stay informed—it's a cruel world out there.

The easiest way to alter many of these problems is to identify the issue, analyze its current status and then decide what can be done about it. The following list is not complete, and "policies in need of change" is an evolving exercise that will forever be grist for the mill of reaction. But for the purposes of this book, these issues should be recognized as the weak foundation of current business practices and promptly acted upon.

1. <u>The dual role of chief executive officer and chairman of the board.</u> It has been a common practice for the CEO of a company to also fill the role of chairman of its board of directors. It's one thing for one of the company's senior representatives, such as the CEO, to be a member of the board of directors to supply the flow of information to enable the directors to properly assess and act upon the affairs of the company. But it's entirely out of order for the CEO, or a senior officer, to serve on the board as its chairman. The conflict of interest is only too obvious.
2. <u>The board of directors should have final approval of senior officer compensation</u>. It's entirely in the province of the chairman and an independent board to decide on salaries, bonuses, perks, vacations, pensions, job retention matters, retirement terms, golden parachutes, golden coffins and other executive compensation in conjunction with the compensation committee of the company.

   The board also should award fringe benefits such as club memberships, paid vacations, use of company airplanes, company seats or boxes at sporting events, tickets for art or science exhibitions, tables at charity functions or other entertainments.

   Likewise, the board has the duty to decide appropriate related outside activities for the CEO and senior officers such as: sitting on board of other companies, trade associations and not-for-profits; accepting honorary positions; or undertaking activities that consume the time and energy of the officer involved.

3. <u>No employee of the company ever has the authority to commit the board of directors to any action</u>.
4. <u>The board of directors must have its responsibilities clearly set forth</u>: continual transparency of investments; selection of the slate of new directors for eventual election by shareholders; the establishment of future major policies and directions of the company; the selection and hiring of successive CEOs; the maintenance of a tight but fair rein on the CEO; the approval of shareholder communications; and the monitoring of the state of the company and its operations are all appropriate functions of an independent board of directors.

    After all, the board of directors represents the shareholders, and the shareholders are the owners of the company—facts not to be forgotten.
5. <u>The company should have an independent outside auditor</u>. The full-time independent outside auditor works closely with the company's internal auditor and the company's outside accounting firm. He or she reports regularly to the chairman of the board and periodically to the SEC. The company contracts with the independent outside auditor for services and compensation. The contract can be negotiated to allow the outside auditor access to company health plans and employee perks and benefits, but the auditor should never be an employee.

    The company's independent outside auditor must be qualified at the highest level and must be trained to comply with all SEC rules and regulations.
6. <u>The board of directors should consist of an unequal number of independent members to avoid tie votes</u>. The senior company officer on the board does not have a vote on matters that concern him or her.

7. <u>The board of directors should have a super-majority of its members from outside the company and all should be truly independent.</u>
8. <u>The company should never make personal loans or salary advances to employees or senior officers</u>. The practice of making loans to senior employees to pay taxes on bonuses, to exercise stock options for optimal profits or to reimburse employees for market losses when exercising an option should be forbidden.
9. <u>Corporate risk management must be transparent</u>. In too many instances, risks taken by senior management (or sometimes junior management) have not been properly disclosed to auditors or the board of directors. Thorough risk appraisal may be compromised by attractive returns on high-risk investments or the desire to close a deal quickly. The age of corporate meltdowns is full of expediency and neglect of risk assessment—with dire results.
10. <u>SEC and other governmental rules and regulations must be fully understood</u>. At least one person in the company should be a compliance officer who is expert in understanding and applying applicable rules and regulations—both those in force and those under consideration.
11. <u>The prime duties of the CEO and the board of a company are to operate a clean "ship" on behalf of its owners—the shareholders</u>. The basis of good corporate governance is sound business ethics, accountability, efficiency and growth in value.
12. <u>Suggestions for bonus policies</u>:
    a. Award a bonus only when there is a reason that it has been earned.
    b. Congress should enact a federal tax of 50% on the amount of the bonus over a certain amount, such

as $40,000. High bonus babies will scream to the high heavens, but look at the net after tax—is it still worth it? Probably, yes.
c. Give the bonus in the ratio of 10 percent cash to 90 percent company stock. The shares should be valued at the exchange closing price on the day prior to issuance.
d. The company stock should be "lettered," with takeout dates of two, three and five years from issuance. Share value on the exercise date is the same as the share value on the bonus issuance date.
e. Any other terms and conditions of a bonus must be valued and treated for future value as in (d).
f. Bonus stock options cannot be sold, transferred or used as collateral in any way. Bonus stock is of value only when vesting dates approach and its market value is established.

13. <u>If the terms of an investment are too good to be true, then they probably are not true! Beware!</u>
14. <u>There are NO free lunches.</u>
15. <u>Whatever you do, dig into and understand the details of a possible investment</u>. A proverb says, "The devil is in the details." Be knowledgeable. Scams and schemes are everywhere. Get good advice.
16. <u>To summarize: the shareholders, the board of directors and each and every employee of a company are part of the whole; each is a valued member of the team</u>. One person or a few at the top deserve their good fortune only because of the team. Without the team backup, what could they have accomplished? Compensation throughout the company should be fair and balanced.

As society evolves beyond business and commerce, it impacts on corporate culture. Don't ignore the character of the individual shareholder or investor. As our future economic structure evolves, the persona and role of the shareholder will change. The "shareholder" won't be a hodge-podge of many individuals, but rather a few large institutional or individual investors with major holdings that may be very much like the corporation itself.

Be aware that the United States Supreme Court has ruled that a corporation has "personhood." Rules and regulations, including taxation, apply to a corporation in ways similar to an individual. Regard a corporation as one very large and imposing person who is a stranger to you—try to get to know it before you place your money with it. In an early chapter of this book, the term "paternalism" was used to describe how Uncle Sam—our government—came to the rescue of banks, insurance companies and automakers with TARP funds. Both our government acting as a shareholder and the corporations revived with government oversight are new and major entities going forward.

The financial experiences of the past five years emphasized a trend that will become even more prevalent. The creation of enormous wealth through the use of innovative commercial paper abounds in our financial institutions. High-risk, high-return hedge funds have created overnight billionaires. Investment banks have netted billions of dollars per quarter using credit swaps and derivatives (and ultimately lost so much value that government bailouts were necessary to save the financial system of the country).

China has purchased such a volume of U. S. Treasury bills that it would be a real threat to the stability of our financial system if a major percentage of China's holdings were placed on the market. The total value of all hedge funds is near $15 trillion, a sum greater than the gross national product of the United States at the end of 2009. What value stands behind these investments and supports them?

Stand back and ask yourself who really owns or controls our country? Who wields the power to influence Congress? Who pays hundreds of millions of dollars annually to lobby our lawmakers? Why aren't there laws to forestall takeovers by greedsters from Wall Street to Main Street?

We are living in a new financial world. Never have so many "smart" managers traded among themselves, driving up prices and pocketing hundreds of millions in profit without making any product or service that society needs and uses. Even the robber barons of the 1800s made their fortunes with mineral and energy resources, industrial commodities and transportation networks. Today's robber barons wheel and deal mostly with "paper"—buying and selling securities like CDOs, credit and debt swaps and the infamous derivatives, some of which have less value than the paper the deals are printed on.

When billions of dollars are made, billions of dollars are lost—it's a zero sum game. For every dollar made, somebody out there has lost a dollar. As in energy and water, dollars are neither created nor destroyed. They just go from one condition to another—but frequently become degraded in the process.

When you come right down to it, our country's financial markets and government are masterminding and executing a giant Ponzi scheme using income from investors and taxpayers to service a mountain of debt with no underlying assets—and there is no end in sight. Entitlements are another Ponzi—current payouts depend on future payroll taxes—and it's an *inverted* pyramid based on decreasing numbers of wage earners at the bottom.

As a final suggestion, pay attention to what is happening. Follow the news, do your own research, consult honest and competent experts and make informed decisions. Take nothing for granted in the financial world. In the financial game, those that rule the roost don't know you, and you don't know them. Don't play the part of a chicken to them—because you know what happens to chickens.

Good luck!

SELECTED GLOSSARY

The following list covers many of the terms and words used in *The Greedsters*. It is a selected list and is by no means intended to be an exhaustive financial glossary. Each definition may have various aspects of interpretation or technical meaning beyond the scope of this glossary.

- Alpha – an investment's risk-adjusted measure of actual returns over time
- AMT – Alternative Minimum Tax: income tax rate computed at 26 or 28 percent for individuals and 20 percent for corporations
- Annuity – an insurance company contract purchased by an investor to guarantee distribution of income over time
- ARM – Adjustable-Rate Mortgage: a loan with an interest rate that changes over time
- Balance Sheet – a financial statement showing assets, liabilities and ownership equity
- Basel Accord – representatives of central banks meet in Basel, Switzerland to agree and establish international levels of capital for banks

- Bear — pessimistic or negative view of the stock market; downward market trend
- Beta — the volatility of an investment's value when compared to the volatility of the overall market
- Blue Chip — highly-rated stock of an established company with stable earnings
- Bond - investment security with a fixed annual interest rate return and term (principal repaid on maturity)
- Bull — optimistic view of the stock market; upward market trend
- Call — issuer may redeem bonds at will if interest rates fall; a financial contract where the buyer has the right, but not the obligation, to buy a security at a certain price at a future date and pays the seller a premium for that right
- CDO — Collateralized Debt Obligation: an asset-backed security whose value and return are based on a portfolio of similar securities
- CDS — Credit Default Swap: a contractual agreement where the buyer is protected against default of a fixed rate security and the seller guarantees the credit worthiness of the product
- CMO — Collateralized Mortgage Obligation: a mortgage-backed security that pays investors from a pool of underlying assets
- Commercial Paper — corporate short-term IOUs
- CPI — Consumer Price Index: measure of price change on specific goods due to inflation
- Compound Interest — interest earned on an investment's principal and accumulated earnings
- Default — failure to abide or pay per the terms of an agreement
- Derivative — a security whose value depends upon one or more underlying assets

- Discount Window – imaginary teller window where banks borrow from the Federal Reserve
- Dividend – a percentage return per share paid to stockholders based upon a company's earnings
- Downgrade – a rating agency lowering the bond rating of investment securities based on the issuer's financial strength and ability to honor the obligation
- Dow Jones Industrial Average – an index of 30 major American companies
- Equity – total assets minus total liabilities of a company; ownership of common stocks of companies is called an "equity" investment
- ETF – Exchange-Traded Fund: an investment fund traded like a stock; typically an ETF is a basket of stocks engaged in a similar industry; ETFs can be actively managed or an index of all stocks in a particular business sector
- Fannie Mae – Federal National Mortgage Association: provides financial products to allow affordable housing mortgages for low-income to moderate-income borrowers
- Fed Funds Rate – interest rate on funds when a bank borrows from the Federal Reserve or another bank
- FHA – Federal Housing Administration: federal agency that provides mortgage insurance on loans made by approved FHA lenders
- Fiscal Year - a declared consecutive twelve months period of operation for purposes of financial accounting and preparation of financial statements
- FOMC – Federal Open Market Committee: an arm of the Federal Reserve system which makes decisions regarding interest rates and money supply

- Front-end Load – fee paid up front on a mutual fund purchase
- Futures – a contract to trade a commodity on a set future date at a set price
- GAO – Government Accountability Office: audit and financial evaluation arm of the U. S. Congress
- GDP – Gross Domestic Product: measure of a country's overall economic output
- Ginny Mae – Government National Mortgage Association: a wholly-owned government corporation within the Department of Housing and Urban Development which provides capital to the nation's housing finance market
- Hedge Fund – aggressive private investment fund with high risk and without significant federal regulation at this time. Requires a large minimum investment and up-front fee but attempts to generate high returns
- Hoot and Holler Phone – open circuit telecommunications system
- HUD – U .S. Department of Housing and Urban Development
- IMF – International Monetary Fund: an organization of over 180 countries interested in global monetary cooperation and stability
- IRA (Traditional) – Individual Retirement Arrangement—an investment retirement account with deferred tax savings
- Junk Bond –a bond rated "BB" or lower denoting high returns and high default risk
- LBO – Leveraged Buy-Out—the use of a company's assets as collateral for borrowing the capital to acquire the company
- Leverage –using borrowed capital to underwrite a financial transaction

SELECTED GLOSSARY

- LIBOR – London Interbank Offered Rate – rate at which banks borrow unsecured funds from other banks
- Liquidity – an asset's ability to be bought or sold easily without affecting the price
- Long-term capital gains – profit on a security held long enough to gain special tax treatment when sold
- Long – stock or commodity position which anticipates a rising market
- Margin – an investment term for the amount of equity contributed by a customer as a percentage of the current market value of the securities held in a "margin account"
- Mark-to-Market – assets on the books are priced at current market value
- MERC – Chicago Mercantile Exchange
- Money Market – short-term financial securities with higher interest rate than savings accounts
- Mortgage – A long-term borrowing usually secured by real estate
- Municipal Bond ("Muni") – bonds issued by states, counties and cities which offer the advantage of paying tax-free returns to the investor
- Mutual Fund – a pool of stocks treated as one security to diversify exposure for the small investor and to achieve a specific financial objective
- NASDAQ – National Association of Securities Dealers
- NAV – net asset value
- NEC – National Economic Council: a government agency which is part of the Executive Office of the President of the United States
- Ninja loan – a loan procured with no income, job or assets.
- No-load fund – no up-front fee when purchasing shares of a mutual fund

- Non-Qualified Stock Option – A stock option where income tax is paid only on the difference between the grant price and the market price when exercised
- Off Balance Sheet – an item not required to be disclosed in the company's financial statement
- Option – the right to buy or sell a security on terms specified as to date, time and value
- OTC – Over the Counter (stock not traded through an exchange)
- P/E - Price to earnings ratio of a stock
- PIK – Payment-in-Kind
- Probate – resolving claims and distributing assets of a deceased person according to their legal will filed in probate court
- Prospectus – A detailed summary of a proposed purchase or sale
- Put – An options contract giving a right to sell stock at a certain price
- Quant – A quantitative analyst
- Repo – Right of a lien holder to repossess property due to the default of the borrower
- Return on Equity – Monetary gain on a positive asset
- Run on a Bank – Depositors withdraw their deposits en masse
- S&P 500 – Standard & Poor's Index of 500 large-cap equities
- Savings Bond – debt securities issued by the U. S. government with a specified term and interest rate and considered a conservative and risk-free investment
- SEC – Securities and Exchange Commission: U. S. regulatory agency which oversees investor safety and safe, efficient markets

- Short Positions – selling a security you don't own speculating that you will be able to buy it at a lower price and make a profit on the difference
- Shortfall – A less than expected return on an investment
- Stock – a certificate of equity ownership in a corporation
- Subprime – less than optimal credit worthiness
- Swaps – a derivative that exchanges the benefits of one financial instrument for that of another as in interest rate, currency, equity, credit default or commodity swaps
- Systemic Risk – risk of the collapse of an entire financial system or market
- TARP – Troubled Assets Relief Program
- Time Deposit – a deposit made for a specified length of time
- Total Return – a calculation when measuring performance of the actual rate of return on a specific investment
- Treasury Bills – interest-bearing certificates issued by the U. S. Treasury
- Tranche – "slice" in French – portion of a contract or of a CDO or CMO
- Underwriter – a financial service provider in a debt offering that accepts some of the risk and reward
- Variable Annuity – Annuity which has certain variable terms
- Volatility – the rise and fall of the value of an asset
- Zero-Sum market – a system whereby all gains to one party are offset by equal losses of another

SELECTED BIBLIOGRAPHY

The following list of sources of research for *The Greedsters* forms a bibliography of sorts. Over the past four years of reading about individual and corporate greed, a bewildering mass of data, both past and present, was available to be used as "grist for the mill" in writing this book. Facts about individuals, companies and events were verified by searching many responsible sources as background.

The primary sources for gathering much of the information for this book were written by many capable authors and were widely available from any book dealer or library. The following books from my personal library were especially helpful:

Barnes, Craig. Democracy at the Crossroads: The Struggle for the Rule of Law. Golden, CO: Fulcrum Press, 2009.

Cohan, William. House of Cards: A Tale of Hubris and Wretched Excess on Wall Street. New York: Doubleday, 2010.

Cruver, Brian. Anatomy of Greed: The Unshredded Truth from an Enron Insider. New York: Carroll & Graf, 2002.

Florida, Richard. The Rise of the Creative Class: And How It's Transforming Work, Leisure, Community and Everyday Life. New York: Basic Books, 2002.

Friedman, Thomas L. Hot, Flat and Crowded: Global Warming and America's Wandering. New York: Farrar, Straus & Giroux, 2008.

Gasparino, Charles. The Sellout: How Three Decades of Wall Street Greed and Government Mismanagement Destroyed the Global Financial System. New York: HarperCollins Publishers, 2009.

Gross, Daniel. Dumb Money: The United States Fiscal Crisis of 2007-2009. New York: Simon & Schuster Inc., 2009.

Karmin, Craig. Biography of the Dollar: How the U. S. Dollar is Valued and Manipulated. New York: Crown Business Press, 2009.

Huffington, Arianna. Pigs at the Trough: Excessive Executive Compensations. New York: Crown Publishers, 2003.

Johnson, Simon and James Kwak. 13 Bankers: The Wall Street Takeover and the Next Financial Meltdown. New York: Pantheon Books, 2010.

Krugman, Paul. The Return of Depression Economics and the Crisis of 2008. New York: W.W. Norton & Co., 2009.

Lewis, Michael. The Big Short: The Rise and Fall of the Real Estate Bubble. New York: W.W. Norton & Co., 2010.

_____. Liar's Poker: The Demise of Salomon Brothers. New York: W.W. Norton & Co., 2010.

_____. Panic: The Story of Modern Financial Insanity. New York: W. W. Norton & Co., 2009.

Lowenstein, Roger. The End of Wall Street: It Started with the Bankruptcy of Lehman Brothers. New York: Penguin Press, 2010.

Markopolos, Harry. No One Would Listen. Hoboken, NJ: John Wiley & Sons, 2010.

McPhee, Martha. Dear Money: A Novel of Bond Trading and Greed. New York: Houghton Mifflin Harcourt, 2010.

Morris, Charles R. Two Trillion Dollar Meltdown: Easy Money, High Rollers and the Great Credit Crash. New York: Public Affairs, 2008.

Paulson, Henry M., Jr. On the Brink: Stopping the Global Financial System Collapse. New York: Grand Central Publishing, 2010.

Phillips, Evin. Bad Money: Economic policies and the American Debt. New York: Penguin Group Publishers, 2008.

Reich, Robert B. Supercapitalism: The Transformation of Business, Democracy and Everyday Life. New York: Alfred A. Knopf, 2007.

Schiff, Pete. How an Economy Grows and Why It Crashes. Hoboken, NJ: John Wiley & Sons, 2010.

Stern, Gary and Ron J. Feldman. Too Big to Fail: The Hazards of Bank Bailouts. Washington, D. C.: The Brookings Institution, 2004.

Stone, Dan G. April Fools: An Insider's Account of the Rise and Collapse of Drexel Burnham. New York: Donald I. Fine, 1990.

Tett, Gillian. Fool's Gold: The Inside Story of J. P. Morgan and How Wall Street Greed Corrupted its Bold Dream and Created a Financial Catastrophe. New York, Simon & Schuster Inc., 2009.

In addition to books, other outstanding media were constantly monitored: newspapers, magazines, television and the Internet. All had major articles and up-to-date data for me to "fill in the holes" of any and all individuals, companies and situations.

I wish to acknowledge in particular the following:

Newspapers:
- The New York Times
- Wall Street Journal
- Denver Post
- Minneapolis Star-Tribune
- Arizona Republic
- Los Angeles Times
- USA Today
- Barrons

Magazines:
> The New Yorker
> Time
> Vanity Fair
> Newsweek

Internet:
> Various Internet news reports as cited in the text of this book
> Separate reports from websites on individuals and companies' websites

Television
> Financial news reports—PBS, CNBC and other financial networks
> Meet the Press—NBC Network
> > CNN

The object of viewing and reading the media is to be objective, complete, impartial, timely and informative. I play no favorites. What you read is a consensus of all facts as well as of opinions. I have no reason to take sides. I wish to report what happens in the world and how we all think about events.

INDEX

A

AB Asesores (Spain), 236
Adams Express, 34
Adelphia Communications Corporation, 297-299, 329-330
adjustable rate mortgage (definition), 217-219
Aetna Insurance Company, 230, 279
affinity fraud, 93-94, 99
Agriprocessors, Inc., 38
AIG, 23, 53-54, 96, 214, 216, 218, 221, 240, 254, 280, 321, 328, 335-336, 339, 345
A. I. Williams Insurance Co, 279
alchemists, 24
Alcoa, 41, 232
Alexander the Great, 20, 24, 51
Allegheny International, 306
Alpern, Ruth, 130
altruism, 51
Amcare, 287
American Continental Homes, 314
American Energy Resources, 66
Anti-monopoly, 33, 41
Antitrust, 39, 41, 219
Aristotle 24, 27
auditor, independent outside, 258
auditor, internal, 288, 345, 352, 367
automated trade, 189

B

Babylon, 14, 24, 26, 29
back-dating, stock options, 185, 257
Balance Sheet, Federal Reserve System, 256, 363
balloon chase, 38, 62-64
Bank of America, 162-163, 174, 198, 214, 218-226, 234, 237-240, 259, 269, 295, 331, 382, 345
Bank of Italy, 162, 219
Bank of New York, 170, 232-234, 248
Bank of New York Mellon Corporation, 155, 169, 170, 209, 232-234, 248
Bank Holding Company Act of 1933, 215, 219

Banking system, 1, 48, 198, 205,
   215, 228, 355, 358-361
Bank Menatep, 41, 61
Bank notes, 154, 205-206
Bankruptcies, 42, 253, 325, 360
Barbuda Island, 138, 183, 184, 187
Barron's Magazine, 196
Barron's Newsletter, 54, 83, 85, 136,
   232, 276, 383
Bartz, Carol, 226, 321
Baxter, J. Clifford, Vice-Chair,
   Enron, 215, 302-303
BDO Seidman International, 35, 57
"Be short," 164, 224
Bear Stearns Company, 186, 194,
   227, 256, 260, 261-262, 272,
   278, 280
Bennett, John G., Jr., 116
Madoff, Bernard, 83, 125-142
Best Buy, 40, 64-65, 114
Beyond Asset Management Corporation, 210, 296
Bird, Lester, Prime Minister of Antigua and Barbuda, 87, 140
Black Monday Crash (October 19, 1989), 360
Blankfein, Lloyd, 222-223, 337
Bloomberg, Michael, 176, 243
Bloomberg News, 142, 174, 190,
   239, 271, 272, 276-277
BMW, 47, 76
Board Committees, 2, 13, 337-338,
   334-345, 351-352
Board Compensation Committee,
   257, 344, 366
Board conflicts, 239, 338
Board of Governors, Federal Reserve
   System 252, 253, 351

Board meetings, 232, 328
Board of Directors, 9, 185, 258,
   325-353
Board oversight, 9, 237, 243, 334
Boesky, Ivan Frederick, 192, 269
Boger, Danny, 149, 201
Bogle, John, 9, 13, 175, 241
bonds, asset-based, 272
   Euro, 231
   High-yield, 274
   Junk, 203, 275, 315
   Municipal, 261
   Mortgage-backed, 272
   Non-investment grade, 274
Boston Scientific, 321
Bottom-feeders, 254, 360
Bower, Frederick, 76
brain drain, 158, 214
Brokered deposits, 218
Brunswick Group, LLC, 190, 265
Buffett, Warren E., 47, 224, 333
Bundled securities, 196, 274
Bureau of Engraving and Printing, 358
Bureau of Labor Statistics, 255, 362
Bureau of the Mint, 358
Burlington Rail Lines, 23, 38
Burke, Stephen, 227
Burnham and Company, 196
Business magazine, 192
Bush, President George W., 13, 141,
   214, 234
Business magazine, 268
Business cycle, 26

C

CBS, 322
Caesar, Julius Gaius, 10, 14, 15, 20,
   24-25

"call", 374
Campbell Soup Company, 240, 333, 339
Canadian Pacific Railway, 38
Canary Wharf Group, 236
cardinal sins, 30, 45, 49
Carlucci, Frank, 210, 296
Carnegie, Andrew, 18, 20, 30, 33-35, 118
Carnegie Mellon, 70
Carnegie Steel, 35
capitalism, 29, 203, 383
Carey, Dennis, 333
Cassatt & Company, 173, 238
caveat emptor, 62, 98
Caynes, James E., 186, 260-262
celebrex, 34, 55
Central Intelligence Agency, 66
certificate of deposit, 14, 181, 186, 197, 207, 292
Chambers, John T., 236, 333
Chase Investment Service, 231
Chase, Salman, 36
Chenault, Kenneth, 235, 332
chief executive officer, 157, 231, 255, 257-258
  duties, 259, 285, 329, 331
chief financial officer, 348, 352
Chin, Judge Denny, 104, 125, 139-140, 142-143, 165-166
China Investment Corp., 236
Churchill, Winston, 29, 49
Cioffi, Ralph, 193, 271-273
Citi Holdings, 169
City Bank, N. A., 168, 229
City Bank of New York, 229
Citigroup, Inc. (Citicorp), 186, 278-280, 336 155, 169, 198, 214, 223, 226, 229-232, 238, 240, 259, 278-280, 309, 335
  Global markets, 168
Comcast, 298, 322
commercial banking, 207, 226-227, 233
commercial credit, 230, 278-279
commercial paper, 222-223, 370, 374
Communist Manifesto, 29
compensation, excessive, 14, 283, 310
Comptroller of the Currency, 154, 202, 207
Computer Associates, International, 208, 292
Conant, Douglas R., 233
Clark, E. W., 22, 36
clawbacks, 86, 135
Clayton Antitrust Act, 41, 162, 219
CIG, 85, 134
Clinton, Hilary, 43, 74, 120
Clinton, President William J., 89, 140, 190
CNN, 384
collateral, 15, 26, 217, 224, 242, 304-305, 369, 376
Consumer Price Index, 362
Control Data Corporation, 230, 278, 387
Cooke, Jay, 30, 35-37
Cooley, Dean Thomas, 344
corporate bylaws, 326-327
Cosmo, Nicholas, 121-123
corporate personhood, 41, 370
Countrywide Financial, 162, 206, 208, 220-221, 293-295
Crachiolo, James M., 323
Cranston, Senator Alan, 316

creative accounting, 284
credit default swap, 209, 217, 374
Credit Suisse Bank, 73, 76, 248
credit union, 207
cricket, 181-182, 187, 191-194
Crocker, Charles, 30
crude oil, 33, 301

D
D-Mo Investors, 111
Dark Knight, The, 193, 200-201
Davis, Governor Gray, 185
Davis, James, 195-196
Dean, Witter, Reynolds, 236, 280
DeConcini, Senator Dennis, 316
deficits, 47
Deikel, Ted, 102
DeLay, Tom, 190, 228
Deloitte, Touche & Tohmatsu, 57
democrats, 134, 359
derivatives, 48, 224, 256, 261, 370-371
Deutsche Bank, 57, 234, 248
Devlin, Matthew and Nina, 265-266
Dimon, James, 226-228, 319
DiPascali, Frank, 141
discount rate, 207
Dodd, Senator Christopher, 209, 295
Doheny, Edward, 30
Dow Jones & Company, 48, 99, 339, 375
Dragon Oil, 228
Dreier, Marc, 57, 90-91
Drew, Daniel, 31
Drexel, Burnham & Lambert, 274, 360, 383
Drexel, Harriman & Ripley, 274
Droney, Judge Christoper, 53

Douman, Philippe, 322
Duke Family, 20
Duke, James Buchanan, 30
Dunlap, Albert, 217, 306-307
Durham, Timothy "Bull", 74
Dwyer, Brian, 30

E
Ear Electrics, 65
Ebbers, Bernard John, 303-305
Economic Policy Institute, 254
E. F. Hutton, 276
Elliot, J. Raymond, 321
Empire Sports Network, 212, 298
Empire Trust Company, 170, 232
England & Wales Cricket Board (E.C.B.), 192
enhanced leverage fund, 272
Enron, 299-303
Erie Railroad, 39
Ernst & Young, 57
ethics, Preface, 55, 131, 316, 368
Euronext N.V., 189, 207, 259, 264, 290
Executive Committee, 351-352
Exxon-Mobil Corporation, 300

F
Fairfield Greenwich Group, 137
False Claim Act, 70
Fannie Mae, 240
Fannin, David, 217, 307
Fastow, Andrew, 301
Federal Banking Districts, 358
Federal Bureau of Investigation, 59, 120, 122, 196, 273, 288
Federal Deposit Insurance Corporation, 96, 186, 207, 215, 218

Federal Home Loan Bank Board, 315
Federal Open Market Committee, 358, 362, 375
Federal Power Commission, 300
Federal Reserve Act of 1913, 355
Federal Reserve Bank, 209, 274, 358, 360-361
Federal Trade Commission, 41
feeder funds, 137-138, 177
financial markets, 48, 212, 214, 227, 371
First Bank of the United States, 355
Fisk, James, 31
Flagler, Henry Morrison, 31
FleetBoston, 220, 280
flipping ownership, 195
Florida Gas, 300
Foggo, Kyle, 45, 65-66
Forbes Magazine, 60, 261, 273, 279, 280, 287
Forciea, Pat, 46, 54-55
Ford Motor Company, 222, 254
Ford, Gerald M., 13, 342
foreclosure, 26, 28, 294
Forte, Joseph S., LP, 109
Fortune Magazine, 268, 274, 291, 305, 308, 314-315, 351
Foshay Company, 87
Foshay, Tower, 87, 89, 90
Foshay, Wilbur, 87-90
fraud, 86, 123
Freddie Mac, 240, 242, 280
Free Bank era, 359
Frick, Henry Clay, 31
Friedman, Stephen, 223
Friends of Angelo, 294-295
Froelke, Robert, 13
Fuld, Richard Severin, 275

G

G-7, 48
Garand, Christopher, 93
Garaventa, Richard, Jr., 68
gas bank, 301
Gates, Bill, 47, 73
Gelb, Peter, 322
General Electric, 223, 308
General Mills, 13
General Re, 45, 52
General Motors, 48, 213, 214, 254, 267, 326, 335-336, 340-341, 345-348
Gen-See Capital Corporation, 94
Giannini, Amadeo, 219
Gibraltar Securities, 130
Glass-Steagall Act of 1934, 41, 215, 216, 235
Glickman, Jeremy, 68
gold, 21, 23-24, 26, 206, 223
Gold Exchange, 154
Golden Eagle, 187
golden coffin, 244, 257, 283, 327, 366
golden parachute, 186, 192, 244, 259, 269, 283, 327, 366
golden commode, 258
Goldman Sachs, 222-225, 236-237, 256, 288, 332, 333
goldsmith, 26, 206
Goodin, John, 74
Gorman, James, 235
Gotham Capital LP, 106
Gould, Jason ("Jay"), 31, 38-39
Gramm, Phil, 190, 216
Gramm-Leach-Bliley Act, 216
Grasso, Richard A., 262-265
Great Northern Railroad, 23, 37-38

Great Northern Steamship Company, 38
Greenberg, Allan, 261
Greenwood, Paul, 69-70
Grim, Judge Arthur, 64
Gross, Bill, 48
Gulf Insurance, 278

H
H & M Petroleum, 66
HNG Internorth, 301
Hammurabi, 16, 26
Harriman, Edward Henry, 31, 274
Hawkes, Daniel M., 109
HBV Services, 97
HealthSouth, 288
Heard, Leon S., 110-113
Heard, Moore and Helfgott, 110-113
hedge fund, 61, 90, 116, 129, 138, 169, 242, 260-261, 370
Heene, Mayumi and Richard, 63
Henderson, Frederic "Fritz", 346
Hershey, Milton S., 31
Hewlett & Tuttle, 82
High Grade Structural Credit Strategies, 272
Hill, James J., 31, 37-38
hiring bonuses, 257
hockey, 46, 54, 256, 298, 305, 321, 330
Hopkins, Mark, 31
House Banking Committee, 190
House of Commons, 75
Houston Chronicle, 189, 198
Houston Natural Gas, 300
Howe, Sara, 83
Hsu, Norman Yuen, 118
Huffman, J. V., 114-115

Hull Trading Company, 223
Humphrey, Hubert and Muriel 13, 328, 343

I
International Business Machines, 41, 235, 332
International Postal Reply Coupon, 54
indemnification, board of directors, 328, 339, 345, 351
independent directors, 107, 134, 200, 213, 218, 257, 259, 283-285, 291-295, 301, 303, 305-307, 323-354, 358, 360, 365-369
Independent Treasury System, 359
initial public offering (IPO), 222-223, 235-236
insider, boardroom, 241, 341
institutional investor, 217, 234, 272, 277
International Banking Corporation, 229
Internorth, 300-301
investment banking, 207-208, 216, 224, 237

J
Jackson, Philip, 32
Jacobs, Irving, 269
Jay Cooke & Co., 30-31, 35-37
Jordan, Michael, 289
Justice, Department of, 58, 76, 120

K
Keating, Charles, 313-315, 318
Keating "Five", 316
Keystone Bridgeworks, 35

Khodorkovsky, Mikhail Borisovich, 67-68
kickbacks, 64, 71
  legal, 131
Killinger, Kerry, 334-335
King, LeRoy, 198-199
Komuro, Tetsuya, 56
Korn/Ferry, 335, 351
Kotz, H. David, 125, 138-139
Koufax, Sandy, 132
KPMG, 57
Kraushaar, Judah, 280-281
Krugman, Paul, 243, 382
Kuhn, Loeb & Co, 276
Kumar, Sanjay, 292-293
Kyle, Judge Richard H., 104

L
labor exploitation, 40
Laird, Melvin, 13
Lautenberg, Sen. Frank, 132
Lay, Dr. Kenneth Lee, 299-303
LDDS (Long Distance Discount Service), 304
Le Nature, Inc. 76-77
Lehman Brothers, 76, 216, 230, 240-241, 256, 265-267, 275-277, 280, 382
Lewis, Al, 48, 99
Lewis, Kenneth D., 220-221, 240, 259, 295, 332
Levy, Reynold, 322
Liability, Board of Directors, 325-354
Lifemark Corporation, 286-287
Lincoln Savings & Loan Association, 313
Lindner, Carl, 314
Lipstick Building, 72, 133

Lord's Cricket Grounds, 191-193
Lyondell Chemical Company, 326

M
Madoff, Andrew, 132-135, 141
Madoff, Bernard, 127-180
Madoff, Mark, 132, 141, 166
Madoff, Peter, 132, 134, 141
Madoff, Shana, 132, 134, 171
Markopolos, Harry, 138-139, 382
Mars Family, 47
Marx, Karl, 28
Mavrodi, Sergei, 91-93
McCain, John, 316
McGuire, Dr. William, 308
McKenzie & Company, 339
Meinl Bank, 76-77
Mellon National Bank & Trust, 232-233
Merckle, Adolph, 60
Merkin, Jacob Ezra, 105-108
Merrill Lynch & Company, 112, 220-221, 237-240, 258-260, 267, 268, 331, 345
Merriman, Shawn R., 98-100
Miami Herald, 194, 196
Microsoft, 41, 223
Miller, William, 83
Milken, Michael Robert, 273-275
Mitsubishi UFD Financial Group, 236
MMM Bank, 92-93
MMM Investments, 92-93
moneychangers, 25, 27, 212
money laundering, 58-59, 64, 72, 96, 103, 117, 141, 165, 190, 199, 289, 290
Monrad, Elizabeth, 45, 53
Morgan, J. P. 168, 218, 226-228, 234-235, 260, 319

Morgan Stanley, 68, 224, 234-237, 256, 280, 296
Morgan Stanley Dean Witter, 236, 280
mortgage products, 28, 217
Morton, Rogers, 300
Moynihan, Brian T., 219-222, 237
Mozilo, Angelo R., 293-295

N

Nacchio, Joseph, 311-312
National Association of Corporation Directors, 347
National Association of Securities Dealers Automated Quotations (NASDAQ), 131, 134, 177, 178, 231, 287, 334, 377
national banks, 208, 215, 354, 358-360
National Securities Telecommunications Advisory Committee, 305, 312
NationsBank, 220
natural gas, 301-302
Nemazee, Hasaam, 74
Nester, John, 266
Network Reliability and Interoperability Council, 312
network, "old-boy", 342
Neuberger Berman, 277
Neurorehabilitation Systems of America, 287
Neutron Jack, 308
New Era Philanthropy, 116-118
New Era Technologies (NETECH), 59
New Frontier Bank, 218-219
New York Daily News, 96

New York Life Insurance Company, 232
New York Stock Exchange, 131, 222, 224, 228, 232, 238, 262, 264, 334
New York Times, The, 57-58, 62, 70, 167, 197, 237, 241, 243, 263, 278, 309
New York World, 33
New Yorker, The, 187, 299
New York Transfer Company, 68
Newman, Paul, 70
Ney, Sen. Robert Ney, 190
Nine, Big, 235
Nike, 319, 320
ninja loan, 377
Noel, Walter M., Jr., 137
non-fraudulent greed, 52
non-revenue category, 210
non-producing assets, 228
non-tangible assets, 255
non-strategic assets, 279
Northern Pacific Railroad, 37-38
"Not Quite Cricket", 187
notes, bank (see bank notes)
notes, promissory (see promissory notes)
nuisance position, 269
number of board meetings, 347
number of board members, 336

O

Obama, President Barack 74, 214, 253, 341
obscene bonuses, 211, 327
Occidental Petroleum, 321
offshore banks, 207
"old boy" network, 342, 348

Omnibus Budget Reconciliation Act, 204, 287
O'Neal, Earnest Stanley, 267-269
Open Seasons, 15
options, 136, 172, 173, 178, 208, 213, 238, 256-257, 259, 261, 264, 268, 294, 308, 333-334, 368-369, 378
Ossie, James G., 100
OTC (over-the-counter), 131, 294, 378

P
Pandit, Vikram, 229
Pang, Danny, 296-297
paper profits, 256, 283
Parker, Mark, 319
Parmigiani, Ted, 266
Pass Words, 14
Pass Words for All Seasons, 14,
patsies, 48
Paul, Weiss, Rifkind, Wharton & Garrison, LLP, 141
Paulson, Henry, 223-224, 383
Pearce, E. A. & Company, 238
Pearce, Harry, 335
Pearce, Thomas, 272
Pearlman, Louis J., 95, 97
Pendergest-Holt, Laura, 196-197
Penn Central Railroad, 223
penny stock, 130
Pennsylvania Railroad, 34-35
pension funds, 212, 217, 243, 272
Perez, George, 72
performance bonuses, 204, 257, 327
perpetrator, 43, 56, 71, 75, 82, 110, 135, 182
personhood, corporate, 41, 370

Pepsico, 13
perks (perquisites), 238, 241, 244, 251, 253, 254, 256-257, 259, 280-281, 300-310, 327, 366-367
petroleum oil, refined, 32, 40, 66
Petters, Thomas S., 101-105
    Petters Company, 102
    Petters Group Worldwide, 102-103
Pfizer, 55
phantom billing, 71
philanthropy, 20, 33, 51, 116, 118, 189
Phoenician, The, 316
Picard, Irving, 108, 132, 135, 142, 167-168
Piccoli, Richard S., 93-94
Picower Foundation, and Picower, Jeffry, 135, 167
Pickens, E. Boone, 269
"Pigs at the Trough", 330, 382
PIMCO, 48
Piper, Harry (Bobby) and Virginia Lewis, 35
pirates, 19, 184
Pittsburgh Post Gazette, 330
pleonexia, 21
Podlucky, 76-77
Polaroid Holding Company, 102-103
Ponzi, Carlo Pietro Giovanni Guglielmo Tebaldo, 84-87
Ponzi nation, 48
Ponzi scheme, 14, 46, 48, 61, 72, 75, 77-78, 123, 125, 127-170, 181-202, 256, 266, 296-297, 371
Porsche, 60, 104, 266
Poses, Frederic M., 332

Postal Service, U. S., 65, 85-86, 94, 113-114, 122, 311-312, 314, 318, 370
Potter, Earl, III, 322
power misused, 45, 50-51
predatory lending, 281
President of the United States, 253, 300, 342, 358, 362, 377
Price Waterhouse, 57, 291
Primerica Corporation 230, 279
Private Equity Management Group, 297
promissory notes, 97
promissory notes, fake, 90-91
prudent oversight, 256
public accounting reform, 344
public stock corporation, 324
"puts", 136, 261, 378
Putnam, George, 13
pyramid scheme, 79, 81-82, 84-85, 119, 128, 181, 201, 371

Q
Qwest Communication, 311-312

R
railroad cartel, 32
Raju, Ramalinga, 290-292
raptor, 302
Reagan Administration, 315
red umbrella, 230
Redstone, Sumner, 322
reinsurance, 53
Real Estate Investment Trust (REIT), 223
retention bonuses, 204, 211, 244, 251, 257, 327, 366
Reuters, 189

Revenue Acts of 1934 and 1935, 41
Rigas, Family, 297-299, 329-330
robber "boomer" barons, 30
robber baron, 20, 29, 30-31, 35, 38-39, 40-41, 371

S
Sacramento News, 70, 185
Salomon Inc., 230, 279, 382
Sarbanes-Oxley Act, 135, 288, 344
Satyam Computer, 290-292
Savings & Loans, 207, 314-315
Schumer, Sen. Charles, 134, 243
Schwab, Charles, 220, 280
Schwartkopf, Norman, 307
Scrushy, Richard M., 286-290
Securities and Exchange Commission, 109, 171, 265, 378
Securities Exchange Act of 1934, 41
securities fraud, 61, 76, 110-111, 141, 165, 199, 271, 273, 289, 292-293, 297, 298, 303, 330
self-aggrandizement, 44, 50-52
seven deadly sins, 45, 49-50
Sinegal, James, 333
Shakespeare, William, 27, 34
Shark, 70
Sherman Antitrust Act, 41
"short" positions, 224, 264, 379
Siegelman, Don, 290
silversmith, 206
Silverado Savings & Loan, 75
Sinclair, Harry L., 31
Skilling, Jeffrey, 301-302
Smith Barney, 230, 279
social security, 48
"Son of Sam" laws, 97
Sotomayor, Justice Sonia, 140

Sousa, John Phillip, 89
Sprint Communications, 304
stagecoach, Wells Fargo, 225
State Street Bank & Trust Company, 233-235
Standard Oil of Ohio, 32-33
Standard Oil trust, 33
Stanford Championship Cricket Tournament, 193
Stanford Eagle, 189
Stanford Financial Group, 194, 198, 201-202
Stanford International Bank, 185, 193, 197
Stanford, Leland, 31, 185
Stanford, R. Allen, 14, 79, 181-202
Stanford, Sir Allen, 181, 183-184, 187, 189, 193, 197, 200-201
Stanford Superstars, 192
Stanford University, 185
Stanford "Watch", 198
Steiff teddy bears, 70
Stock Market Crash of 1929 ("Black Monday"), 360
sub-prime mortgages, 203, 209, 224, 242, 256, 275
Sunbeam Oster corporation, 306-307
Supreme Court, U. S., 28, 38, 41, 107, 140, 263, 290, 299

T

tally sticks, 27
Tannin, Matthew, 272
tax evasion, 57, 67, 76, 92
tax shelter, 57, 190
Tea Pot Dome scandal, 31, 40
ten deadly sins, 45
Test Cricket, 191-192

Thain, John, 228-240, 258-260, 331
Third National Bank, 355
"thundering herd", 238
Time Warner Cable, 298
"Too Big to Fail", 203, 222, 229, 244, 340, 383
toxic assets, 204-209, 218, 240, 242, 243, 262, 273, 275, 318
Transmerica Corporation, 219
Travelers Insurance, 229-230, 279
Treasury, U. S. Secretary of, 234
Treasury, U. S. bills, 116, 379
Treasury, U. S. Department of, 36, 74, 190, 223-225, 228, 231, 233-236, 239, 302, 358-359, 370
Troubled Asset Relief Program ("TARP"), 135, 216, 221, 224, 228, 231, 233-237, 239, 240, 260, 335, 345-346, 370, 379
T. Rowe Price, 13
Truman, President Harry, 89
Twenty20 cricket, 190-192

U

Union army, 37
United Health Group, 308
United States banking crisis (1933), 359
U. S. Steel, 35, 235
usury, 26-28, 215

V

Valero Energy, 340
Vanderbilt, Cornelius, 31, 39, 106
Volkswagen, 60
Volcker Rule, 243

W

Wachovia Corporation, 218, 225-226
Wagoner, Rick, 341, 346
Walker, Professor Pinkney, 300-301
Wall Street Journal, The, 73, 105, 120-121, 136, 239, 242, 258, 275, 280, 321, 341, 351, 383
Wang Laboratories, 70, 292
Washington Mutual (WAMU), 218, 227, 240, 280, 334
Ways and Means Committee, 58

Wells Fargo, 218, 220, 225, 226, 280
Wealth Tax Act of 1936 (Securities and Exchange Act of 1934), 41
Wegman, Danny, 94
Weill, Sanford, 229-232, 278-281, 336
Welch, John Francis, 308-310

Wellstone, Paul, 54
W G Trading Company, 70
Wharton School of Business, University of Pennsylvania, 119, 260, 274
Whitacre, Edward E., Jr., 341-346
Winnick, Gary, 330-331
wire fraud, 59, 66, 73, 96, 100, 110, 111, 121, 141, 165, 303
World Trade Center, 127, 236, 268
WorldCom, Inc., 303-305
Wriston, Walter, 230

X

Y

Z

Zero-Max, 13
Ziarossi, Luigi, 84
Zucker, Michael D., 61

ACKNOWLEDGEMENTS

I wish to acknowledge the invaluable assistance in thought and process for this book that Dr. Marion Downs and Mr. Robert Sheets, both of Denver, Colorado, contributed to this book.

Laura Burns of Corrales, New Mexico, served as an incomparable copyeditor, and her experiences in the banking and financial world made my writing job easier and more accurate. Author Sara Voorhees, also of Corrales, New Mexico, not only steered Laura Burns to me, but also aided greatly in preparing the manuscript for publication.

My son, Steven S. Gray, of Plymouth, Minnesota, kept me going on my computer. He was an honor graduate in 1968 from the Control Data Institute, where he learned the intricate byways of modern computers and has kept up with the astounding strides of computer development.

My thanks to Dr. Dayton Voorhees, Sara Voorhees, and Blyth B. Brookman for their kind endorsements and a special recognition of my friend, Dr. Alfred E. Kahn, now deceased, for his wise and considerate appraisals of *The Greedsters: When Enough is Never Enough.* Dozens of others from all walks of life played parts of influence on my beliefs and decisions.

A general acknowledgement to the media is in order for their timely reporting of world-shaking current financial events, frauds and misdeeds of greed. The period of 2007 to 2012 is one of the unprecedented financial hardships, profits, mergers, acquisitions and schemes. In other words, it has been a playground for greedsters.